Archaeometry and Aphrodite

Proceedings of the seminar
13th June 2013 CNR Rome

edited by
Maria Rosaria Belgiorno

Alessandra Lazzari: Ricordo dell'amico silenzioso.
CV. Alessandro Lentini (CNR archive).
Maria Rosaria Belgiorno: Subject Presentation: Pyrgos/Mavroraki.
Gianfranco Todisco: The ingredients of the Cypriot Prehistory.
 in the cosmetics of the 3rd Millennium.
Maria Rosaria Belgiorno: Cosmetics.
Alessandro Lentini: Archaeometry.
Federica Gonzato & Alessandro Lentini: Textiles quality and spindle whorls type.
Angelo Bartoli & Concetta Cappelletti: Experimental Archaeology for Pyrgos/Mavroraki
Angelo Bartoli & Marco Romeo Pitone: Experimental Archaeometallurgy at Pyrgos-Mavroraki.
Francesca Ceci: The house of the Goddess, Coins tell the Cypriot Aphrodite myth.

Bianca Cornale: photo pag. iv

Antonio De Strobel:
Computer processing of all illustrations
© Photographs and elaborations:
pages x, 3, 4, 5, 7, 8, 10, 12, 15, 16, 17,
19, 20, 22, 25, 26, 27, 28, 30, 49, 53, 54,
55, 56, 57, 58, 61, 64, 67, 69, 71, 72, 73,
74, 75, 76, 77, 79, 82, 83, 128, 146, 154,
155, 156, 157, 158, 159, 160, 162, 163,
164, 165, 171, 172, 173, 174, 175, 176,
182, 184, and hard cover.

Simone Jacomini: maps pags. 13, 14, 23

Copyright © 2017 M R Belgiorno

All rights reserved.

ISBN: 978-9963-2448-0-5
Edited by Maria Rosaria Belgiorno

Alessandro Lentini dedicata

Ricordo dell'Amico Silenzioso

Solo la sua porta in fondo al corridoio, ostinatamente chiusa, mi ricorda che Alessandro non c'è. È talmente forte la sua presenza che ho l'impressione di vedermelo ancora accanto, al binario 9 e 3/4 in direzione della nostra collina, ai confini delle terre conosciute. Un lungo pezzo di vita lavorativa e non trascorso insieme, accanto al suo silenzio – un silenzio pienissimo e rumoroso.

Ho sempre ammirato la sua lenta e testarda crescita professionale, nell'ombra di personaggi spigolosi ma anche piena di incontri importanti, da cui ha tratto conoscenze ed esperienze notevoli. Raramente ne parlava ma le sue fotografie in luoghi sorprendenti ne rivelavano l'importanza, di quei viaggi, di quei paesaggi inusuali. Ne rivedo l'atteggiamento appartato, seduto un poco in disparte, le braccia strette alla borsa, e allo stesso tempo era capace di stare, di ascoltare, di apprendere, di comprendere, di adattarsi come ha fatto nelle sue tante esperienze di lavoro sul campo.

Il silenzio di Alessandro non era mai vuoto: scivolava nel sorriso, nell'ironia, nella curiosità, ed incontrando lo sguardo ci sorprendevamo di come non fosse evidente anche agli altri quanto ci faceva ridere, arrabbiare, sbeffeggiare ... Scriveva, inventava con la stessa attenzione con cui si impegnava a fare propri gli ardui cammini della conoscenza scientifica, imparando, annotando, riempiendo sistematicamente i suoi quaderni di lavoro o di creazione. Lo vedevo sempre assorto in questa attenta metodologia pratica che ne faceva un coscienzioso lavoratore della scienza.

Alessandro era un tecnico del CNR: una concreta esperienza di laboratorio nell'ambito delle analisi e dello studio dei materiali archeologici, con una spiccata propensione allo studio della bio-archeologia; aveva una lunga abitudine all'esperienza sul campo, anche in paesi poco accoglienti ma pieni di fascino storico ed umano. Aveva comunicativa, nonostante la sua timidezza, o forse era solo riserbo; sapeva insegnare, e tutti coloro che lo hanno avuto accanto nello studio e nell'esperienza di laboratorio hanno potuto apprezzare la sua capacità di "accudimento" didattico.

Era una persona timida, soprattutto riservata; un collega attento ai suoi compiti e alle sue responsabilità, e questa non è una definizione riduttiva ma un indice di doti morali ammirevoli. Era l'amico silenzioso, dalle battute fulminanti. Il rammarico è anche di non poter ormai condividere quel sogno a lungo discusso, descritto, immaginato fra noi colleghi, di sinecura, di un ipotetico centro di ricerca su un'isola del Mediterraneo, con un tempo infinito dedicato al mare e al sole. Così lo voglio pensare, che riposa al sole, su di una spiaggia dell'anima... ...

Alessandra Lazzari

ALESSANDRO LENTINI C.V. (CNR archive)

Was born in Rome on 13/03/1955, where he died on 10/3/ 2016.

He has attended various specializations courses at the Institute of Mathematics, in Rome University "La Sapienza" for programming languages in Basic and Fortran 77, at the European Space Agency in Frascati (Rome) for scientific literature searches online. During the years 1988 - 1991 has attended various courses at the Modena University for Palynology and Sedimentology Mediterranean basin, then at the Perugia University has attended the Fifth European Course in Basic Palynology.

Photo by Bianca Cornale

He always had support activities in archaeological excavations, with the development of paleopalynology and sedimentological techniques applied to archaeological stratigraphic sections. Also in the field of biology of primary production, has develops some techniques of flotation and dry screening of archaeological sediments for the recovery of seeds, plant macroremains, charcoal and textile fibers.

In archaeometrical research has configured some methods for chemical analysis of archaeological materials (lithic industry, pottery, metals, glass and sediments) through a plasma spectrometer (ICP-AES). While for the organic residues are some methods in preparation for HPLC analysis.

1985 - 1986 collaborated with their work for the preparation and traveling exhibition "*Aphrodite's Scents*", organized by the Ministry of Foreign Affairs and the Italian National Research Council, in the National Museum of Ireland, Dublin (IRL) and Allard Pierson Museum, Amsterdam (NL). Participation with their work for the preparation of exhibitions organized by CNR - itabc: :"*Pyrgos Mavrorachi Advanced Technology in Bronze Age Cyprus*", Nicosia (CY- 2004),"*Cyprus Aromata - I Profumi di Cipro*" L'olio di oliva nei profumi e nei medicinali nella Cipro del 2000 a.C, Museo Storia dell'Olivo, Trevi (2006), "*I profumi di Afrodite e il segreto dell'olio*" Musei Capitolini, Roma (2007), "*Mavrorachi - Dal 2000 a.C. ad oggi quattromila anni di profumo*" Complesso di Santa Maria Novella - Firenze (2008) and "*Cipro un sito di 4000 anni fa e l?archeologia Sperimentale, l'Olio, i Profumi, i Tessili di Pyrgos Mavrorachi*", Viterbo (2009), Museo Nazionale Etrusco - Rocca Albornoz.

1987 - 1999 collaborated with Ministry of Foreign Affairs and the Italian Institute for the Middle East for the Joint Italian and French Archaeological Mission (UMR 9993) in Baluchistan (Pakistan), in the archaeological sites of Merghart, Nausharo, Pirak and Miri Kalat, with geobotanical surveys, selection and plant macroremains study, selection of archaeological sediments for physic, chemical and palynological analysis, setting up a collection of comparison (palynology section).

2000 - 2002 collaborated with the Italian Archaeological Mission in Sistan (IsIAO) and Iranian Culture Heritage Organization at the archaeological site of Shahr-e Sukhteh (Iran), with selection of plant macroremains, seeds and textile fibers, collaborator of the Joint Archaeological Mission of the University of Bologna and Lecce in Egypt (Fayyum), with selection of archaeobotanists materials.

Since 2004 he is member of the Italian Archaeological Mission of CNR-ITABC at Pyrgos Mavroruchi (Cyprus), for archaeometric and archaeobotany investigations and geobotanical surveys on the territory. In Italy has participated in several archaeological excavations in Prehistoric sites Riparo Salvini and the Capre cave (LT), Neolithic villages, Ripa Tetta (FG), Torre Sabea (LE) and Scamuso (BA), Mycenaeans, Vivara (Procida), Phoenician, Tharros (OR) and Nora (Pula - CA), Etruscan and Roman, Pisa San Rossore (PI), Roman Empire, *Portus Tiberinus ad Emporium* and Garlands Hypogeum *Ad Decimum* (Grottaferrata RM).

1996 - 2001 collaborated with Istituto Universitario Suor Orsola Benincasa (Naples) for didactic stage in archaeological sedimentology and natural landscape for students in Cultural Heritage Conservation.

He worked in several museums in Italy, France, Pakistan and Cyprus, including the Guimet Museum (Paris), National Museum of Pakistan (Karachi), Archaeological National Museum (Nicosia), Archaeological Museum (Limassol), Cyprus Wine Museum (Erimi), Capitoline Museums (Rome), National Museum of Oriental Art G. Tucci (Rome), History Museum of the Olive (Trevi), National Museum of Cerite (Cerveteri), monumental complex of Santa Maria Novella (Florence) and National Museum of Etruscan, Rocca Albornoz (Viterbo). He has published about one hundred articles on national and international journals and contributions to scientific books, participated with communications and posters at national and international conferences. It is also a memberships of Italian Association of Archaeometry and the Italian Botanical Society.

http://www.cnr.it/eventi/index/evento/id/13302:

C.N.R.
EVENTO

Archeometria e Afrodite: ricerche e novità dal sito di Pyrgos a Cipro

Il 13/06/2013 ore 15.30 - 19.30

Cnr sede, Aula Bisogno

La Missione Archeologica del Cnr a Pyrgos-Cipro, che ha scoperto (2003) e indagato con sistemi archeometrici (Mostra Il profumo di Afrodite e il segreto dell'Olio, Roma Musei Capitolini 2007) la più antica fabbrica del profumo risalente alla prima metà del II millennio a.C., presenta i risultati della campagna di scavo del 2012, durante la quale è stato portato alla luce un laboratorio di cosmetici e piccoli gioielli in picrolite, simbolicamente connessi alla lavorazione delle fibre tessili di cui si è rinvenuta ampia testimonianza in diversi ambienti di Pyrgos. L'insieme delle indagini condotte in 9 anni fa emergere il ruolo preminente della donna cipriota già all'inizio del II millennio a.C. e la sua padronanza dell'impianto industriale scoperto a Pyrgos; facendo nascere l'ipotesi che il mito di Afrodite, dea della bellezza e dell'amore sia da riferirsi proprio alla produzione dei beni di lusso come profumi, cosmetici, gioielli e tessuti preziosi di cui Pyrgos ha restituito un repertorio che ad oggi non trova confronti. Il seminario si conclude con un cenno all'uso ancora attuale degli ingredienti rinvenuti a Pyrgos, nella composizione dei profumi e dei cosmetici naturali.

Organizzato da:
CNR
MIBACT: Direzione Generale Antichità

Referente organizzativo:
Alessandro Lentini
Area Ricerca Roma, via Salaria km 29,300
alessandro.lentini@itabc.cnr.it
0690672368

Archaeometry and Aphrodite

June 13, 2013, CNR- Rome, P. le Aldo Moro 1, Room "Bisogno". 15,30-19,30.

The seminar has been organised for the 90th years of CNR.
The Italian Archaeological Mission of ITABC-CNR at Pyrgos/Mavroraki in Cyprus, which in 2001 started investigating with Archaeometry methodologies the archaeological material, presents the results of the 2012 archaeological season, during which it has been brought to light a laboratory of cosmetics and small jewels, including picrolite and shells, with all the instrumental equipment.
The room in which the laboratory was set up has an unusual plant like a mini cloister. The large opening of the roof, supported by inner structures, illuminated entirely the working environment distributed on the four sides of the room.

The archaeological and Archaeometry investigations, bring out the prominent role of the Cypriot woman at the beginning of the second millennium BC and her masterful management of the industrial complex discovered at Pyrgos, giving rise to the hypothesis that the myth of Aphrodite, goddess of beauty and love, is to be referred to the Cyprus' reputation to produce luxury goods since the Bronze Age: such as perfumes, cosmetics, jewels and precious textiles. Of these industries Pyrgos returned a repertoire that has no comparison.

The collaboration with "Antiquitates" Centre for Experimental Archaeology of Blera (Vt) helped to clarify many suggestions born during the excavations regarding the main activities performed in the workshops of the industrial area. Archaeometry analyses have provided useful elements for reconstruction, through experimentation, technologies performed at Pyrgos 4000 BP. Replicas of stone tools, useful, curated pottery and botanical species recognized after the Archaeometry investigations have been utilized for experimentations. The research on loom weights started after the discovery in 2006 of a furnace still containing 76 loom weights made of simple pressed earth, shaped as the weights found at Pyrgos in the workshop for textiles together with the remains of a loom and many spindle whorls.

Regarding metallurgy, the peculiarity of Pyrgos' context is the proximity between the coppersmith workshops, the Olive press room and the storage area full of huge pithos jars.

This fact produced some considerations about the nature of the fuel employed in the metallurgical process, suggesting a possible use of the olive oil. The preliminary experimental study carried out on underlined the great potential of the research addressed on the use of olive oil in the Bronze age.

As has been the case in Mediterranean civilisations, for the use and dissemination of manufactured metal, Cyprus has been deeply involved in the social development agreement based on common interests that caused the expansion of settlements and gradual transition from the simple food production of a more organized domestication of plants and animals.

In later periods coinage was one of the most powerful resources of propaganda for images of the ancient world, and Rome knew how to use this wisely. This also happened in Cyprus, which became a Roman province in the 58 BC keeping as a rule its religious institutions, first the ancient worship of Aphrodite-Wanassa at Palaeo Paphos administered by a great priest, who played a pan-political function as a recognized symbol of identity of the island.

The seminar concludes with nods about the presence of the same ingredients found at Pyrgos in the composition of modern perfumes and cosmetics. The history of Cyprus is deeply linked to the most ancient production of items to improve the beauty. And perhaps it is not a case that today the island is at the third place in the world for the consumption of cosmetics *pro capite*.

CONTENTS:

1. Subject Presentation: Pyrgos/Mavroraki
   Maria Rosaria Belgiorno — *1-34*

2. The ingredients of the Cypriot Prehistory in the cosmetics of the 3rd Millennium
   Gianfranco Todisco — *35-44*

3. Cosmetics
   Maria Rosaria Belgiorno — *45-93*

4. Archaeometry
   Alessandro Lentini — *95-143*

5. Textiles quality and spindle whorls type: New data about spinning techniques in Cypriot Middle Bronze Age.
   Federica Gonzato & Alessandro Lentini — *145-152*

6. Experimental Archaeology for Pyrgos/Mavroraki and the research on loom weights.
   Angelo Bartoli & Concetta Cappelletti — *153-166*

7. Experimental Archaeometallurgy at Pyrgos-Mavroraki: the pilot-experiments.
   Angelo Bartoli & Marco Romeo Pitone — *167-179*

8. The house of the Goddess. Coins tell the Cypriot Aphrodite myth.
   Francesca Ceci — *181-190*

Giovedì
13 Giugno 2013

CNR
P.le Aldo Moro 1
ROMA

Aula Bisogno
Ore 15,30

ARCHEOMETRIA e AFRODITE
*ricerche e novità
dal sito di Pyrgos a Cipro*

La missione italiana di Pyrgos opera in collaborazione con il Dipartimento delle Antichità di Cipro, cofinanziata da:

1. SUBJECT PRESENTATION: PYRGOS/MAVRORAKI

Maria Rosaria Belgiorno

Pyrgos/Mavroraki:
environment, archaeology, archaeometry and social aspects

Environment.

1. Cyprus is for extending (in extension) the third island of the Mediterranean (Fig.1). As the other larger islands, Sicilia, Sardinia and Corsica, its position on the marine trade routes and proximity to different countries and civilizations determined its history and cultural evolution. She is in a privileged position, encircled by the coasts of Anatolia (East), Syria and Palestine (South), Egypt (West) and Crete (North): countries where some of the most important Mediterranean civilizations born. The true distance from the coasts of bordering countries played an important role in the inhabitation of the island. It lies about 264 miles from Egypt, 76 miles from the Syrian coast and 43 miles from the shores of Anatolia.

However, considering the short distance from the Syrian and Anatolian coasts, we can assume that people from these lands could sail to the island in about a day. From remote antiquity to present day, this situation has determined coming of people, knowledge, religion, and technology.

In the past Cyprus was known as the green island for its vast forests, which reached the shores of the Sea. The rains were abundant, although seasonal, but many marshlands existed along the coast at the mouth of the streams.

Those larger, of Hala Sultan Tekke and Akrotiri on the southeast coast, still exist, but many more were scattered as small pools near the sea around the island.

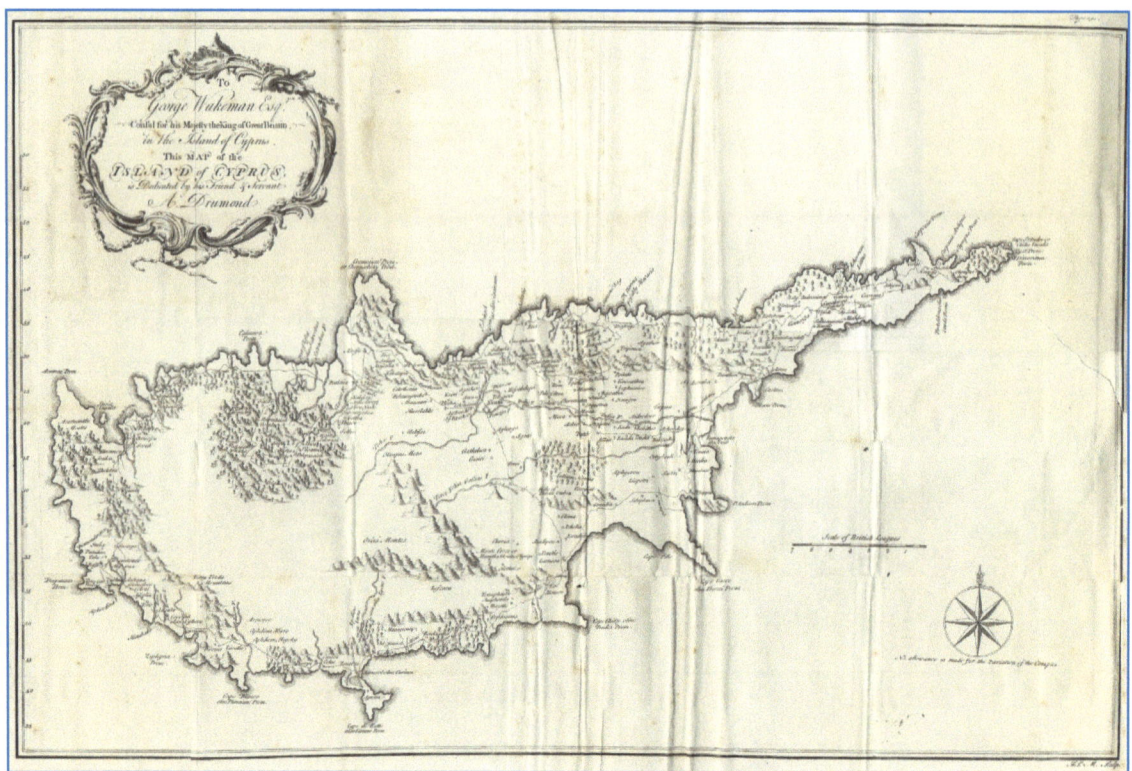

Fig. 1: Map of the island of Cyprus, Drummond Alexander 1754

They hosted a rich flora and fauna, which is now almost completely disappeared, but that, in ancient times, has played a very important role in providing food, basketry and textile resource (Fig.2). Furthermore, looking at the geography of the island, we notice that the western portion is divided into opposite coastal regions by a large mountain, the Troodos, while the east by a smaller mountain the Pentadactilo. In between a large plain, the Mesaoria acts as an element of connection and communication of the two coasts.

People, still involved in the pre-Neolithic revolution occupied the island around the 10th millennium BC, including Cyprus in the phenomenon that started from high Mesopotamia and Ararat slopes and transformed the communities of hunters and gatherers in sedentary farmers and livestock breeders. These people had knowledge of navigation and knew how to make boats to transport people and animals. Archaeologists found evidence of the coming of these people, who first colonized the island, not only along the coasts but also in the inland. This indicates that they were a consistent number, probably different tribes; however, it is not possible to identify the country from which they came.

What they found would have been a land with few animals, lacking in enemies or dangerous beasts, and with a luxuriant forest that descended to the seashores. The mountain that grows up to 2000 meters provides water to innumerable streams, while the sides and small valleys among the foothills near the sea were full of pools and marsh plants. Eastward, larger rivers traversed the interior of the island. Most of the wild forest consisted of Mediterranean Flora, enriched by subtropical species that could survive due to the temperate and warm climate.

Fig. 2: A glimpse of wild forest, Paphos district.

High Cedars of Lebanon, Pine trees, Cypresses, Junipers, Mastic trees, Tamarisk shrubs, Pistacia terebinths and Myrtle perfumed the air with their aromatic resins, leaves and berries. An incredible number of flowers and plants covered the brushwood, and grappled with the scent of superb centenary conifers. At that time, Cyprus was like a small-uncontaminated Eden

The colonisers brought with them domestic animals and seeds to cultivate grains and vegetables, starting to transform the environment of the island by including new flora and fauna. Cyprus gradually became a crucial exchange point in the trade networks of the Eastern Mediterranean, and its civilization appears from the start as part of a cultural subsystem related to a larger whole through maritime trade.

However, during the Neolithic a sort of natural or intentional division created two individual cultures influenced by trades and associations with different countries. Otherwise, it is possible that this cultural duality has been also the result of a complex of different economies and territorial organizations encompassing the North and the South.

In EBA, the difference between Northern and Southern sites is mainly perceptible through their pottery typology, but also through their architecture and settlement patterns: all the available evidences suggest contrasting subsistence strategies as well as differing managements of authority.

The coexistence in Early-Middle Bronze Age Cyprus of sites owing individual cultures, «commercial» North opposed to «industrial» South is a reality more than a hypothesis. Limited the evidence may be, similar trends started to appear during the Chalcolithic, in the fourth millennium BC, giving Cyprus a character of «Cultural duality» which in the limits of historical dimension and political division is still alive.

2. Geomorphology.

Pyrgos is located on the Southern coast in Limassol district, one of the six districts in which the island was divided before the 1974.

Furthermore, the region includes some of the most ancient pre-Neolithic sites: Akrotiri Aetokremnos (the earliest site of Cyprus associated with extinct endemic Pleistocene fauna), Parekklisha Shillourokambos (at 3 km West of Pyrgos, where was found the most ancient cat buried with a human, 9th millennium BC) and Ayios Tychonas Klimonas (9th millennium BC, 5 km West of Pyrgos), and a number of Neolithic and Chalcolithic small sitse located 1-5 kms West of Pyrgos during the survey made by the France Archaeological Mission at Amathunte in 1989[1]. More Neolithic sites (Early and Middle Neolithic) are along the line of the river Kouris, which descends from the Olympic mountain, crossing the Western territory of Limassol district. Most important is Erimi where Porfirios Dikaios in '30 years excavated a late Neolithic site, whose pottery typology underlines a chronological step in the evolution of Cyprus culture. Among the others, there is the chalcolithic site of Souskiou, famous to produce picrolite pendants shaped as anthropomorphic cruciform idols (Fig.3).

Fig. 3: South west Neolithic sites close to the Pyrgos village

3. Occupation.

However, numerous are the sites of Bronze age distribute in correspondence of modern villages, demonstrating the uninterrupted continuity of occupation of comfortable places to inhabit, thanks the mineral wealth of the territory, the natural resources, and the presence of hydrological facility.

---

[1] C. Petit, C. Dieulafait, E. Guillet, P.-Y. Péchoux BCH 1989, 889-899.

Water is the driving element in the past that justifies the presence or absence of a settlement. If it is true that the presence of wells indicates an advanced level of human organization, the complete absence of wells or pipes indicates that the site had natural water resources in close proximity. The archaeological evidence indicates that since the Neolithic villages were on the sides of the rivers flowing down from the Troodos. Many of them are now dry, because the water has been intercepted before reaching the valley, and is collected in dams of different sizes, built in the last century to create drinking water reserves.

In antiquity, the problem of scarcity of rain was less severe than today, and the Greek geographers describe the island covered by a blanket of forests that reached the sea. In the case of Pyrgos, the settlement was developing along the confluence of three arms of a stream (Pyrgos), which joins other streams before reaching the sea after 4 km. The water catchment of Pyrgos in fact includes a vast array of streams that descend from the Troodos passing through one of the richest areas of the island for mineral and natural resources.

Considering the geographical position of Pyrgos and the geomorphology of its territory, we found that the site, in terms of metal ore possessions, is in a privileged position.

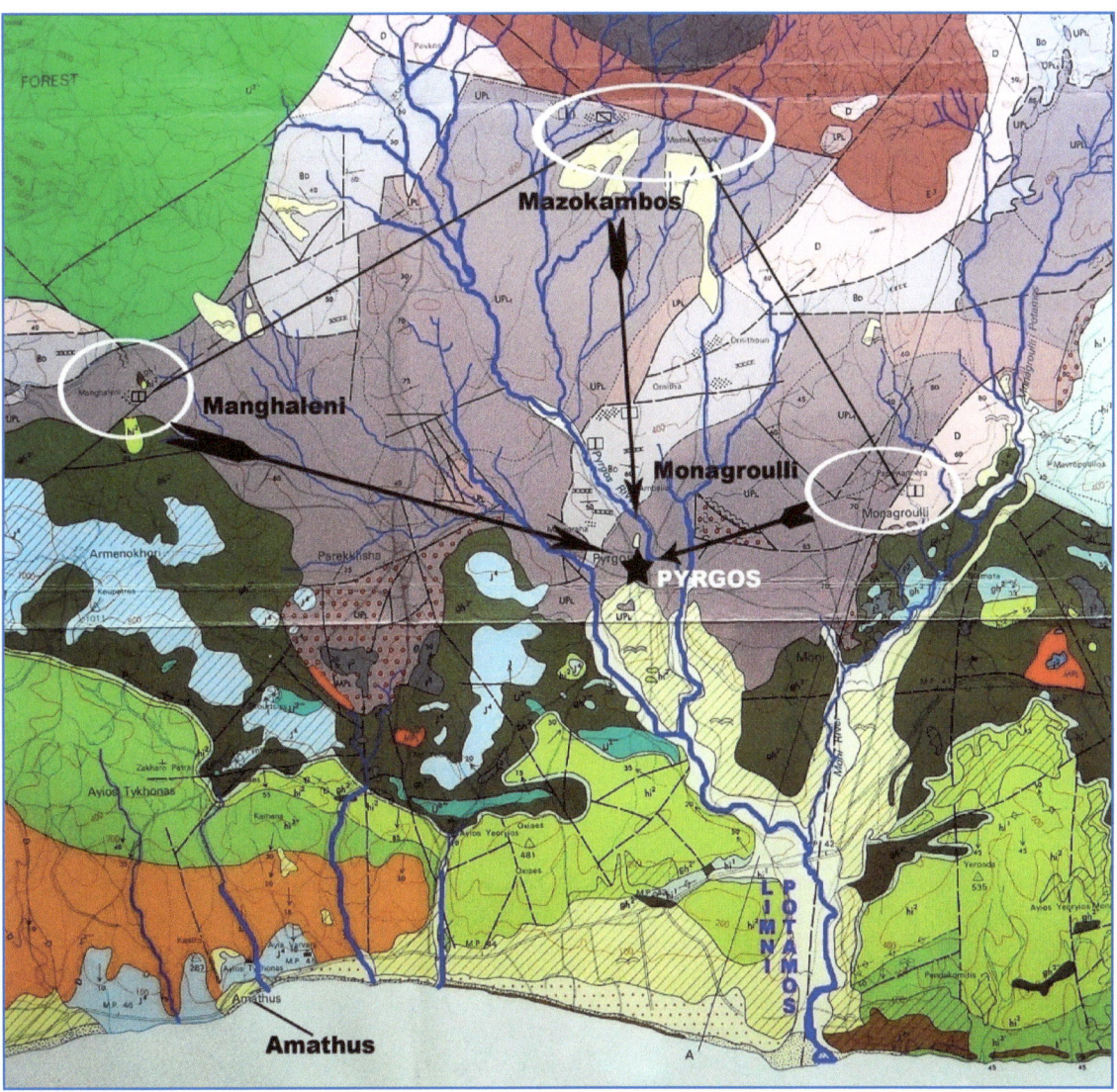

Fig. 4: Pyrgos geological map, including the alluvial Limni cone.

The prehistoric site is situated in the heart of the Limni large alluvial cone, positioned between the Pharmakas and Kalavassos villages[2]. The geological structure of the Pharmakas - Kalavasos area is one of the richest in minerals of the island for its mineral formations and rare morphologies, studied by many researchers (Fig. 4). Since Maestrichtian a long history of lifting and erosion of soil has shaped the land. Many cycles of sedimentation, formed by running water, have produced special coastal morphologies.

Among them, the most debated is the Monì Formation[3], which occupies a belt of 2 km between the villages of Armenochori and Monagroulli. Pantakis described in detail the geomorphology of the area in 1978. Gaudry in 1862, Bellamy and Jukes-Brown (1905), Henson, Browne and McGinty (1949) published previous geological maps. Moussoulos (1957) and Schmidt (1960) have studied the geological composition and distribution of minerals. In 1963, Bear completed a detailed geological map of Cyprus including all available geological information at the time about the Pharmakas-Kalavasos zone.

The area is the lowest of the Troodos Mountains close to the southern coast; minerals morphologies composed of many litho-outcrops form it. The region is located where the Troodos Ophiolite complex combines Circum Troodos sedimentary succession. Its formation dates to the middle Cretaceous, beginning with the oldest Arakapas Ophiolite sequence. While the final formation of sedimentary levels slips back to upper Miocene. Millenarian erosion of rainwater left a sedimentary area between the mountains and the sea, principally composed of quartziferous serpentine sandstone and clay matrix.

The Millenary erosion made by the very aggressive waters of the numerous seasonal streams is particularly marked around Pyrgos, whereas mineral outcrops of copper and iron surface in the deep cuttings left by running water

4. Anchorages. The Monì cement factory, which is located at the mouth of Limni, faces the coastal limestone rocks of Monì formation. The tributaries of Limni worked as lines of communication between the ancient villages and the sea during the dry season. Even today, the road that runs from the village of Pyrgos straight to the sea follows an ancient path bordering a stream, which originates from the western branches of Pyrgos.

At the end, there is a small port, a luxury marina for private yachts, which worked until a recent past for fishing port. Other two anchorages are still in use; one is a terminal for the oil supply of the "Monì power station" that provides electricity to the Limassol district; the second is the support base of the Lofitis fishing farm (Fig. 5). Along the coast, some remains of marshes formed by ancient flows are still visible. Meanwhile, a stone arch (almost hidden by the new coastal road) points the place where one time there was a structure for the bath of sheep before shearing.

---

[2] Eventually was not only the copper which suggested to the people to settle here, but the abundance of water brought down by the numerous streams which form the Pyrgos and the Monì and make this valley particularly fertile. We do not have to forget that the abundance of water played in the antiquity the most important role for every domestic and industrial activity. In turn, the "Limassol Forest", which characterizes the inland landscape of the region, produced at the time plentiful combustible for metallurgy and pottery.

[3] "Monì formation" has been investigated by Pantakis first (1967) and Robertson (1977) and later included in the geological papers of the volume "South Troodos Transform Fault Zone", (Nicosia 1994) published by IG Gass, CJ MacLeod, BJ Murton, A. Panayiotou KO Simonian and C. Xenophontos". Gass, MacLeod, Murton, Panayotou, Simonian and Xenophontos reconsidered the area (1994), examining the possibility of economic mineral resources. A detailed map of the territory is included in "The geology of the area Parekklisha map (Morel 1964)".

Fig. 5: Position of anchorages at 4 km far from Pyrgos/Mavroraki

The sheep baths were organized around some freshwater pools formed near the sea by the waters coming from the Troodos Mountains. According to the memory of old people, wool clipping was a traditional event and the opportunity to organize a kind of an agricultural fair. This event gave people the opportunity to buy seasonally and sell fish, livestock, agricultural products, and tools. The old tradition corresponding to the morphology of the territory, justifies the existence, within walking distance of three anchors on the coast. It is highly probable that one of the three was an ancient trading port, which began working after the prehistoric economy of Pyrgos/Mavroraki.

5. The archaeological site of Pyrgos: Mavroraki (Mavrorachi per Greek maps) is a low hill 145m high, to the west of the village, on the left bank of the Pyrgos. According to Cypriot dialect the name means black shoulder (rocks), probably referring to the colour of basalt malachite and chrysocolle veins emerging on the surface. The hill, on its south side, hosts part of the prehistoric settlement.

Regarding the presence of mineral resources, it is important to note large formations of pillow lava outcrop along the western edges of the territory. Meanwhile the entrance of an old mine gallery is still visible in the Pyrgos riverbed, 600 meters North East from the site (Fig. 6) probably pertaining investigations of Hephaestus Mining Company. After a short entrance, the gallery branches out in different directions and water is usually present according to the season.

Straight to the river source of Pyrgos, 5km inland, there is Mazokambos, the abandoned mining village where the Hellenic Mining Company exploited gold minerals until 70 years ago.

Moreover, on page 95 of 1st Bulletin, published by the Geological Survey Department of Cyprus in 1963 (Bear 1963), there is a description of the mineral occurrences of the Pyrgos territory reported at number 70 of the Map:

"The most promising mineralization in the Pyrgos area lies in Basal Group rocks, immediately to the north and northeast of the village. Discontinuous screens of pillow lava of varying widths (from two feet to 30 feet) have formed iron-stained zones through the oxidation of their disseminated pyrite content, but the proportion of

pillow lava to dyke material is low. Malachite and Azurite staining is not uncommon, but jarosite, silica and gypsum were not observed. Some of the gossans have been superficially explored by means of shallow pits and trenches, but without giving a particularly encouraging result. A sample from Ambeli averaged 8.0 percent sulphur, 22.0 percent iron and 0.3 percent copper, and specimens of leached material from gossans assayed 0.40 dwts gold per ton and 2.0 dwts silver per ton."

Fig. 6: A mine entrance still visible in Pyrgos' river bed.

In turn, the results of a geophysical survey carried out in 1957 by the mentioned Hephaestus Mining Company, a subsidiary of Cybarco Limited, gave disappointing results for modern economic exploiting. It should also be considered that the North-West branch of the river Pyrgos, that flows for 700 meters through the centre of the prehistoric settlement, crosses the Ampeli area bordering the Mavroraki hill west. Along all these 700 meters, and on both sides of the river, it is possible to find lumps of copper slag and fragments of Early and Middle Bronze Age pottery. Considering that the slag nuggets (nucleus of reduction) are an index of copper, metallurgical activity, it is hard not to relate the outcrops of Ambeli and Mavroraki to the prehistoric copper production of Pyrgos.

Nevertheless, northeast of the village, in the territory of Monagroulli, only 3km away, there is another interesting mineral area at Papayiannena, 1 mile west of the village. Samples from the mineralized zone at Papayiannena were assayed for precious metals and averaged 0.1dwts per ton gold and 4.3-5.9 dwts per ton silver.

Regarding the presence of gold minerals in the area, we have to remind the finding gold artefacts from Philia facies, around 2500-2000 BC, gold production must have taken place in the Early Bronze Age Cyprus. Until recently, the question was whether that gold was the first acquired by sporadic nuggets occasionally found in streams, or intentionally exploited from mineral outcrops. The analysis of the most important mining regions of Cyprus (Skouriotissa and Kalavassos) indicates anomalous, 1-5 p.m., concentrations of Au in silicified umbers of ophiolite complexes (Prichard & Malliotis 1998). The analyses demonstrated that the silicified umber is often auriferous with hundreds of thousands of ppb Au. Minerals from Mangaleni (the mine area, 4kms from Pyrgos was transformed in a recreational park in 2000' years), Perapedhi, Asgata, Pyrga and Kokkinovounaro have high Au values, but most anomalous Au concentrations in silicified umbers occur in Mangaleni, Pyrga and Kokkinovounaro.

At Asgata (12 Km East of Pyrgos) values of 440 ppb and 220 ppb Au occur in two silicified umbers taken by the massive silicified umbers vein near the base of umber deposit. Slightly enriched Au values of 10 ppb occur in unsilicified umbers at Asgata compared to typical umbers elsewhere in Cyprus which have an average of 5 ppb and sheared and basal umbers adjacent to the underlying pillow cobbles have higher Au concentrations of up to 165 ppb. Au presence is well known in several deposits, including Skouriotissa, where it is often associated with silicification. From 1937 until 1940, 26673 tonnes of gold and silver-bearing ore were mined from Mitsero Agrokipia mines in the district of Nicosia, where it is estimated that 395 kilos of gold and 2002 kg of silver were produced.

In turn, no evidence for ancient exploitations has been observed as the modern activities completely overturned the minerary territory. This data suggests that the whole region around Pyrgos is an important resource of minerals possibly exploited in the past, as the small percentages of arsenic, lead, gold and silver found in the bronzes of the Early-Middle Bronze Age suggest (Craddok and S. Swiny 1986).

6. Pyrgos village in the Bronze Age: the picture of the Bronze Age Pyrgos is like most of the Eastern Mediterranean villages of the time: a long line of houses constructed with mud bricks on stone foundations bordering the sides of a seasonal stream.

The homes were roughly rectangular, some with an open court, generally of one story; the roof was constructed with wooden beams and mats of reeds, sealed with a thick layer of mud. It was often utilized for domestic purposes as to dry fruits and vegetables and it was accessible via a wooden stair positioned inside the house in a corner corresponding with an opening in the ceiling. Other wooden beams were used for doors, windows, outdoor sheds, under which, large stone mills, and mortars were often placed.

Few streets run across the villages as the houses were leaning against each other. Whereas no evidence of stables has been found among the dwellings (including the other contemporary sites archaeologically investigated), we can assume that the animals were placed outside the village, probably in pens.

The surrounding environment was quite different from today, because the climate was more humid and green fields, forest, ponds, and several smaller streams surrounded the village.

However, going along the centuries, the visual aspect of the village has not changed substantially until 1954, when Pyrgos had some public fountains in the streets and the first houses with electricity.

The industrial complex is in the middle of the prehistoric settlement, which has an extension of approximately 35 hectares. Most of the Bronze Age remains, and structures are underneath the houses recently built.

The Bronze Age necropolis extend to the East, tombs running under the houses of the modern village distributed as a large arch including the church, the school and the main street of the village (Fig. 7).

Mavrorachi hill hosts part of the settlement and presents on the surface interesting copper veins of chrysocolle and malachite probably exploited as primary mineral resource by the industrial site.

Fig. 7: Google earth view of Pyrgos village with Early/Middle Bronze age tomb distribution

Pieces of minerals, copper reduction nuggets, querns and pestles of different type and dimensions are scattered on the surface everywhere. This material helped the finding of the settlement in 1995. The size and distribution of the site were calculated and mapped in 1999-2000. Plain surveys revealed that the settlement extended along the western branch of the river Pyrgos, for a length of 700 metres, between the localities of Kolla and Perivolia, including the small terrace Aulaki, positioned on the southern side of Mavrorachi, 500 metres west to the old *koriò*. The number of stone tools and fragments of ceramics (including many fragments of Red Polished storage vessels) led estimation of the extension (GIS made by Emeri Farinetti).

The industrial area of Pyrgos, located in the middle, has a delay of about 8000 sq. m., calculated by resistivity testing applied to an area of 70 by 70 meters. The excavations brought to light only part of the area devoted to the industrial activities. Still today we cannot affirm that the industrial organisation of the place belongs to the Middle Bronze Age or to the first emplacement of the Early Bronze Age (Philia facies), around the end of the III millennium BC, as the diagnostic fragments of pottery suggest. They correspond to the ceramics found in the tomb located under the houses of the village, which date back from the Early Bronze to the Middle Bronze II[4].

7. Abandon and recent history. At the end of the Middle Bronze Age II, Pyrgos was abandoned as many other settlements of Cyprus, probably for a sequence of seismic events followed by other calamities.

Then, until the end of the Bronze Age, the area seems seasonally frequented but not regularly inhabited. From the beginning of the 1st millennium[5] until today the settlement moved to the East, where there is the modern Pyrgos village, becoming an important agricultural centre.

Though mentioned after 1500 as *Byrgo*, it seems that the village would not have acquired its name due to the existence of a tower (Pyrgos) or a castle, but after a noble Italian knight, *Pietro da Perego*[6] who arrived in Cyprus in the wake of the Lusignans (Guido and Almerico I) in the late twelfth century (1190 approx).

In the chronicles of the time, we find a *Pietro da Perego* belonging to the noble family "De Perego", recorded in the list "Matricola Nobilium, Familiorum", established in 1277 by Othone Visconti Archbishop of Milan.

The name of the Italian noble family coincides with the name of the village, "Peregus, which occurs in the papal autograph letter of 17th August 1224 by Pope Honorius the 3rd to William de Rivet, in the diocese of Nicosia, regarding a dispute over the feudal assignment of "Casale Peregi or Perogi" (Casale = farmhouse-feud. Peregi Latin genitive of Peregus, after "Perego"), donation of Queen Alice widow of Hugh I of Lusignan[7].

We also find "Casale Peregi" mentioned in the list of dealers of commanderies, feudal lords forced to annual donations (animals and earth products). In the list mentioned in the thesis of Evangelia Skoufari (a) there is the manager of Casale Per(e)ogi in 1316: Antonio da Monì of "Casale Perogi" (Monì is the name of the village bordering Pyrgos 2 km East)[8]. In turn the actual name Pyrgos seems to be the local dialect transformation of the Latin name "Peregus".

---

[4] Later tombs date back to the Geometric and Archaic periods.

[5] The people of the beginning of 1st millennium BC who reoccupied after centuries the site didn't possess any memory of the prehistoric village and decided to build their houses on the location of the Early and Middle Bronze Age cemetery ignoring the presence of the tombs. The foundations of their houses have been reused for numberless times in the following periods and form today the hearth of the ancient "choriò". Geometric, archaic, Hellenistic and roman remains scattered everywhere and reused in buildings, together with a number of inscribed funerary *cippi* used as embellishment in private gardens, and pottery of different periods sparse everywhere testify the uninterrupted life of the village until today.

[6] About Pietro da Perego, chronicles report that in addition to considerable organizational skills, Peter had great success in the conversions of the Cathars, which can cause or accelerate the extinction of the Cathar dioceses located next Concorezzo church. As Pietro da Perego, the Cathar bishop Desire in 1235 modified his dualist positions to smooth the friction with the Catholic Church. Following this, Raniero Sacconi, doctor Cathar belonging for seventeen years to Concorezzo church, abjured in 1245 and devoted himself to composing the Summa de Heresis, a memory of the doctrine he professed. Since 1241, the anti-heretical ecclesiastical institution's commitment reinforced in Milan thanks to another member of the Perego family, the archbishop Leone da Perego (1241-1257), former provincial minister of the Franciscan order of Lombardy, concisely judged by Salimbene de Adam: "He was famous and solemn preacher and great persecutor of heretics."

[7] Golubovich P.G. 1906: *Biblioteca bio-bibliografica della Terra Santa dell'Oriente Francescano*, vol. I, Firenze, 372-8; Shabel C. 2000: Frankish Pyrgos and the Cistercians, in *RDAC* 349-358.

[8] Skoufari E. 2008: phd tesis: *Il Regno della Repubblica, continuità istituzionali e scambi interculturali a Cipro*, Gennaio, Università degli studi di Padova, p. 248.

The abundance of water and the geomorphological peculiarities of the territory, suitable for agriculture activities had attracted the attention of the Cistercians, who founded in Pyrgos a monastery in the XII century. The Cistercian organisation an urban centre, according their famous system of building long-way channels and cisterns to take the water. The system survived for centuries and was utilised by the Pyrgos inhabitants until 1950 (Fig.8), when the Cistercian channels bordering the houses were substituted under the British rules with a new aqueduct (date impressed on public fountains).

Fig. 8: Ruins of the XII cent. Cistercian flour mill. Pyrgos village

Ignoring the Cistercian history, today the people believe that the name of Pyrgos comes from the "Pyrgui Righena" (a legendary queen), a sort of gallery or cave deeply sunk in the local *havara* and located in the very centre of the ancient "Chorio", where runs the "Righena odòs". Today its entrance has been unfortunately closed, but the people memory reminds that the "Pirgui" had a large entrance and was furnished with a staircase going down into a sub terrain road used by the queen Righena to reach in the night (on a gold chariot) her lover in Amathunte. If the "Pirgui" was the entrance of a secret gallery used for private affairs, or the "dromos" of a monumental tomb, or the main Cistercian channel[9], or the entrance of an ancient copper mine, we will never know, as it was sealed definitively in 1994, under a cement carpet to build a private

---

[9] Which collected the water coming from the large stone ashlars cistern at the North of the village with the basilica, partially included in the church of modern cemetery.

garage. This has hidden forever the monument that, for popular tradition, gave the name to the village.

After the 1500 we find *Byrgo* on geographical and nautical maps among few referent geographical points of southern Cyprus (like Amathunte, Polemidhia, Episkopi and Erimi) followed by the symbol of a monastery.

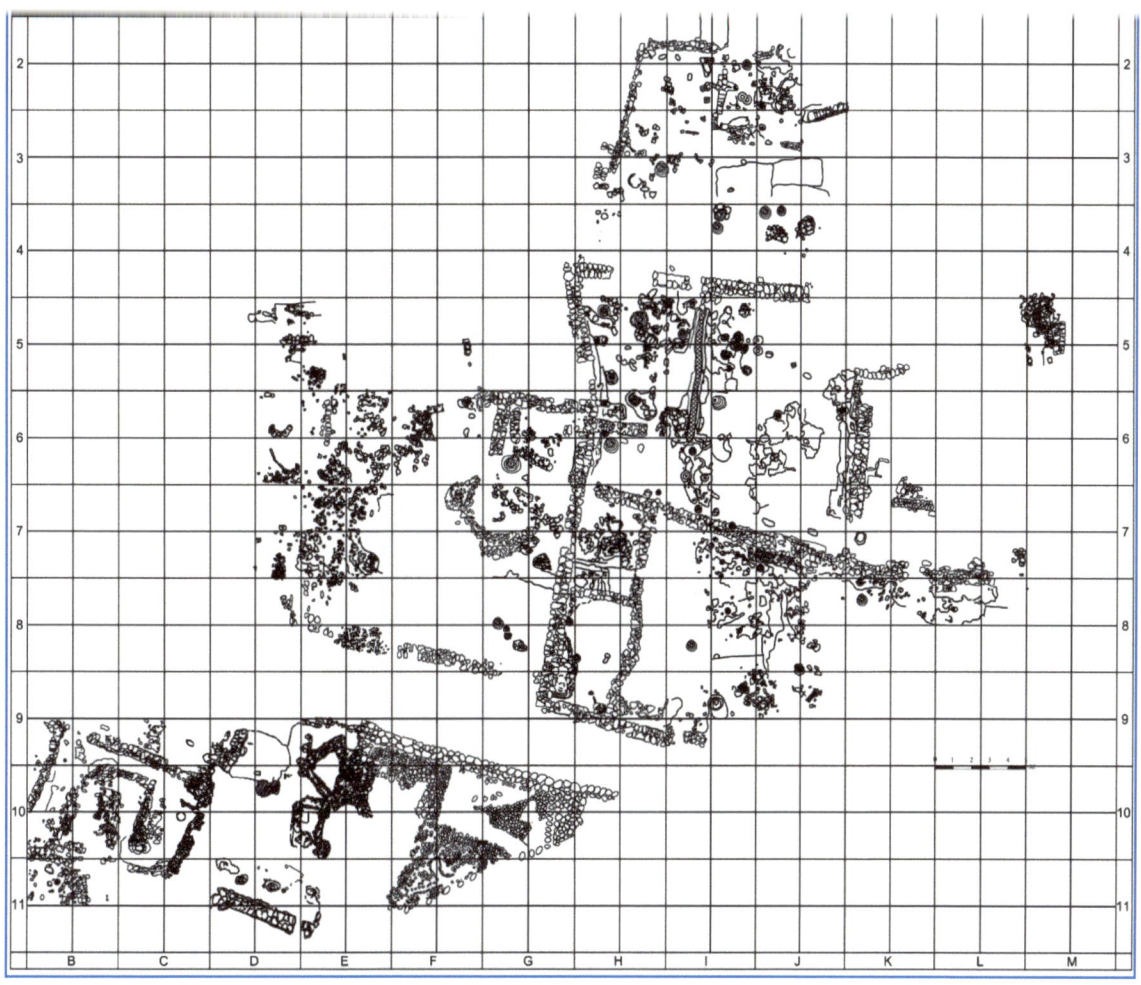

Fig. 9: Excavation map of Pyrgos/Mavroraki

Archaeology

1. The area investigated (Fig.9) has in the middle a large olive press-room furnished with ten storage jars and a laboratory for extracting olive oil scents. On the western adjacent room, there is a large room for dyeing and weaving textiles. To the North and South there are two courtyards full of implements and facilities to produce metal objects. The structures are characteristic of a unitary building with a specific industrial destination. The olive press-room and its storage area, was the fulcrum of the industrial quarter, communicating on three sides with courtyards and workshops for the copper industry.

This peculiar position has suggested an extra employ of the olive oil for metallurgy, such as the fuel for running the furnaces and forges.

The olive press-room was divided in two parts by a central bench made to control the beam of the press. The western section was wholly devoted to store the jars for the olive oil;

meanwhile a small perfume factory was arranged in the Eastern sector, close to the central bench. It consisted of a battery of 14 ground pits (each hosting a jug on coal) and several stone tools, vases, flints and various implements for preparing, blending and conserving the scents (Fig.10).

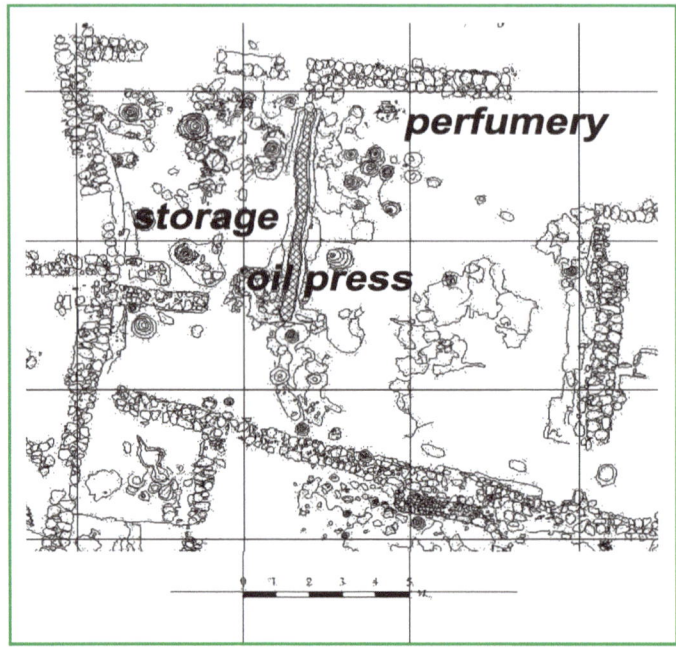

Fig. 10: Detailed map of olive oil press-room

For all its length, (18m) the Southern wall of the olive press room runs adjacent to copper working places. Near the Western corner there was a small passage of 80 cm, that led into a small rectangular room, which on the West related to the textile area. The large court for the processing of copper borders the southern wall and its Eastern extension, as the wall continues straight to the East for over 15m, including two sectors that seem to be part of the same metallurgical area. A second, smaller room on Western side was found equipped with 2 rough basins built of small stones and earth against the western wall, 2 storage jars, 7 large basins and a paraphernalia of other 25 vases. The remains of tartaric acid in many vessels and basins, and the presence of seeds of grapes suggest that the room was for storing wine. Eventually, according to the seasons, it is possible that the room was utilized for making more operations regarding winemaking.

2. A detached building, discovered and brought to light in 2008, south the olive press-room, has the same axial orientation. It is located between two roads that run in the industrial area. It has a triangular plan (Fig.11), perhaps due to a recovery episode of older structures partially collapsed or removed when a new road was opened in the direction of the Bronze Age necropolis. This evidence would explain the absence of a hypothetical continuation of the original walls, set directly on the bedrocks, which would be totally removed to preserve half of the building. In this case, the building should have been rectangular, including a small squared cell.

During the episode of rebuilding an entrance was created cutting the South-East corner (G10c) to maintain the triangular perimeter of the building. The first implant could date back to the end of the third millennium BC, as suggested by the two Philia earrings, ceramics diagnostic and axes of Neolithic type found there. The diagonal cut (hypotenuse), connecting the two ends of the triangle, emphasizes the massive appearance of the inner walls, creating a triangular niche effect, whereas the foundations of stones, set directly on the rock are a meter thick[10].

Fig. 11: A view of the triangular plan.

However, the comparison with other triangular structures used for worship in Cyprus and in Greece, leave open the possibility that the building was deliberately set in a triangular layout.

In Cyprus, we have the Aghia Irini (Kyrenia) Temenos famous for the 2000 clay figurines found around its altar, which was arranged in a triangular space, later close on one side to stop the flow of the stream. According to the report of the excavations, the most ancient altar of the Aghia Irini's Temenos was triangular.

The area investigated is included in a grid: squares B-M x 2-11, extending on natural terraces of basaltic pillow-lava, which originally stretched to 500 meters between the eastern bank of the river and the hill of Mavroraki.

Two parallel roads, which connect Pyrgos, with the village of Parrekklisha, joining west, border north and south the investigated area; meanwhile East and West there are two large villas. According to the different architectural remains, distribution of walls, diagnostic pottery, stone tools and fragments of stone vases, it seems that the area was first occupied during the end of the Neolithic period. After this episode, it was probably abandoned and reoccupied at the very end of the Chalcolithic until the end of the Middle Bronze II.

In establishing a relative chronology of Pyrgos it is important to note that for the full extension of the investigated area there are no structures that may be traced to episodes of resettlement

---

[10] A more detailed description is reported in: Belgiorno M.R. 2009: Progetto Pyrame: Pyrgos Ricerche Archeologiche e Archeometallurgiche, lo stato dell'arte a dicembre 2008, 87-97; in M.R. Belgiorno *Cipro all'Inizio dell'età del Bronzo*. 14-106. Gangemi Roma

after the abandonment of the site around 1700 BC. It therefore seems probable that the prehistoric site was never rebuilt after that event.

Moreover, material and structures dating back to Philia facies and Early Bronze Age I-III (2500-2000 BC) have been found under the ruins of the Middle Bronze age. Most interesting are the bronze objects characteristic of Philia facies, which represent most the metal objects found. The evidence suggests that the site probably inherited the technologies of Philia culture, perhaps together with its peculiar industrial organization. In the Middle Bronze Age, the site was completely reorganized, superimposing buildings on previous dwellings. In that period the village reached its maximum extension, becoming one of the largest in the Limassol area. The artefacts and stone tools testify to a continuous occupation of the site, with reuse of facilities and objects. Of course, the ruins brought to light belong mainly to the last occupation.

3. The natural terrace formed by merging blocks of pillow lava and basalt (Fig.12), which holds the site, spans only 6 meters over the southern limits of the expropriated area, as some years ago, the works to asphalt the road to Parrekklisha, lowered the level of two meters, destroying part of the ancient settlement.

Fig. 12: Pillow lava and basalt bedrocks close the remains of a circular building. Grid C11a.

On the preserved portion of the terrace, in 2009, embedded into the emerging basalt blocks of the bedrocks, have been found post holes, pits and remains of circular structures like the rounded remains of the walls brought to light in G 6-7 and K 5-6.

The new room found in 2009 seemed to belong to the very beginning of Middle Bronze Age and abandoned before the settlement. The huge dimensions of the stone foundations of the Eastern and Northern (a portion of 2 meters) walls suggested that the building was of some importance and that it was entirely detached from the triangular buildings previously highlighted on its East side.

The purpose of the excavation in 2012 was to complete the setting considering the room a normal house, not a workshop. On the contrary, it was found that the room belonged to a building used and reused for a long time for different activities. In fact, the large number of stone tools found in the room leaves no doubt on the industrial destination of the room, whose main entrance was on the western continuation of the inner road that separates the cult place by the industrial area.

4. The investigated sector is on the limits of the main road that bringing from Pyrgos to Parekklisha cancelled a large portion of the settlement.

Due to the exceptional rainy season that has flooded many times the site in autumn 2012, only one of the two rooms the Northwestern corner of the building was not excavated.

The main room (8x6 meters) is cloister shaped, with the roof missing in the middle. The stones of the foundations insist directly on the bedrock, composed of emerging basalt rocks and pillow lava. Contents comprise a different artefactual assemblage from that found elsewhere, mainly addressed in the production of cosmetics and jewellery.

5. Earthquake and Archaeometry. The intact archaeological layer, sealed by the collapsing of the structures due to the earthquake, together with the absence of later rebuilding, gave the possibility of systematic archaeometric investigations to find organic and inorganic material used in industrial activities (Fig.13).

Fig. 13: Alessandro Lentini at work in the ITABC-CNR laboratory

The investigations use X-Ray Fluorescence (XRF), Infrared Spectroscopy (IR), Chromatography, Fengel test (sulfuric acid +Dinaphthol under ultraviolet light), Gas-Chromatography, chemical, toxicological tests (the Halphen-Grimaldi method, the Bloor mixture, the Liebermann, Marquis, Bellier, Chen, Vitali, Bechi and McNally reactions and toxicological tests) for organic remains.

Meanwhile Optical Microscope observation, Ignate Coupled Plasma (ICP, Optical Spectrometer Perkins Elmer mod. 40), Energy Dispersive X-Ray Fluorescence (ED-XRF), X-Ray Diffraction (XRD), Scanning Electron Microscope observation (SEM) and Fourier Transform Spectroscopy (FTIR) are used in metals investigations. All the treated material, are conserved in the archive of ITABC-CNR, after consolidating for future investigations.

A program of Radiocarbon Calibration analyses (C 14) for the absolute chronology database is in progress, 9 samples of carbonized materials analysed by G. Calderoni of the University "La Sapienza" of Rome, gave a chronological range between the 1900-1800 B.C., and one between the 2350-2200 B.C.

Patterns of Metallurgy activity

1. Metallurgical industrial sites have specific characteristics and accessories. The amount of material on metallurgical sites can give an estimation of their importance in terms of time, number of people employed, local use and trade in objects and metal products. In short, six different components should be present to identify a site as "an industrial metallurgical site":

1) The proximity or availability of mineral resources and water.
2) The presence on the surface of a significant number of processed and unprocessed ore fragments (cracked, natural, partially roasted, roasted and glassy slag.)
3) The remains of objects and structures for the processing of copper such as crucibles, slagged pot sherds, nozzles, tuyeres, furnaces, bellows, benches, barriers to protect people from fire, and water channels.
4) The presence of stone tools, such as grinders, querns, mortars and pestles to crush ore and copper nuggets.
5) The presence of special tools to melt and refine objects such as moulds, anvils, hammers and burnishers.
6) Furthermore, regarding the importance of the relation between religion and copper production in Cypriot Late Bronze Age, the proximity to a cult building should be considered the 6th component.

2. By accident, the excavations at Pyrgos started from a sector (North on the map) where superimposed floors of pit furnaces, benches, querns, stone tools, mortars and slag showed the metallurgical destination of the place (Fig.14).

In primis, was considered that the place could belong to a coppersmith's house. However, the hypothesis falls soon, after discovering that the copper processing installations superimposed on earlier dwellings and directly connected with an olive press-room, as a second area completely equipped for copper production was found in 2005 adjacent the southern wall of the same olive press-room.

The total extension destined to the copper working was almost 600 sq. metres. In addition, the distribution of the reduction copper nuggets suggested the existence, of more rooms devoted to the same activity (Fig.18).

Regarding the number and distribution of the working places and implements, we realize that at Pyrgos there was an uncommon community well organized to produce artefacts of copper and bronze. To give an idea of the number of people involved I will try briefly to sum up the procedure to work the copper according with the evidence found at Pyrgos.

Fig. 14: A glimpse of the North metallurgical area. Grid I2d-I3b+J2c-J3a

3. After the mining of the ores, the first operation to obtain metal was the enrichment of the minerals. It consisted in crushing ores to facilitate the selection of the best pieces and reduce them in powder for the smelting. Numerous andesite querns and heavy pestles for this operation have been found, including heavy stone rings chipped all around the rim (appendix. Pontieri). However, any heap of waste remains has been found. The selection of the best pieces was important, as the percentage of the metal is proportional to the richness of the mineral smelted. The furnaces found in the Northern sector are of three types.

1) A large (1.80x 1, 80 metres circa) squared low depth (25 centimetres) cavity carved on the floor and bordered by 2 joined lines of small stones.
2) A cylindrical oven (base: 1 metre outside, 45 cm inside) built with stones disposed in superimposed circles, opened by side, and plastered inside.
3) A pit furnace (dim 30 cm inside) made of calcarenite earth, plaster, and very small stones.

4. In the central metallurgical area (Fig.15), the situation is quite different and all the evidence indicates that the main activities were the casting and refining of the copper objects.

The area is organised in a peculiar manner: a large quantity of calcarenite soil forms a sort of artificial heap in the centre of the room, and a large low bench built of small stones and plaster occupies two thirds of the back wall of the olive press-room starting from the East corner.

In front of this bench there is a battery of small ovens (pit furnaces) arranged inside the calcarenite heap. Each oven was found covered by a flat stone. The inside diameter of these ovens does not exceed twenty centimetres for a depth of thirty centimetres circa.

Fig. 15: Central metallurgical area. Grid I7c-d+I8a-b

More pit furnaces of the same dimensions are distributed irregularly on the top of the calcarenite heap. The ovens are covered in soil up to the top, and a large stone slab covers an opening of ten centimetres at the top. A small jug broken on the side, positioned upside down with the mouth pointed inside the oven, was found on two occasions close to the wall structure of the pit furnace (Fig.16).

Fig. 16: Small jug half burned, with a side spout (missing) found positioned on an oven I,8 b.

No fragments of clay tuyeres have been found, only of nozzles. On the Western side and on the Southern corner a labyrinth of small underground galleries suggests a pipeline connection to supply another line of small ovens. The area includes several ground stone tools (querns, pestles, hammers, rub stones, axes and anvils) found in the pits, on the bench and the floor. Two intact clay moulds for axes (23 and 20 centimetres in length) have been found in two adjacent different ovens in front of the main bench. A swage andesite anvil for shaping swords, with its hammers has been found near a sort of forging in the Eastern corner. More remains of metallurgical activity, including fragments of crucibles and copper reduction nuggets have been found scattered everywhere (Fig. 18). Two large jugs and three long spouted amphoriskoi together with ladle cups have been found collected in two groups near the bench and in the South-Western corner of the court. Some spindle whorls have been found on the bench together with small vases and two askoi. A further three spindle whorls were nearby the ovens on the West side.

4. Olive oil as fuel.

The material used as fuel by the ancient metallurgists is an important topic, as it involves many environmental, cultural, and social aspects. Up to the present little attention has been paid to the identification of possible different fuels used in prehistoric times, assuming that the charcoal has been the universal fuel used by all the coppersmiths. The traditional formula of Tylecote $CO+CuCO_3= 2CO_2 +Cu$ which explains the chemical reaction of the smelting of copper carbonates using the charcoal is not *a condition sine qua non*, and was not the only system known to smelt the copper in the Bronze Age. It is enough to remember the use of Bitumen in Sumerian civilisation since 3500 BC.

Even today, there are etno archaeological examples of the use of different fuels in the absence of charcoals in desert environments.

Probably, in finding copper furnaces remains there could have been a misunderstanding in the interpretation of the remains of wood (eventually carbonised) believed charcoal prepared in advance. Probably small pieces of dry wood (usually of olive trees) were used to start on the fire, but the pyroclastic procedure was carried on with the addition of a high calorific fuel to achieve the melting point. Necessity is the mother of invention and it is logical that all people had used the most available fuel resource. Probably, in Cyprus, at the beginning of the II millennium BC, what could be simpler that to make and use olive oil rather than charcoal, considering the difficulties of cutting down the trees with stone tools.

At Pyrgos, the peculiar distribution of the copper-working areas around the olive press-room, suggested from the beginning that there should have been some specific relation between the olive oil and the metallurgical activity.

In addition, there were few remains of charcoal inside and around the furnaces. Considering the amount of charcoal necessary to reach and maintain the copper smelting temperature and the number of the pit furnaces found, the remains are almost inconsistent.

Moreover, the small dimensions and the structure of the southern court ovens make difficult to fill up them with pieces of charcoal during the melting operation. However, it was very easy to fill them with olive oil, using a long reed inserted in a small jug positioned upside down or using a holed holding stone with a clay nozzle at the end of the reed. The use of olive oil has been confirmed by the analyses of the burned soil found in the furnaces and in many vases nearby.

To understand how the system worked and calculate how much olive oil was necessary for each operation, a series of archaeological experiments have been made at Pyrgos and in Italy in cooperation with Angelo Bartoli and his team of the Centre of Experimental Archaeology

"Antiquitates" of Blera. The furnaces have been reconstructed with the similar material, respecting dimension, and position of the bellows, connected with simple reeds covered by mud. Moreover, a small jug broken at the base has been embedded at the top of the oven, and used to drop the olive oil in the furnace using a long reed, which leaves the operator to stay far from the fire.

The experiments show that the system worked perfectly, and, regarding the use of olive oil as fuel, it is possible (after starting the fire with small pieces of dry wood) that olive oil was employed to reach and maintain the temperature to smelt or melt the metal. Normally 5 litres of oil are enough for a furnace of thirty cm in diameter (and a temperature of 1100 degrees). However, it is possible to reach a temperature of 1300 degrees with less (temperatures monitored with a thermocouple of chrome, aluminium) as demonstrated by a later proves made by Dr Livio Pontieri with a group of students coming from the Istituto Orientale di Napoli in 2010 (Fig. 17).

Fig.17: Livio Pontieri furnace working with olive oil: experimental season at Pyrgos in 2010.

The first laboratory analyses and the smelting experiments (made using the waste remains of the ores found around the furnaces) gave the following results.

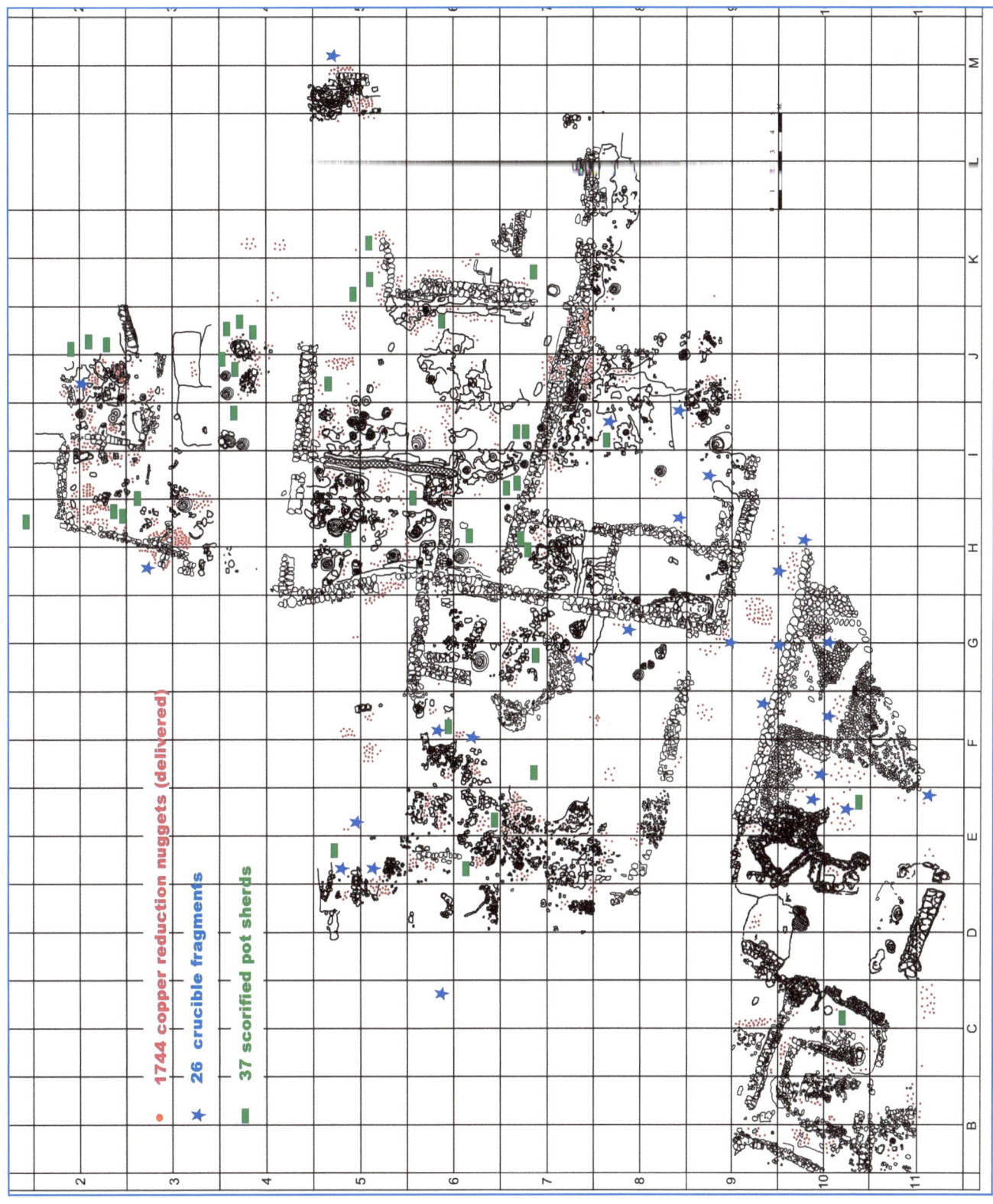

Fig. 18: Position of copper reduction nuggets, fragments of crucible and slagged pot fragments.

1) The ores come probably from Mavrorachi outcrops, as their mineral composition (in order of percentage of copper, iron, tin, arsenic, zinc, nickel and antimony) are very similar to the lumps of chrysocolle and malachite recovered on the slopes of Mavrorachi.

2) The powdered ores smelted at 900 degrees to produce a slag that includes many copper prills.

3) This slag smelted a second time produces a small quantity of copper and soft matrix rich in spherical copper inclusions that it is easy to recover crushing the lumps. At the end of the process, it is possible to obtain from 420 grams of ores 150 grams of slag and 30 grams of copper.

4) The slag found in the excavations (1500 lumps delivered to the Limassol Museum) have the same composition of the ores, and contain still a high percentage of copper. They are as hard as the slag product obtained after the first smelting in our experiments and melt at a low temperature, around 950 degrees.

5) A piece of slag (110 grams, officially exported in 2006) smelt in a crucible gives a second product of 30 grams consisting in a soft matrix slag imprisoning spherical drops of copper, like the second slag produced by our experiments, as easy to crush to collect the copper as the ores.

This does not demonstrate that the copper used at Pyrgos was smelted directly inside the industrial complex as the absence of large vast material suggests.

Anvil lithic packet.

1. The working stations set up with furnaces, benches and stone tools have been recovered in an abandoned state, as if something had suddenly forced people to leave. Some implements offer, the possibility to reconstruct the process of the making of bronze axes and knives, as well as other items refined by hammering.

The most functional objects found on these stations are the stone tools, mainly shaped by the user. Currently Pyrgos is the first Cypriot metallurgical site, which returned a complete set of these instruments.

The lithic repertoire does not differ greatly from the Neolithic period, apart from a new implement, the anvil, which we find in connection with the final hammering and refining of the metal objects. Axes and adzes are the elective tools often recycled from a previous use.

The appointive use was the cutting of the metal burbs after the casting, and the hammering of the blades before the final sharpening. The hammers are few in comparison with stone axes. For the sharpening, it was invented a new type of whetstone consisting of a curated bar perforated at one extremity. For this latter, there are close comparisons in the kit of Tomb 21 of Pyrgos believed to belong to a blacksmith of the Middle Bronze age.

Different from the Neolithic anvils used for breaking stone nuclei and chipping flints, the Coppersmith anvils of Pyrgos has a completely different texture and shape. The elective material is basalt and Gabbro, volcanic stones resistant to high temperatures (melt over 1450 °C while granite melts at 600-700 °C), largely present on territory in the form of large pebbles or boulders, often smoothed by atmospheric agents.

The shape of the anvil is usually a rectangular prism, the surface carefully smoothed for not leaving streaks and imprints on metal objects, during the working. Their shape is different according the use. For this reason, we have divided the repertoire in six typologies.

1 - **Portable anvil** (n°1462, kg 2,300) obtained from a basalt pebble. It is an irregular frusto-pyramidal hexahedron, with four working faces, completely smoothed and rounded (Fig. 19).

Fig.19: Portable anvil, Inv. n. 1462.

2 - **Portable horn handled anvil** (n°1543, kg 1,010) for jewellery or small items, it has a complex and articulate shape. A sturdy oblique foot extends below the rear end, squared in section, with a concave stop underneath the face, which makes possible to insert the object in a support (Fig. 20). The face has both the ends squared, tapering towards the tip, which has the left side slightly longer.

Fig. 20: Portable horn handled anvil, Inv.n.1543.

The anvil was sharpened to facilitate "the transverse volar-grip" of the left hand. The left side on top of the handle has a notch to accommodate the thumb and its carpal. The right side has an underneath recess for the other fingers, specifically made according to the imprints left by the hammering (cm. 9.5 x 14.8 x 6.2 + face 10 x 6> 4).

3 – **Two types of slab anvil:**

a) Flat slab anvil (n°1517, kg 9, 00) with a sort of step on one side to support the wrist or tools (Fig.21). The molten alloy was directly poured on it to obtain a rough bar or sheet, then finished by hammering on the proper anvil (cm 26 x 21 x 6, 7 + cm 11, 38 x 10, 3 x 21).

Fig. 21: Flat slab anvil, Inv. n. 1517.

b) **Flat, squared anvil** (n°3056 kg 1,997), rectangular, almost regular shape with double working faces (Fig.22). The type is very common in Early-Middle Bronze Age Spanish metallurgy (15 x 12-10, 7 x 5, 8).

Fig. 22: Flat squared anvil, Inv. n.3056.

4. Multifunctional anvil (n°409 kg 8, 00). It has a triangular prismatic shape, obtained from a rough triangular block cut and shaped into art (Fig. 23).

Fig. 23: Multifunctional anvil, Inv. n. 409.

It has five usable sides: two triangular faces (A and B) on the wide sides and three rectangular faces (C, D, and E) on the minor's sides. Each side shows several traces of use (cm. 23 x 23 x 20). Comparison with an anvil from La Bastida Spain of the faces A and B the hammering left a central rounded convexity. Face C has a deep and precise transverse groove (3 mm deep, at 9 cm from the one end).

The opposite end bends on the left side with a sort of short rounded horn. On both sides of the groove there is a convexity formed by the hammering, its extension corresponding to 3 cm to one side and 4 cm on the other. The groove and the lateral imprints, match to the shape and dimension of the sword/knives of the Early-Middle Bronze age with rib reinforcement. Face E has an extremely smooth surface on which it is possible to note the characteristic striations left after the burnishing of metal sheets.

5 - Bench anvil (n°87 kg. 6).

Rectangular parallelepiped, with four working faces (Fig. 24).

On the surface are well visible the extensive imprints left by the burnishing and hammering of metal objects (cm 22 x 11 x 12). It was found on the bench in front of the two furnaces containing each a clay mould for axes left in the heat. It was part of a peculiar set including half basalt quern shaped on side to host the anvil forming a multifunctional table to work the metal. It has an interesting comparison with an anvil of the same period, found in a

Coppersmith tomb in Spain containing a clay mould for axe too (T. n°3 Fuente Alamo, Argaric culture EBA). This circumstance suggests that this type of anvil was commonly used to refine the axes.

Fig. 24: Bench anvil, Inv. n. 87.

6 - Self standing anvil (n°188 kg 20,00).

The instrument is obtained from a huge block of basalt. It has a great stability due to the masterful workmanship (Fig. 25). The surface has been carefully hammered and smoothed except the base left rough. The top face is professionally worked to improve functionality. It has a rounded, pointed extremity, meanwhile the opposite ends with a step immediately after a deep groove, where it was possible to locate the rib of swords and knives during the sharpening of the blades (cm37 x 27,46 x12; face cm 21x10,74).

The simple squared types 1, 3b, 4, 5 have strong comparisons with some smaller contemporary Spanish anvils, with any groove.

After 4000 years, the comparison with the modern standard anvil shows the evolution of 3 key elements, which we find in embryonic form in type 4° (n°188) and 6° (n°409).

Fig. 25: Self standing anvil, Inv.n.188.

a- The face, which is the main flat surface, where most of the hammering takes place.
b- The horn on the "front" end of the anvil, which allows the smith to hammer different curves into the piece he is working on.
c- The step just below the face, whose edge is used to "cut" pieces while hammering.

Fig. 26: Particular of deep groove and the step just below.

Regarding the groove for the accommodation of the rib during the hammering, we found in France nice comparisons, which indicate that until a recent past this facility was well known.

Meanwhile, one portable anvil, available on the market, seems the perfect copy of the horn handled anvil n°1543. Considering these elements, Jock Dempsey affirms that an anvil has a face, heel, body, waist and feet as well as biological symmetry. The horn, which developed over time to a stylized yet organic looking rhinoceros horn is often considered a phallic device, but could also be recognizably albeit distractedly female, if we consider the cutting in the middle. This increases the visual identity of the anvil and reminds us that in central Africa the anvil is the "Mother" and the hammer the "Father"[11].

---

[11] Eugenia W. Herbert: Iron, Gender and power: rituals of transformation in African societies. 1993.

Other peculiar classes of metallurgical tools are the emery stones and burnishers for smoothing the metal plates are recognizable from the pyramidal shape and the characteristic base.

4. People involved.

To summarise the dimensions of the rooms devoted to metallurgical activities (in the limits of the area excavated) we have an extension of 600 square metres, which suggests that a considerable number of people were engaged in the processing of the copper. In addition to these activities, we have to consider the number of the people engaged in the exploiting of the copper ores and in the transportation to the factory.

Assuming that the mineral came from Mavrorachi, the distance was irrelevant, but if we consider the possibility that the outcrops exploited were as far as the mines of Mazokampos (6-7 kilometres North) or Kalavassos (25 kilometres North East), we have to calculate the engagement of more people. Moreover, the whole procedure required other people appointed in procuring and preparing food for metallurgists. The scenario is quite unforeseen for the current reconstructions of the Early-Middle Bronze Age society, as the direction and the organisation of such number of people should require more than a patriarchal control to run.

Moreover, it is not possible to estimate what relationships were among women and men in the organisation of the copper line processing, even if the evidence found in the excavations suggests that at Pyrgos the copper processing was not an exclusive male job. In particular, numerous spindle whorls have been found in the metallurgical area, near the working places and the furnaces, suggesting that the women normally frequented the place.

In addition, at Pyrgos we do not have evidence of a coppersmith workshop organised by a master with his own team, but evidence of a group of people working simultaneously on different correlated activities. Considering the possibility of women employed in the copper processing. I would like to point out that until recently women were normally engaged in the smelting process of the metals, employed especially in the choosing of the pieces of minerals after the crashing and in recuperating the drops of metal after the smelting[ii]. Moreover, assuming that the spinning was an exclusively female art and using the presence of the spindle whorls as "fossil index", we can presume that at Pyrgos the women had some roles in the metallurgical industry.

5. Social aspects

In examining the different archaeological and Archaeometry results discussed during the present seminar, I would like to try to give a social interpretation of what we found. First, in 2000 BC Pyrgos, we are witnessing a social evolution that led to the determination of aggregate lines within a community, which create the participation and the emerging of different spheres of social life.

Ideally, we can start from the first spheres that are the largest ones, which in turn contain the smallest: village, food and resource production, cemetery, goods production and trade.

In Neolithic Cyprus, we have the formation of the first community sphere, the village that lives of the territory resources, whose exploitation is the second sphere of aggregation, essential for life and social progress. Both are types of aggregation characteristic of the Neolithic revolution, born from the social extension of the family in the tribe, which, it was assumed to have a patriarchal organisation that managed the social relations of the small community.

Towards the end of the Neolithic period, we are witnessing the gradual evolution of a third sphere of aggregation, the necropolis, in which the living community moved into dead community, maintaining its principles of social gathering and family distinction. We recognize these principles in the typology of grave and funerary ritual that require a background of religious beliefs and superstitions linked to a cultural tradition that unconsciously started to have a cultural identity aware of some historical memory.

What we are discussing, is the existence at Pyrgos of a fourth and fifth sphere of aggregation that of industry and market, linked to the area mainly occupied by workshops producing different goods.

Anchorages, objects coming from the North Cyprus and abroad, small objects used to count and register the production as (tokens, cretulae ecc ecc) suggest the existence of the fifth sphere. What includes different economic interests and requires the employ of a number of organised people that appear as the real innovation of Pyrgos.

The industrial complex may belong to the Middle Bronze Age, even if the chronology is relative, as we do not know if the industrial area started to be organised in the Early Bronze age. The complex seems not organised according to the general parameters of the time. It was not common the people going to work far from home, in a collective determined area if they are not under a precise organisation, power, or control, such as a "Palace" administration.

The mere existence of the industrial area inside a large settlement, suggests that at Pyrgos the nature of the central organisation of labour had some ideological aspects.

Fig.27: Pyrgos' scenic vase, Tomb 35, Inv.n.16-17, Limassol Archaeological Museum.

We have evidence in other cultures of industrial area organised within the temple and palace complexes suggesting the existence of a control system over production of luxuries and commodities. In Pyrgos there is any evidence of this kind of control. A detail that points to the absence of a ground ideology linked to the idea of luxury items produced by a central organisation of labour, in contrast with the opinion of some scholars (Oppenheim and Crawford in regarding Mesopotamia) who see in the production of luxuries the employ of surpluses, under a sort of ideology far from economic interests.

Again, I must remind the absence at Pyrgos of any administrative evidence or structural control over people or commodities at their various stages of production. We do not have any idea about the number of people involved in various jobs, or any reference to the hierarchy position within the community, except for the representation on the famous Pyrgos' vase (from Tomb n° 35) of a gentleman in the chair positioned in the middle of people busy in different jobs. We can only argue that each production required a trained clear-cut organised workforce and a well-controlled agriculture production, probably involving most of the inhabitants at certain times of the year for sowing and reaping. Overall, the presence of a storage room inside the perimeter of the olive press, suggests that could be a redistribution of goods, in this case the olive oil, addressed to domestic and industrial uses (per Bottero theory).

In any case, the model is far from the common degrees of power represented by the temple or palace economies. It belongs to an institution, which does not differ from the extended-family unit. A community which produced surpluses and exchanged luxury items not owing any form of power control or administration, which requires the exhibition of violence in administrating the power that seems completely unknown in Cypriote communities, as it was never represented in coroplastic models. The male person often reproduced on a chair, seems to have more an ideological power, such as that of a wise aging man, that the power of life and death of people in subjection.

It seems that Pyrgos' organisation was addressed to specific productions that did not need a monumental structure to run, but a space organised and unitary to arrange working places for several people. Situation even more interesting when you consider that there are all the elements of a medieval alchemical laboratory[12].

The architecture of the complex, in which the people used to go to work together, was linked with many common facilities, which included disposability of stone tools, irrigation, extensive agriculture, gathering, transporting and provision of organic and inorganic material from land and sea. One of the main facilities seems to have been the central olive press-room, that represents an index of a system born by economic and cooperative motives.

---

[12] If we compare the material of the alchemical laboratory found in 1980 at Kirchberg am Wagram in Austrian Oberstockstall we can identify the Pyrgos industrial complex as a proto alchemical community area: Sigrid von Osten, "Das Alchemistenlaboratorium Oberstockstall. Ein Fundcomplex des 16. Jahrhunderts aus Niederosterreich" PhD dissertation Universitata Wien 1992; Rudolf Werner Soukup and Helmut Mayer, Alchemistisches . Martelli M. 2011: Greek Alchemists at Work: 'Alchemical Laboratory' in the Greco-Roman Egypt, Nuncius 26, 271–311. Martinon-Torres M. 2012: The Archaeology of Alchemy and Chemistry in the Early Modern World: An Afterthought in Archaeology International No. 15, 2011-2012, 33-36.

Furthermore, in the absence of any evidence of centralised power we wonder which kind of ideology is behind the creation of the industrial complex of Pyrgos. Probably we can find a suggestion in Cypriot coroplastic of the time, which seems addressed to underline the level of knowledge of the island giving it a plastic body after the representations. The power and pride of the reached level are clearly expressed in them, together with the necessity to trade and preserve that knowledge for future generations using imagining of it. The iconographic motives become a transfer of technological knowledge from past to future, suggesting methodologies, social organisation, identities, and religious implications. In this regards the role of artisans and the organisation of the Pyrgos industrial area takes form and we can start understanding the ideology behind it. Even if it remains to understand completely the social organization of the artisans and their identities, dealing with interconnections between crafts, society, and arts, it appears evident their attachment to an independent status or elite, and concern to transmit of the knowledge over time.

According to the chronology of models and vase decorations representing objects, implements and moments of life, this happened in a relatively short span of time, around the end of Early Bronze age and the beginning of Middle Bronze age. On these objects, we can find the need and pride to testify and transmit the knowledge of an acquired level of life and technology, we will not find anything of similar before or after[13] this period, which approximately find the same end of Pyrgos' settlement at the close of Middle Bronze age II.

REFERENCES

-Bear L.M. 1963: Geological Map of Cyprus, scale: 1: 250,000. *The Mineral Resources and Mining Industry of Cyprus. Geological Survey Department of Cyprus. Bulletin n°1.* Nicosia.

-Belgiorno M.R. 1999: Preliminary report on Pyrgos excavation 1996-1997, in *Report of the Department of Antiquities,* Cyprus. Nicosia.

-Belgiorno M.R. 2000: Project "Pyrame" 1998-99, Archaeological, Metallurgical and Historical Evidence at Pyrgos (Limassol), in *Report of the Department of Antiquities, Cyprus,* Nicosia, 1-17.

-Belgiorno M.R. 2001: Rescue Excavated Tombs of the Early and Middle Bronze Age from Pyrgos (Limassol). Part I. in *Report of the Department of Antiquities, Cyprus* Nicosia 2000, 34-70.

-Belgiorno M.R., A. Lentini & G. Scala 2006: The textile industry (2000 BC) of Pyrgos-Mavroraki (Cyprus), in *Archaeological Textiles Newsletter 2006.* Copenhagen, 25.30.

-Belgiorno M.R. 2008: El aceite de oliva en la prehistoria mediterrànea: el caso de Chipre, in: *Tierras del Olivo exposiciòn en Jaen, Baeza, Ubeda, Baema. Diciembre 2007-April 2008.* Immaculada Cortes, Carmen Pozuelo de, (El Legado Andalusi, Espana, 35-51.

-Belgiorno M.R., A. Lentini 2008: A. Paleoethnobotany investigations at the site of Pyrgos-Mavroraki, Cyprus, *International Symposium on Archaeometry*, Kars H., Meyers P. and Wagner C.A. Editors, 37. Siena, 296-297.

-Belgiorno M.R., A. Lentini 2008: Image Analysis and Measurement Applied to the Archaeological Material from Pyrgos (Cyprus), in *Remote Sensing in Archaeology and the Management*

---

[13] Later similar representations are linked to cult place and ritual offerings.

of Cultural Heritage, Lasaponara R. and Masini N. Eds, Aracne Editrice, Roma. 419-423.

-Belgiorno M.R. 2008: Lana e olio d'oliva binomio vincente nell'industria tessile, in *Atti del II° Convegno Nazionale di Etnoarcheologia, Mondaino 17-19 marzo 2004,* Francesca Lugli, Alessandra Assunta Stoppiello eds. BAR 184, Archeo Press. international series, 48-54.

-Belgiorno M.R. 2009: New suggestions from Pyrgos/Mavrorachi on Cypriote 2000 BC proto-industrial society and its gender perspective, *Proceedings from the International Conference "Finds and Results from the Swedish Cyprus Expedition 1927-1931: A Gender Perspective"* March 31- April 2, 2006, Medelhavsmuseet, Stockholm, Sweden. Medelhavsmuseet Focus on the Mediterranean V, Stockholm, 50-63.

-Belgiorno M.R. 2009: Progetto Pyrame: Pyrgos Ricerche Archeologiche e Archeometallurgiche, lo stato dell'arte a dicembre 2008, in: M.R. Belgiorno ed. *Cipro all'inizio dell'Eta' del Bronzo: Realtà sconosciute della comunità industriale di Pyrgos/Mavroraki,* Gangemi ed. Roma, 13-105.

-Bottero J. 1967: The First Semitic Empire, in J. Bottero (ed.), The Near East: Early Civilisations. London; 110-18.

-Craddock P.T. 1986: Report on the Composition of Bronzes Excavated from the Middle Cypriot Site at Episkopi Phaneromeni and Some Comparative Cypriot Bronze Age Metalwork, in The Kent State University Expedition to Episkopi Phaneromeni.Part II, S. Swiny ed. SIMA 74 (2), Nicosia, 153-158.

-Crawford H. 1973: Mesopotamia's Invisible Exports in 3rd Millennium BC, World Archaeology 5(2): 232-241.

-Calderoni G. 2009: Diagrammi di calibrazione per le età C-14 convenzionali misurate per il sito di Pyrgos-Mavroraki, Cipro, in M.R. Belgiorno a cura di, *Cipro all'inizio dell'Eta' del Bronzo: Realtà sconosciute della comunità industriale di Pyrgos/Mavroraki,* Gangemi, Roma. 188-194.

-Dothan T. and A. Ben-Tor 1983: Excavations at Atheniou, Cyprus 1971-1972. Jerusalem: Ahva Press.

-Gabrielli R., Iuliano T., Mauriello P., Peloso P. & D. Monna 2004: Application of resistivity survey in the Mediterranean area, *ISAP News Issue No. 1, May,* Shrewsbury, Shropshire. SY5 6WH UK. 10-11.

-Gass I.G., Macleod C.J., Murton B.J., Panayiotou A., Simonian K.O., Xenophontos C. 1994: The Geology of the Southern Troodos Transform Fault Zone. *Geological Survey Department of Cyprus Memoir. 9,* Nicosia.

-Giardino C. 2000: Prehistoric copper activity at Pyrgos, in *Report of the Department of Antiquities of Cyprus, Nicosia,* 19-32.

-Giardino C., G.E. Gigante, S. Ridolfi 2002: Archaeometallurgical investigations on the Early-Middle Bronze Age finds from the area of Pyrgos (Limassol), in: *Report of the Department of Antiquities of Cyprus. Nicosia,* 33-48.

-Giardino C. & S. Rovira 2007: Pyrgos-Mavroraki (Cyprus): copper smelting slag of the beginning of second Millennium B.C., *Proceedings of the 2nd International Conference "Archaeometallurgy in Europe 2007,* AIM Milano, file 153 eBook.

-Henson F.R.S., Browne R.V. & J. Mc Ginty 1949: A synopsis of the stratigraphy and geological history of Cyprus, in *Quarterly Journal of the Geological Society*; v. 105; issue.1-4; Dorchester, 1-41.

-Lentini A. & G. SCALA 2006: Aromatic and therapeutic substances from the prehistoric site of Pyrgos-Mavrorachi (Cyprus), in: Belgiorno M.R. ed. *Cyprus Aromata, Olive Oil in Perfumery and Medicaments in Cyprus 2000 B.C.*, Edizioni Eranuova, Perugia 2006, 219-243.

-Lentini A. 2009: Tra Archeologia e Archeometria, Archeologia ePaesaggio Naturale: Indagini archeobotaniche e fisico chimiche, in Belgiorno M.R. ed. *Cipro all'inizio dell'Età del Bronzo, Realtà Sconosciute della Comunità Industriale di Pyrgos Mavrorachi*, Gangemi Editore, Roma, 129 - 187.

-Maddin R.J.D. Muhly and T.S. Wheeler. 1983: Metalworking. in Excavations at Atheniou, Cyprus, 1971-1972, edited by T. Dothan and A. Ben-Tor 132-8. Qedem Monographs of the Institute of Archaeology, Hebrew University, Jerusalem. Jerusalem: Hebrew University

-Morel S.W. 1964: The geology of Parekklisha area. Unpublished Cyprus Geological Survey Department Report, Nicosia.

-Moussolos L. 1957: Contribution A l'etude des gisements de pyrite cuivreuse de l'ile de Chypre. Recherches geologiques et mineres dans le region de Kalavassos, *Annales Geol. Pays Helleniques [Athens], ser. 1*, Athens, 269-ff.

-Oppenheim A. 1954: 'The Seafaring Merchants of Ur', Journal of the American Oriental Society 74: 6-17.

-Pantazis T.M. 1967: The geology and mineral resources of the Pharmakas-Kalavasos Area. *Memoires. Geological Survey Department Cyprus, 8*. Nicosia.

-Pantazis T.M. 1978: Cyprus Evaporates. Initial Reports of the Deepsea Drilling Project, Washington 42, U.S. Government Printing Office Washington, 1185-1194.

-Prichard H.M. & Maliotis G. 1998: Gold mineralization associated with low temperature, off-axis, fluid activity in the Troodos Ophiolite, Cyprus, in *Journal of the Geological Society*, 155, London. 223-231.

-Schmidt W.F. 1960: Zur Struktur und Tektonik der Insel Cypern, *Geologische Rundschau*, Berlin/Heidelberg, v.50, n°1, Berlin 1960, 375-395.

-Swiny S. 1986: *The Kent State University Expedition to Episkopi Phaneromeni, Part II*. Studies in Mediterranean Archaeology, 74:2. Nicosia: Paul Astrom Forlag, Goteborg 1986.

2 THE INGREDIENTS OF THE CYPRIOT PREHISTORY IN THE COSMETICS OF THE 3rd MILLENNIUM

Gianfranco Todisco

We will now try to glimpse the possible connections which link present cosmetics to the cosmetics of Pyrgos such as researchers and archaeologists describe it.

To do so, we will trace a rather bold itinerary by intentionally maximising every possible slight connection between two ages so distant from one another. So distant that the whole reference system to which what we now identify as "cosmetics" used to belong has entirely changed, causing frustration to any possible linear reconstruction.

We can summarize by saying – with a word that belongs to semiology – that cosmetics has deeply altered its significance.

By doing so, cosmetics has opened its way, as we will see, to vaster and basically laic scenery. Research of a guideline that would let us approach – in a less daring way – the problems that occur when considering two ages so distant between each other, has lead me to consider the etymology of the word "cosmetic".

We will have the opportunity – during our time travel – to recall a character who is closely concerned with cosmetics and with cosmetic powders.

In fact, next year it will be the 180th anniversary of the first modern non-toxic mascara and the person from whom I'll borrow the definition of cosmetics is Eugène Rimmel, (fig.1) the man who, at the peak of the chemistry revolution, produced the first modern non-toxic synthetic mascara. Therefore, he did not invent anything new. The Egyptians used their kohl a few millenniums before him.

Fig.1: Eugene Rimmel

Rimmel (Fig.1) lead the word "cosmetics" back to Cosmos allowing suggestions that the term may etymologically refer to an original concept of adorning, arranging, sorting.

It is of course, as we know, the Gods' duty to arrange and sort the world and its elements, and therefore it is the Gods who manage the affairs that refer to a given order even if these are libertarian and intriguing ones such as beauty, attraction, and sensuality.

Yet, we should not be astonished if in the history of the civilization which originates in the Fertile Crescent, lays the foundations and sets the imprinting of Western culture in the Greek region, the image of beauty is more often bound to Goddesses.

After Inanna and Ishtar, Aphrodite and Venus are the Goddesses who will tell the world of Mediterranean civilisation.

When the eclipse of the Gods and the Goddesses (beaten by consequential traumas) will slowly come to an end, cosmetics (the servant of refined and cherished beauty) will slowly branch out and loose its sacredness to the point that men will claim the right to manage it.

Women, beauty & cosmetics

However, for a long time only women will define beauty and cosmetics. Let me introduce you some other woman linked to cosmetics. Just a little hint to Isabella Cortese, active in Venice, who wrote "The secrets of Lady Isabella Cortese "in 1561 where cosmetics were also prepared through operations of alchemical distillation. Unfortunately, we have no portrait of Isabella Cortese. Before her Caterina de 'Medici, an Italian woman, (Fig.2) diffused increasingly the elegance of perfume in France.

The last one is Anne Marie de Tremouille, wife of Prince of Nerola (Fig.3).

She diffused the orange blossoms fragrance in France. The fragrance we call Neroli.

Fig. 2: Caterina de'Medici

Fig. 3: Anne Marie de Tremouille

In 1828, the world has changed.
Friedrich Wohler (Fig.4) obtained through synthesis a natural substance in his laboratory. But in some ways, the goddesses of the perfume punished him.
The substance that Wohler was able to produce synthetically had a very bad smell. The first product obtained by synthesis was **urea.**
But since then, more or less all the perfumed molecules present in nature have been reproduced synthetically.

Fig. 4: Friedrich Wohler

Beauty and cosmetics

In the last recent decades, the concept of beauty and cosmetics has changed a lot. Let's look at the definition of health given by the World Health Organization.

"Health is a state of complete physical, mental and social well-being and not merely the absence of disease or infirmity."

This way, we can say that feeling beautiful even using cosmetics, has become part of the concept of health. However, which cosmetic today is more close to the natural scents of Pyrgos?

Organic cultivation and cosmetic products

Cosmetic products which are closer to the natural world are currently the ones that, with regard to the plants used, comply with the rules of organic (biological) cultivation.

Many of the perfumes produced in Pyrgos were oleolites. We know that is oils that took the scent of the plants that were left into infusion.

In the modern cosmetics industry oleolites are rare, but essential oils, by contrast, are widely used. Let see what the European Pharmacopoeia says about essential oils.

Essential oils are: "Odorous products, usually of complex composition, obtained from a Botanically defined plant raw material by steam distillation, dry distillation, or a suitable mechanical process without heating". In the United States, they say an even more precise thing: Essential oils .... "They may be distilled with steam and / or water, or mechanically pressed. Oils that are made with chemical processes are not considered true essential oils". *So, the current distillation process is identical to the one used here in Cyprus more or less than four thousand years ago.*

Fig. 5: Replica Pyrgos stiil 50% scale

Distillation:

What you see (Fig.5) is a reconstruction of Pyrgos' still. A modern distiller has few differences compared with the most ancient contrivances built in Cyprus (Fig, 6).

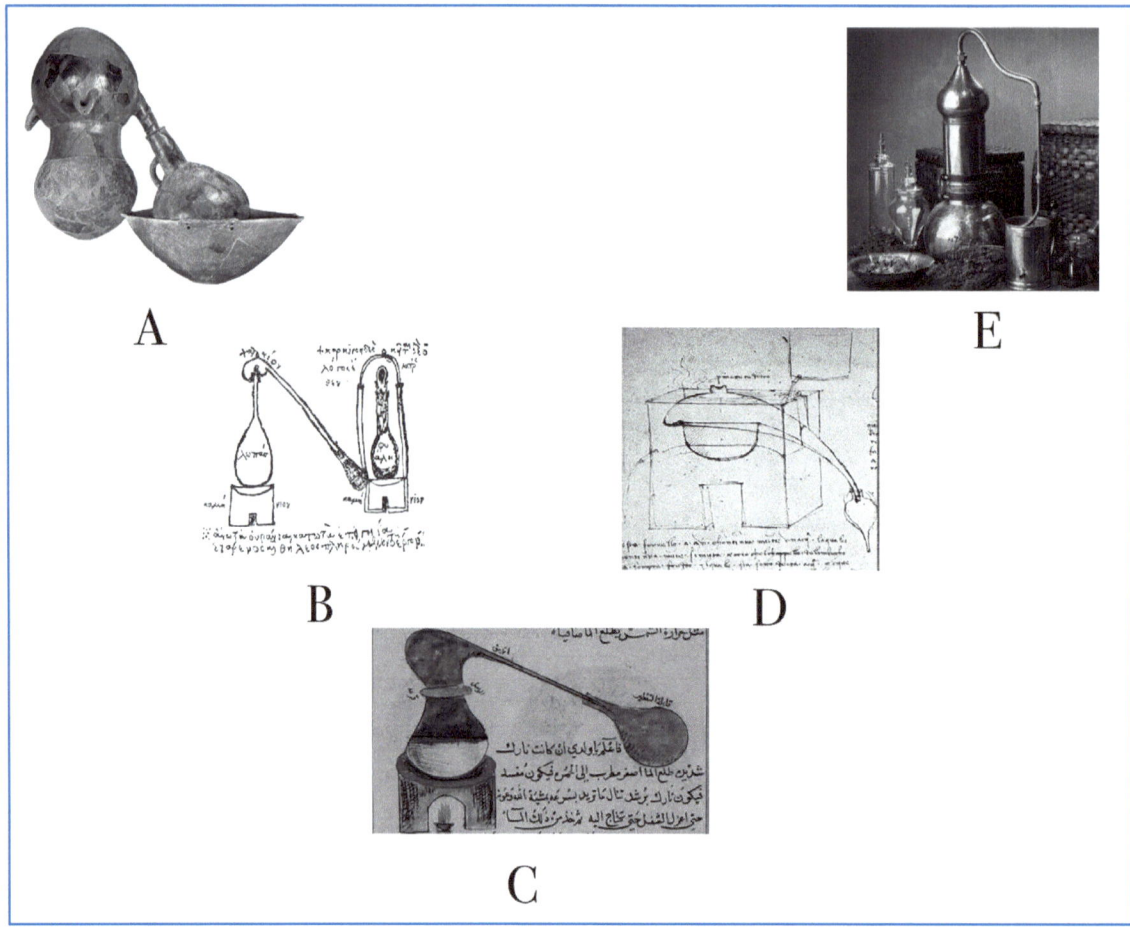

Fig. 6: From left to right: A) Pyrgos still B) the design of the still as it can be found in some Greek manuscripts that talk about distillation C) Arab still D) a drawing of a still by Leonardo da Vinci E) modern copper still; nothing has changed.

Old scents of Pyrgos

Now we can start seeing which plants produced the old "scents" of Pyrgos.

Obviously in Pyrgos they used local plants. To be clear, I have grouped (Fig.7) the plants used in Pyrgos following their botanical classification. We will see later which ones among these fragrances belong to the modern cosmetics.

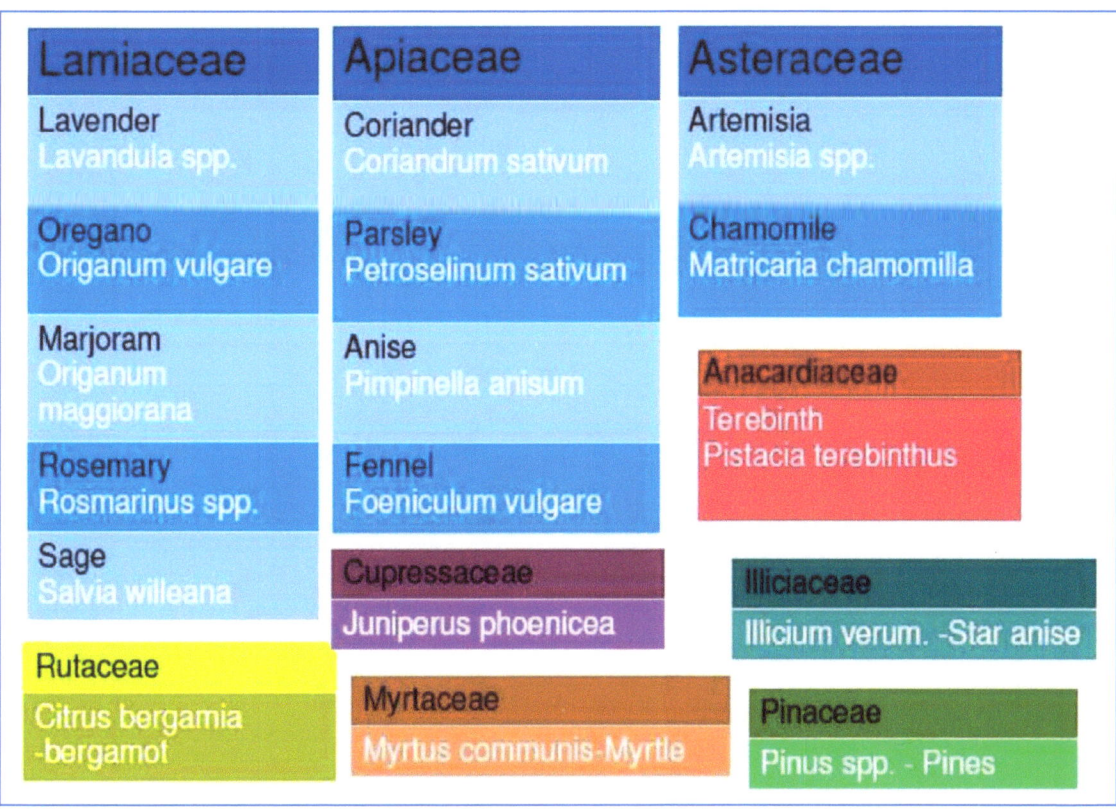

Fig. 12: Plants found at Pyrgos

Fig. 8: Aleppo soap

Among these there is a plant that is among those used in Pyrgos and which is still used mainly in soap manufacture. We must not forget that the soap is the most widely used cosmetic product all over the world. I'm talking about laurel and about the soap of Aleppo. Aleppo soap (Fig.8) is made with olive oil and laurel oil. We know that olive oil was the basic element of every production in Pyrgos.

Lavender

Another plant used was lavender. We can ask ourselves if today while smelling a flower of lavender we feel the same perfume that Cypriots of 3800 years ago felt. Unfortunately, the answer is negative because 99% of lavender used today in the cosmetic product comes from relatively recent hybridizations. (Fig.9)

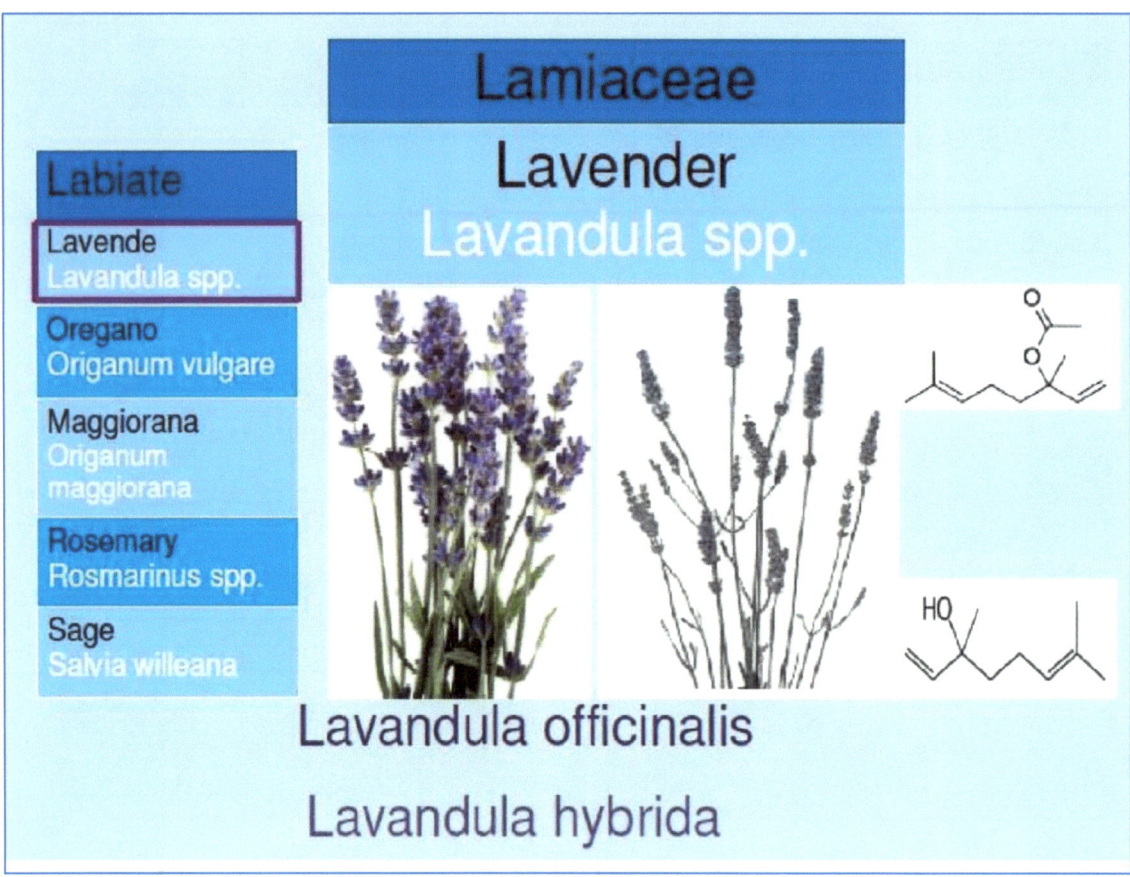

Fig. 9: Lavender

The knowledge of the real and presumed properties of lavender is widespread. There are entire cosmetic lines dedicated to lavender essential oils to which other essential oils are added in lower percentages. The lavender essential oil is part of the composition used in anti-cellulite blends with oregano and thyme.

Oregano

The oregano which is also present in Pyrgos, is used today also in some products to prevent hair loss, even though there is no clear evidence in this regard.

Rosemary

Another important plant present in Pyrgos and is still used today is Rosemary. Today in natural cosmetics we tend to differentiate the essential oil of rosemary according to its composition. (Fig.10)

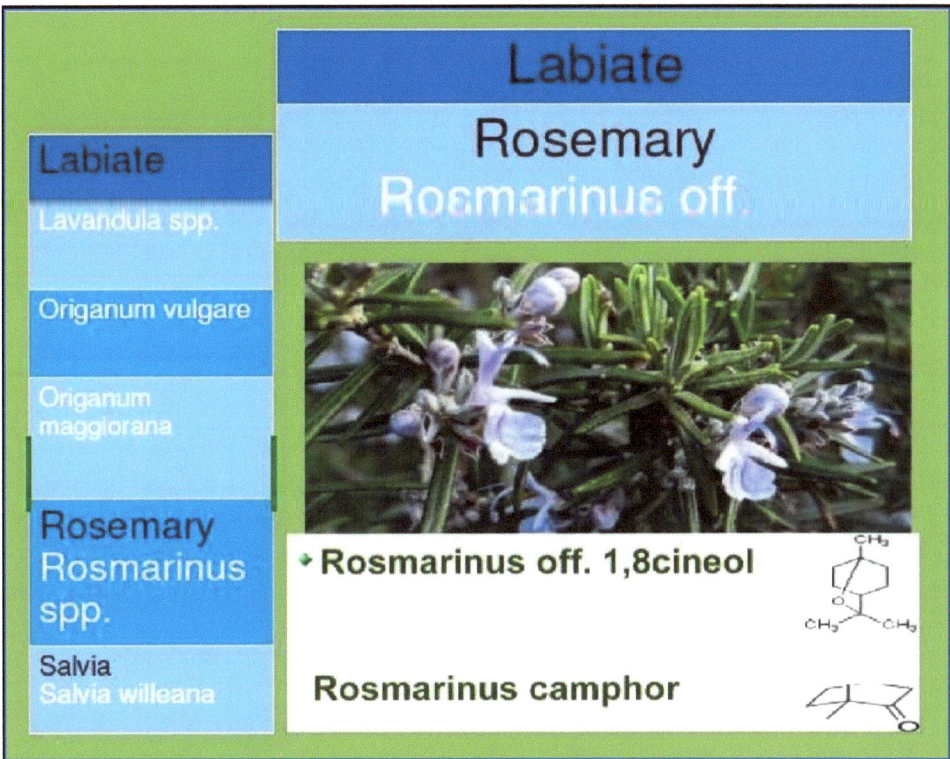

Fig. 10: Rosemary

Sage used at Pyrgos

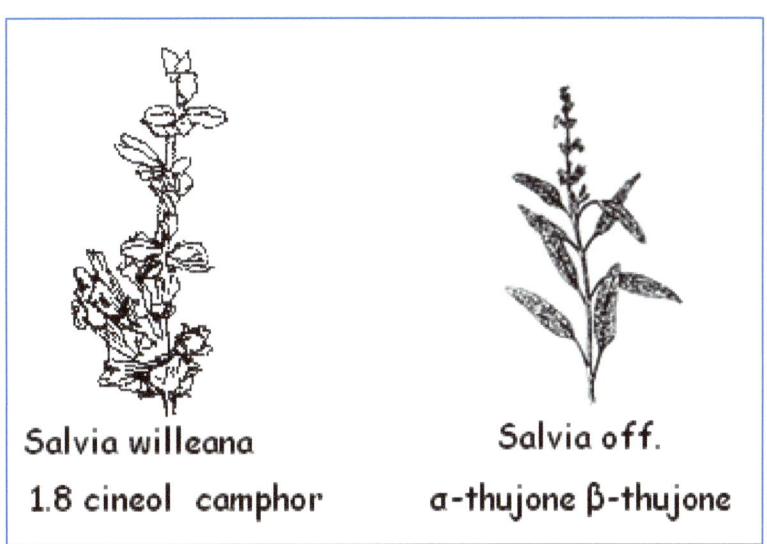

Fig. 11: Comparison between willeana and officinalis

The sage (Salvia willeana) that was used in Pyrgos has an essential oil that is very different from the essential oil of salvia officinalis which is used today in many after shave lotions especially in the U.S. (Fig.11).

Pine trees

If a few decades ago many bath products contained essential oils derived from pine trees, presently bath products contain essential oils extracted from other plants

Before talking about the real perfumes, I would like to add that today, the trend is to put many essential oils in the same product primarily to obtain a pleasant odour.

About organic cosmetic cost, today the price difference between a cosmetic obtained with organic raw materials and a non-organic cosmetic is decreasing and this is a good sign.

The Bergamot

The Bergamot, that researchers tell us that it could be found in Pyrgos, deserves a separate speech. In history, the most important perfume in which bergamot is used is *the eau de cologne Jean Marie Farine* derived from the Zur Stadt Mailand o Aqua mirabilis de Cologne (Koeln) of the seventeenth century.
Today, major perfume companies still use bergamot which is also able to stabilize the various components of certain perfumes. Now we come to our days.

Beginning

More than thirty years ago in the seventies and eighties some perfume companies started using again natural substances (Fig.12). Here are four examples: Aromatics Elixir, Polo by Ralph Lauren, Kouros by Yves Saint Laurent and Egoiste Platinum by Chanel.

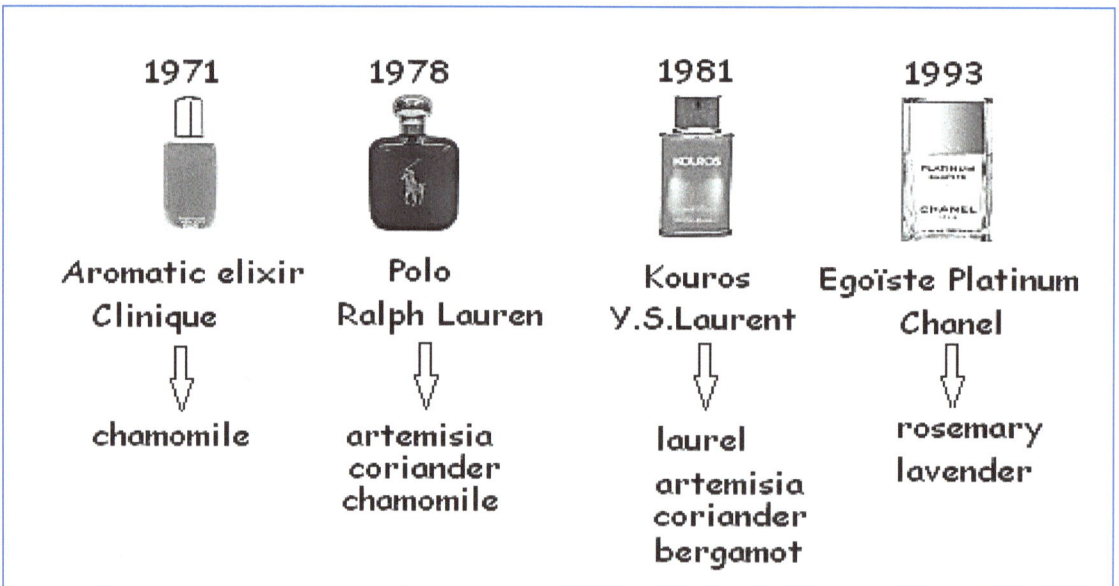

Fig. 12: Example of perfumes with natural substances.

The interesting thing is that for the first time their logic was to use natural scented substances with the intent to produce an overall well-being. We can say that they were working in the logic of aroma-chology. To clarify the term in aroma-chology we can say that that the scent is everything, in aromatherapy the plant is everything. Kouros is also important for another reason:

it is perhaps the first, or at least one of the very few perfumes that also uses fragrances derived from Chamomile.

You're seeing some old perfume, but in recent years it is always the same story (Fig.13).

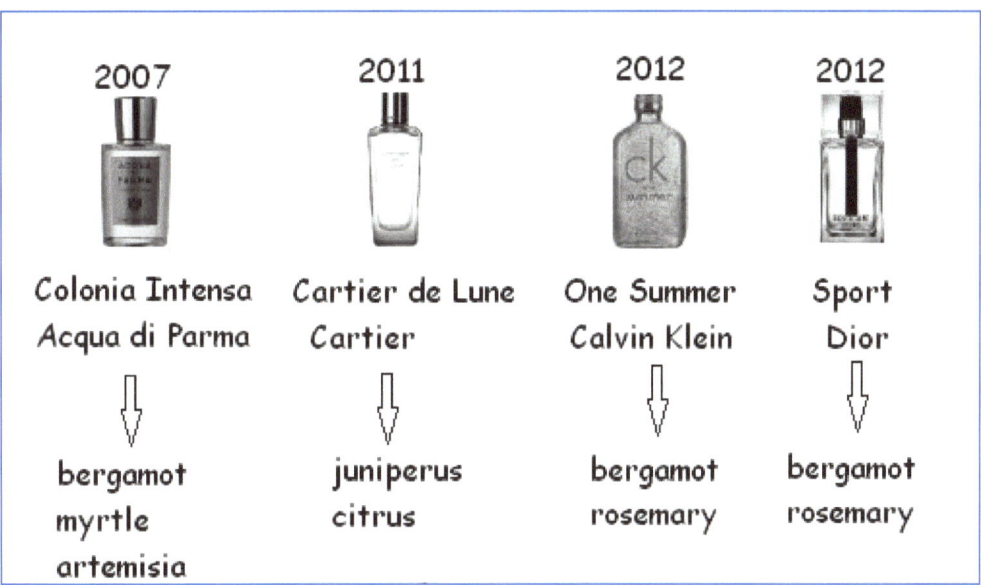

Fig.13: Modern perfumes with natural substances

We do not have a great knowledge regarding the cosmetic properties attributed to plants used in Pyrgos almost four thousand years ago, but we hope that the work of archaeologists and scholars of your island will be able to tell it to us and to the whole world.

REFERENCES

-Bariletto G. 1561: *I Secreti de la Signora Isabella Cortese pe' quali si contengono cose minerali, medicinali, artificiose e alchemiche e molte de l'arte profumatoria appartenenti a ogni gran Signora.* Venezia.

-Belgiorno M.R. 2014: *Il Profumo di Cipro*, Gangemi Roma.

-Bettiol F., Vincieri F. 2009: Manuale delle preparazioni erboristiche, Tecniche Nuove Milano.

-Harris R. 1991: Inana-Ištar as paradox and a coincidence of opposites, in *History of Religions* 30: 261- 78.

-Leick, G. 1994: *Sex and Eroticism in Mesopotamian Literature.* Routledge, London.

-Levey M. 1956: Babylonian chemistry: a study of Arabic and second millennium BC perfumery, in: *Osiris* Vol. 12, 376-389.

-Levey M. 1960: A group of Akkadian texts on perfumery, *Chymia Revue d'histoire des sciences* Vol. 6 (1960), 11-19.

-Leonie F. 2011: *Catherine de Medici: A Biography*. Orion, Hachette UK

-Rimmel E. 1865: *Book of Perfumes*. Chapman and Hall, London.

-Senatore F. 2000: *Oli essenziali. Provenienza, estrazione ed analisi chimica*. EMSI. Roma

3. COSMETICS

Maria Rosaria Belgiorno

"Nature delights in nature,

Nature conquers nature,

Nature controls nature"

*Democritus 200 BC: *Treatise, Physical and Mystical Matters"*[14]

Several elements make Pyrgos a case of production and trade. Among them, we can consider the strategic location, the availability of natural resources and the division of roles, results of a cultural revolution born within the Cypriot society at the beginning of the second millennium BC. During this period, the agricultural production was in fact supported by craft activities dedicated to the production of prestige goods for domestic and foreign trade. It is therefore conceivable, in consideration of the historical and archaeological data, that at the time, many settlements of Cyprus had commercial areas like the Pyrgos' one.

The excavation brought to light workshops producing prestige goods as bronzes, jewellery, fine fabrics, perfumed ointments, pharmaceutical preparations, and cosmetics in an area located at the centre of the settlement. There were all goods in great demand from the Mediterranean market, which found in those products merits of quality that made the island home of wellness and beauty later identified in the native country of Aphrodite goddess of love and eternal youth. In Early Middle Bronze age, we are at the origin of a legend that survived wars, occupations and religions, and still is in charge today when you want to bring to the market a new luxury product, a perfume or a cosmetic that promises miraculous results.

---

[14]Diels H. 1924: *Antike Technik* 3, Leipzig; repr. 1965, Osnabriick 1965, 121-54; Kroll W. 1934: Bolos und Demokritos, *Hermes* 69, 228-32.

1. Meaning of word cosmetics

The use of cosmetics is the result of a critical path towards yourself, which leads to change your appearance through artifices, ornaments, and magic-pharmaceutical remedies. Transformation of your own image according to personal choices, gives you a kind of power-safety in the pleasure of being able to deceive or impress people who look at you.

It is not by chance that the word "cosmetic" refers to the Greek word for beauty, but also conveys ideas of totality and absolute order. Cosmetology, like writing, was a sophisticated technology for organising and managing social interaction, strategically linked to development of early urban civilisation. In ancient times, the cosmetic art precariously swayed between the look-up for the physical well-being and outer beauty: between the security to be and to appear.

Whereas, the role of makeups and ornaments was that to externalize possession of resources, to beautify the appearance and to communicate a visual message on the identity and dignity of the person. You can recognize the search for an aesthetic expression, through both direct outdoor ornaments and decorations, and through jewellery and flashy clothes, in the incised and painted decoration of the Early-Middle Bronze Age pottery).

Tangible and intangible values merge and alternate the cosmetic realm. Tangible materials as the ownership of precious objects and the knowledge of technology point of production and marketing. The intangible values relate to the semantic aspect, beauty, magic, and holistic healing. Both classes of values converge in the same effort of being better than others are[15].

Probably it is not correct to believe that in prehistory, the mere appearance became an end. The amount of different symbolic patterns suggests that a number of them was linked with magic beliefs and religion. The use of natural materials with which it was possible to identify a life or a previous history was essential.

Therefore, when we use the word cosmetic, we do not refer only to "make-up", used to improve the appearance of a person, but also to substances and ornaments that help a person seems not only beautiful, but also healthy and younger[16].

The use of cosmetics represents a status symbol to underline the economic position and/or the belonging to a social class or a leading tribe. For the same reason, we can consider the wearing of personal adornments and the use of tattoos and makeups. Of course, the canons of the time were not so different from today and many cosmetic remedies were pharmaceutical preparations to improve and rejuvenate the appearance. Examples are the wide range of preparations against baldness, wrinkles and cellulite described in the Egyptian papyri. In fact, the division between cosmetics and medicine dates back to the recent past with the birth of pharmaceutical companies, many of which also produce cosmetics.

The current distinction considers make up something that generates temporary aesthetic effects, cosmetics something that produces prolonged or permanent effects and medicines that cure disease. In this research, we have considered "cosmetic product" what refers to any substance or preparation in contact with the human body to change its appearance for beauty or health.

---

[15] The Latin *fascinum*, charm, malefic spell is related to fascia, bandage and to *fascis*, bundle; *ligare*, to tie, and ligature, act of trying also a mean to charm and charm. To bind by a magic charm, by tying a knot. All the etymology confirms the idea that the act of binding is essentially magical.

[16] Walter P. 1995: La peinture des femmes préhistoriques, in *La Dame de Brassempouy*, (*Études et Recherches Archéologiques de l'Université de Liège*) 74 - 259.

2. Beauty pattern of past.

We can find traces of beauty's pattern of past civilizations in the painted representations and incised figurines, which sometimes trade the aesthetic canons of local tradition. It is difficult to look at them with the eyes and imagination of the people who made them, but we know that behind them there are important steps of social and cultural evolution, including clothing, jewellery, makeup, and hairdressing. Even if the canons of fashions, myths and knowledge have changed in the centuries, the principles of charm never changed in the human mind and it is interesting that even the main manners consisting in dressing precious clothes (brands and quality textiles), jewellery, makeup and body care are still the same. Today Aphrodite is still present as an ideology, even if most of the people roughly know that she was a Greek divinity.

Her name is the antonomasia of woman beauty, a myth created by verbal, historical and visual traditions that survived over every later religion, spreading her identity and canons of beauty in the world. Before introducing the case of Pyrgos, I would like to mention the inorganic and organic natural resources existing in Cyprus and the material available to make the instruments to produce for them. We will use some comparison with Egypt as they had the most important knowledge of the time to make cosmetics and medicines, turning the environmental resources in useful compounds. Most of the inorganic had two or three parallel uses: as a colour for make-up, dyeing of textiles and ingredient of pharmaceutical remedy. The same for the organic employed in perfumery, cosmetics, medicines and handcrafts.

2.1 COLOURS

Colours are part of the very essence of the things that surround us. Their composition is endless, as are endless nuances that they can take. It is difficult to copy the reality, but it is perhaps the attempt to reproduce what has contributed to the evolution of technology. Base of multiple beliefs, religions and magic, the colours symbolize life, death and becoming.

Ochre, as a symbol of regeneration and life, is among the oldest colourist ingredient, accompanied by coal, used to capture on cave walls nature, life, and the world around.

The human body was the first available surface where experience colours recovered by nature, before that item, domestic walls, furnishings, and clothing became the surfaces on which testing artistic skills.

At the same time, vegetable parts, which by nature long preserve colours, were the first intertwined to manufacture baskets, mats, mattresses, and bags to collect and store supplies and household goods. In a second time, people used plant and animal fibres and employed the already possessed knowledge to dye. Then, began a real hunt of colours even if their extraction was not so simple. Often, in fact, the colour obtained was very different from the starting material and its transfer of the material or objects did not give the expected results. It then took multiple attempts to get to know and manipulate mineral and organic colours, while experience and tradition, passing down from father to son created a class of experts who knew the most complex dyeing methods.

It is, therefore, easy to imagine how the fabrics and dyed objects were considered valuable, and how much the person who possessed them important, rich and worthy of respect. The oldest written records on the subject, coming from the Mediterranean basin, tell us about gifts, trade and preciousness of these tissues. The "purple" dyed textiles are still considered the most valuable after centuries marked by moral and religious power of the wearer, and made famous the city that was producing the best quality, Tiro.

However, next to professional textile production, it existed and still exists, a "domestic" activity of dyeing intra moenia, often using alternative processes that contributed to evolving the dyeing method, leaving rare evidence of an unknown artistic universe.

2.1.1 Inorganic ingredients [17]

The inorganic pigments, used in painting and cosmetics, come generally from minerals and need to be reduced (and sometimes separated from the matrix) in powder to obtain a product soluble in fat or water[18]: Ochre (Fe_2O_3) Cinnabar (Hgs), Chrysocola ($CuSiO_3 - nH_2O$), Orpiment (As_2S_3), Cerrusite ($PbCO_3$), Galena (Pbs), Realgar (AsS), Magnesium, Talc[19].

---

[17] Pointer S. 2005: *The artifice of beauty: a history and practical guide to perfumes and cosmetics* 11, Stroud ed., Sutton. Gunn F. 1973: *The artificial face: a history of cosmetics,* Hippocrene books, (35, stating that this original lip colour contained white lead). Cohen Ragas M. & K. Kozlowski 1998. *Read my lips: a cultural history of lipstick,* San Francisco, 13. (Stating that this original lip colour contained crushed red rocks). Lipstick first appeared approximately 4,000–5,000 years ago, in ancient Mesopotamia when women ground precious gems into dust to decorate their lips. Such information about ancient lipsticks' components recently became available through gas chromatography, which allows for identification of minute residues extracted from old containers. Pointer, 2005: suggesting the date of first lipstick use closer to 2500 BC - The ingredient identification remains imperfect, however, because: some ingredient compounds have altered or disappeared over time, cosmetics containers often served multiple uses and so contain residues from multiple substances, and the waterproofing treatments used on the cosmetics containers interferes with residue analysis. Fortunately, in some cases, written evidence can help corroborate the chromatographic findings or help fill the informational gaps. Corson R. 2003. *Fashions in Makeup from ancient to modern times*, 25 Peter Owen ed.

[18] Microscopy, X-ray diffraction, SEM analysis, and optical and spectroscopy can be used to discriminate these minerals.

[19] I reproduce below the original text of Alessandro Lentini about the analyses on Pyrgos palette: "*Le analisi hanno rivelato un quantitativo di Piombo, con valori compresi tra il 35 e il 52%, corrispondente ad una percentuale che suggerisce la preparazione di un composto simile alla biacca (PbCO3)2. Pb (OH)2), noto pigmento bianco, inorganico, tossico, a base di piombo. La biacca, oltre ad essere tra i colori più conosciuti e usati nella pittura su tavola e nelle miniature (Zanardi B. et alii, 1984), fu largamente utilizzata nel passato come cosmetico per le sue qualità coprenti nonostante la sua nocività. In alcune palette sono state identificate due tipologie diverse di ocra relative ai colori giallo e rosso (Fig. 3 e 4) prevalentemente costituite da ossido idrato di ferro FeO (OH). n H2O, che si trovano normalmente vicino alle miniere di rame (famose a Cipro quelle di Ambelikou, Apliki, Skouriotissa e Mathiati). Della stessa origine sono le terre rosse e brune, caratteristiche dei sub areali Mediterranei, composte in prevalenza da ematite (Fe2O3 • nH2O). I caratteristici suoli rossi di Cipro indicano la presenza di molte varietà di ossidi di ferro, con diverse proprietà cromatiche relative alla presenza o assenza d'acqua. Depositi di ocra rossa e terra d'ombra (la ben nota "umbra") sono noti in tutta l'isola e furono ampiamente utilizzati come scorificanti nell'estrazione del rame, come dimostra la composizione dei milioni di tonnellate di scorie che caratterizzano il paesaggio circostante le storiche miniere di rame dell'isola.*
Inoltre, durante la prima fase analitica, relativa all'essiccamento in muffola dell'acqua igroscopica presente nei sedimenti selezionati, sono stati osservati alcuni viraggi di colore verde, rosso, blu e bianco. Le prime osservazioni allo stereo microscopio hanno evidenziato per alcuni di questi sedimenti una serie di aggregati con abiti pseudo cristallini, tridimensionali, dalla morfologia cubica o romboidale. I sedimenti presentano vari gradi di sopra saturazione di elementi che hanno nuovamente cristallizzato dei centri (germi) già esistenti, secondo un processo, già noto nelle descrizioni di Aristotele (Brock S., 2000) relative al cloruro di sodio e in quelle di Plinio il vecchio relative al solfato di rame.
Nell'identificazione del pigmento verdastro, i sedimenti flocculati in pseudo reticoli cristallini sono stati portati in soluzione con diversi metodi (acqua deionizzata acidificata - acidi e basi forti a caldo). Nei cristalli di colore bianco si sono notate composizioni diverse: in una è presente il magnesio (MgCl2), nella seconda il sodio (NaCl). I cristalli di colore blu sono caratterizzati dalla presenza di rame (CuSO4), il verde e il rosso da una argilla dalla composizione particolare, ricca di silicati, alluminio, ferro e magnesio (Mg2+ Fe2+ Fe3+ Al3+). Tra le sostanze identificate ci sono due tipi diversi di composizioni saline: il cloruro di sodio normalmente disciolto in acqua di mare, che a Cipro si trova anche sotto forma di salgemma minerale e il cloruro di magnesio presente in natura nelle marcite e nei laghi salati, caratteristici del paesaggio costiero cipriota, nella penisola di Akrotiri, nel golfo di Larnaca e in quello di Famagosta, dove i fiumi stagionali creavano prima della costruzione delle dighe per le riserve d'acqua, lagune e paludi, ricche dei sali minerali, trascinati dal dilavamento delle acque dai giacimenti ofiolitici del massiccio della Troodos. Di particolare interesse è l'utilizzazione dei

In Egypt, malachite and turquoise were extensively used not only to create amulets, but also to compose curative cosmetics, commonly used for green eye shadow to obtain the "cat eye" look. They also used black ointment that derives from galena and cerussite, like Kohl, of which the protective function against the sun's rays, insects and various bacterial diseases of the eyes is well known[20]. Hydrated copper sulphate ($CuSO_4 \cdot 5(H_2O)$), also known as blue vitriol, was one of the best recognised compounds attested by a Sumerian list that in Cyprus occurs as chalcanthite[21] (Crosland 1962, 67).

Along with Dioscurides, Pliny mentions chalcanthite-vitriol (Book XXXIV, section XXXII 3) and its use in medicine, particularly in the eyes. Referring mainly to the substance produced from copper ore deposits in Cyprus, both authors describe the chalcanthite-vitriol forming as white dripstones in caves and along the sides of pits dug into the mine tunnels.

In Egypt, the Smith papyrus (2400 BC) mentions the use of copper as a sterilization agent for drinking water and wounds. Meanwhile the Eber papyrus (1500 BC) recommends the use of copper potions for headaches, burns and itching and that of copper oxide and copper sulphate powder with a mixture of honey and red copper on open wounds.

2.1.2 *Ochre*

Ochre has been the first ingredient for human creativity in paints and cosmetics and a basic component of medicines. Moreover, it has been one of the most ancient suggestions to improve our future.

Fig. 1: Ochre pottery burnisher, Pyrgos Inv.n.1737.

The mineral is composed of iron oxide mixed with clays, silicates and other minerals, and most commonly occurs as sedimentary infill or as the precipitate of iron-rich rock and in deposits of iron oxides that are geochemical distinct from each other[22]. The large family of ochres used in

---

sali di rame CuSO4. 5H2O, esistenti in diverse concentrazioni, ampiamente utilizzati e commerciati per scopi farmaceutici anche nella tarda età imperiale (come testimoniano gli scritti di Zosimo di Panopoli e Galeno) e nel Medioevo, come riporta Francesco Balducci Pegolotti, Gonfaloniere della compagnia dei Bardi a Firenze nel 1300 nel suo trattato "La Pratica della mercatura", dalla quale provengono preziose informazioni anche sulla continuità del commercio delle spezie e delle fragranze cipriote, inclusa la resina del Laudano (Cistus Laudaniferous) simile alla mirra".

[20] Papyrus Eber 346, 355, 367, 368, 383, 393, 407, 416, 423; Nunn J.F. 1996: *Ancient Egyptian Medicine*, London, 198-199; Walter P., Martinetto, G. Tsoucaris, R. Bréniaux, M.A. Lefebvre, G. Richard, J. Talabot & E. Dooryhee 1999: Making make-up in Ancient Egypt, *Nature*, vol. 397; 483-484.

[21] Crosland M.P. 1962: *Historical Studies in the Language of Chemistry*, Heinemann, London, 67.

[22] Constantinou G. and Govett G.J.S. 1972: Genesis of sulphide deposits, ochre and umber of Cyprus, *Transactions of the Institution of Mining and Metallurgy"* 81: 34–46.

antiquity includes yellow ochre, red ochre, purple ochre, Siena, and umber, as it is a mineral composed of "earth" occurring in various shades and colours, generally ranging from light yellow in red and dark brown.

The difference is mainly due to the percentage of iron oxide (Fe2O3) even if lumps of ochre often include traces of gypsum or manganese carbonate. The component of hydrous iron oxide conveys yellow colour and the anhydrous red: the consistence is a sort of natural clay, including various minerals.

It has been used as a pigment since the beginning of prehistory: ochre sticks (crayons) have been found in the graves of *homo erectus* dating to 1.5-1.6 million years. Evidence for old mining dating back 250.000 years has been found in Southern India at Hunsqi. The first employ was probably in the colouring proper body, later as a pigment to draw on natural rock walls and caves for simple decorative purpose (75,000 years ago, Blombos Cave South Africa)[23]

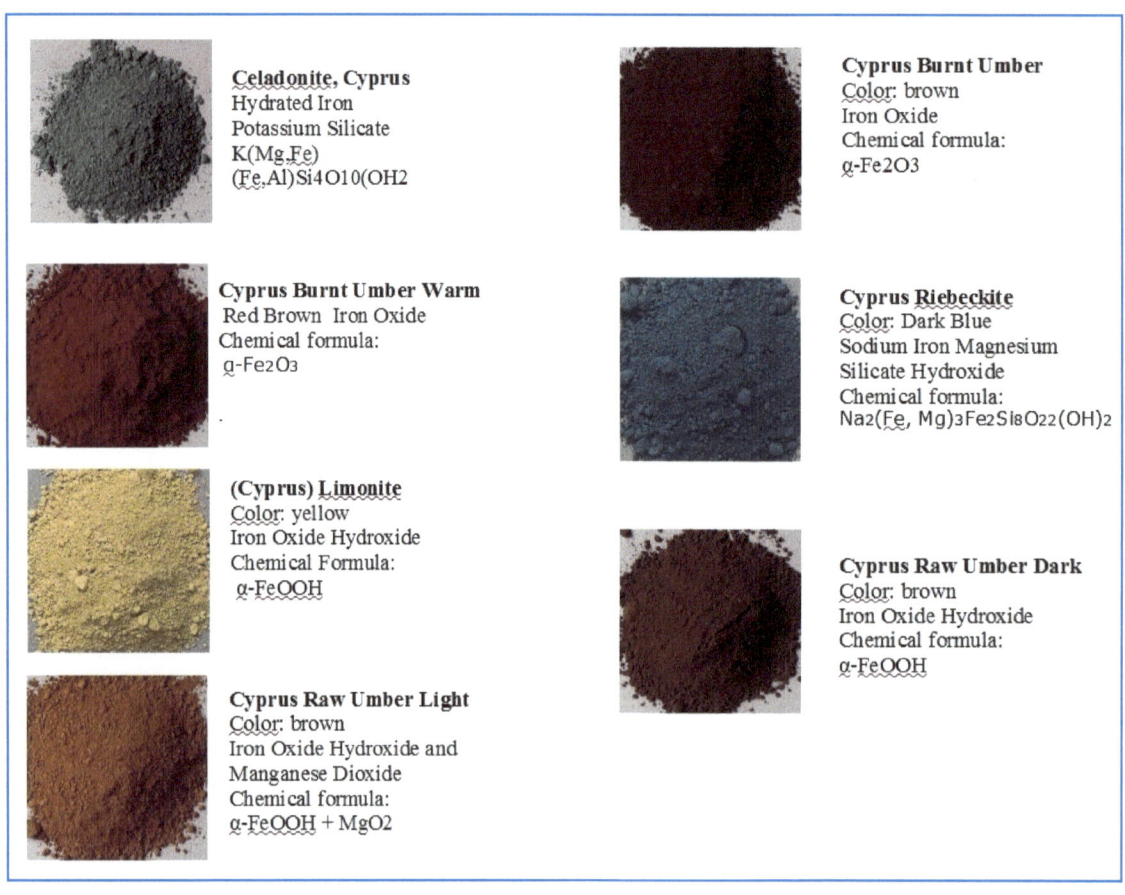

Fig. 2: Official recognised ochres from Cyprus.

Most famous are the painted images of the Neolithic sites at Pech Merle in France (ca. 23,000 BC), the Cave of Altamira in Spain (ca. 15,000-16,500 BC) and the Cave of Lascaux (15,300 BC). It was and is wide used in Africa to protect the skin from the sun, the insects and the

---

[23] http://science.sciencemag.org/content/334/6053/219.

infections. Researches by Photobiology Laboratory prove that ochre protects the skin against ultraviolet (UV) exposure.

Furthermore, despite thousands of years of topical use, there is still much to be learned about the benefits of this traditional mineral pigment and much more about its health benefits as an ingredient in pharmacological compounds. Under these aspects, a project of extensive comparison between the ancient uses of ochre may open new frontiers on a modern employ in natural and **no toxic** cosmetics and in medical therapies. Italy, France and Cyprus are some of the countries that possess an extensive cultural heritage of the use of ochre from the Neolithic period onwards.

Depending upon the colour, the ochre is called red ochre, yellow ochre, green earths, sienna, umber and by various other names.

In addition to red ochre, the red oxide of iron, commonly called 'red oxide', is an important natural pigment. It results from alteration of Hematite and ferruginous laterite and consists essentially of Fe_2O_3 having pigmentary quality. Red oxide usually contains about 70% Fe_2O_3. *Terra Sienna* is brownish-yellow containing about 60% Fe_2O_3, with some quantity of manganese oxide. It is named after the town of Siena in Italy, where a large deposit is located. Sienna is marketed in the raw and burnt (calcined) states.

The Green Sienna is greenish brown containing some 45% Fe_2O_3 and 15% MnO_2. Numerous deposits of colouring earths occur in various parts of Europe: umber of good quality, called *Turkish Umber*, is found on the island of Cyprus.

The medicinal use of ochre in Egypt is extensively described in the Medical Papyri (Eber's Papyrus 1550 BC, E:700). Moreover, its use as a component for makeup, cosmetic and medicinal compound is attested until today all over the world.

2.1.3 *Mercury*

Cinnabar (Cinnabar/is mercury sulphide) HgS (Fig.3) is another mineral that was discovered, processed and used by ancient people in different and distant civilizations and cultures of the world. The first use was as pigment due to the attractive red colour, probably the grinding to obtain the powder was the second step. Among the first evidence we find the ritual painting of human skulls at the Neolithic site of Çatalhöyük in Turkey (7000-8000 BC)[24], the local use including the paintings on the walls. Recent investigations in Spain propose the use of cinnabar as a pigment in the 6th millennium BC.

In the Balkans, including the Serbian sites of Plocnik, Belo Brdo, and Bubanj we find another Neolithic (Vinca culture 4800-3500 BC) use of Cinnabar, exploited in quartz vein from the Suplja Stena mine on Mount Avala, 20 kilometres (12.5 miles) from Vinca (Jovanovic, 1978; Shepherd, 1980; Mioc et al., 2004)[25].

---

[24] Çatalhöyük skull retrieval, curation and reposition: Haddow S.D., Boz B. and B. Glencross 2013: The Human Remains I: Interpreting Community Structure, Health and Diet in Neolithic Çatalhöyük in I. Hodder, *Humans and Landscapes of Catalhoyuk, Reports from 2000- 2008 seasons, The Humans and Their Lifestyles, 2013 Monumenta Archeologica 30*, 339- 396.
[25] Ferber J.J. 1774: Beschreibung des Quecksilberbergwerk zu Idria in *Mittel-Krayn Ch*. F. Himburg, Berlin. Miloi V. 1943: Das vorgeschichtliche Bergwerk, Šuplja Stena am Avalaberg beiBelgrad in Serbien, Wiener Prähistorische

The first documented use in medicine dates to 1500 BC Egypt. Aristotle[26] mentions mercury in an academic text dating back to the 4th century BCE, in which he refers to it as "fluid silver" and "quicksilver, followed by Theophrastus of Eresus (371-286 BC) who includes cinnabar in his treaty "*De Lapidibus*", in which he describes the method to get quicksilver from **cinnabaris**. Later references appear in Vitruvius (1st century BC) and Pliny the Elder (23-79 AD), who was the first to describe mercury poisoning as a disease of slaves working in the mines contaminated with mercury vapour."[27] Among the later medical employ we remind mercury as the earliest known treatment for syphilis, reported by Paracelsus (Philippus Aureolus Theophrastus Bombastus von Hohenheim 1493-1541),[28] Cinnabar was also identified in Cyprus[29].

Fig. 3: Cinnabar

2.1.4 *Chrysocolle*

Chrysocolle $CuSiO_3-nH_2O$, (Cu, Al) $2H2Si2O5$ (OH) $4 \cdot nH2O$ (Fig.4) is a copper phyllosilicate that unlike Azurite and malachite may be used in oil. The name comes from the Greek chrysos, "gold", and cola, "glue", in reference to the name of the material used to solder gold, and was first mentioned by Theophrastus in 315 BC.

It comes from the oxidation of copper ore bodies and is often found in association with minerals of quartz, limonite, azurite, malachite, cuprite, and other secondary copper minerals.

Pliny identifies "*chrysocollè*" as coming from Cyprus, Armenia, Macedonia, and Spain (N.H. 33.4, 86-93, 161; 35.30, 47, 48), mentioning the *chalcosmaragdus* from Cyprus (N.H.37, 74).

Even if its natural colour spans from light green versus cerulean and bluish, under the

---

Zeitschrift XXX, 41-54. Vasi M. 1932: *Preistorijska Vina I, Industrija cinabarita i kosmetika u Vini*, Beograd. Durman A. 2002: The Neolithic settlement in Vina, *IAMS Newsletter*, Institute for Archaeometallurgical Studies, London.
[26] Aristotele, Meterology Book IV, part.8.
[27] Brooks W.E. 2012: Industrial Use of Mercury in the Ancient World, in *Mercury in the Environment: Pattern and Process*, ed. Bank S.Michael, University of California, 19-24.
[28] Phillipus Von Hohenheim (1493-1541), called Paracelsus, was amongst the earliest proponents of mercurial chemotherapy for syphilis. Johann Karl Proksch summarized his extensive writings on the use of mercury in 1828.
[29] http://nora.nerc.ac.uk/7723/2/Jowitt_SGA_2005_Poster.pdf

microscope, it appears pale green nearly amorphous or cryptocrystalline, meanwhile the grounded powder retains the ore colour and may melt in fat or water to be used as a pigment.

Therefore, chrysocolle unlike azurite and malachite is an ingredient more malleable for producing cream and fat cosmetic/medicines or pigment for wall fresco.

Fig. 4: Chrysocolle from Pyrgos

In Egypt chrysocolle was highly estimated as a pharmaceutical component for many diseases. The unguent was commonly used to treat skin problems and wounds. A filling made of resin and Chrysocolle was extensively employed to treat tooth caries referred to as a *worm gnawing a tooth* as early as the Old Kingdom. Liquid drops and ointments containing chrysocolle where daily used to protect the eyes chasing away all kinds of insects and demons that threatened with a variety of eye infections. Egyptian professional ophthalmologists and physicians, carried a special kit that contained ampullas of green chrysocolle (often blending lead sulphide and laudanum) and black kohl[30].

In Cyprus, chrysocolle is present in connection with both the copper carbonates and sulphides. Its by-products, very estimated for the medical properties have been traded since the Bronze Age.

2.1.5 *Arsenic*

Arsenic is a metalloid, which is often combined with other metals, sulphur and oxygen,

---

[30] Jonckheere F. 1952: La 'Mesdemet', cosmétique et médicament égyptien, in *Histoire de la Médecine*, 2° année, no 7, Paris 2-11; Bourghout J. 1973: The evil eye of Apopis, *JEA* 59, 114-150; Sauneron S. 1958: Une recette égyptienne de collyre, *BIFAO* 57, 157-61.

different in colour: Realgar (AsS) red (Fig.5), Orpiment (As_2S_3) yellow (Fig.4), Arsenolite (As_2O_3) white and Arsenopyrite (FeAsS) grey. The two arsenic sulphides mainly used as pigments were Realgar and Orpiment commonly present in Cyprus in copper ore especially in the areas of Laxia tou Lavrou, Dhierona and Pefkos in Limassol.

Fig. 5: Realgar ore from Pefkos region, Cyprus

The word arsenic is derived from the Persian *zarnikh* and Syriac *zarniqa*, later transformed by Greeks as *arsenikon,* which means "male". The medical and poisoning properties of arsenic were known by Hippocrates and Theophrastus in the fourth century BC. At the time, both Realgar and Orpiment were used to treat ulcers and abscesses not only for cosmetic purposes.

In Egypt, a dark-compound for the eyes, with antibacterial properties included lead and arsenic as revealed by a recent study published in *Analytical Chemistry*[31]. It has been for a long time the only pure orange pigment employed in composition of cosmetics, before the people realized its toxicity.

2.1.6 *Lead*

Like Mercury, people since prehistory processed and utilized lead for many alternative uses, including cosmetics, and its history continues to this day. In Egypt, we have evidence of a cosmetic composition, including lead since the first dynasties. Most famous was Kohl, an ancient eye makeup extremely elaborate, employed as early as 4000 BC to create the characteristic unisex almond eye look. The favourite kohl colours were black and green.

---

[31] Tapsoba I., Arbault S., Walter P. and Amatore C. 2010: Finding Out Egyptian Gods' Secret Using Analytical Chemistry: Biomedical Properties of Egyptian Black Makeup Revealed by Amperometry at Single Cells. *Anal. Chem., 82* (2), 457–460.

The main ingredient was galena, a blue-grey lead sulphide mined in the eastern desert at Gebel el-Zeit, mixed with soot dust. Kohl was used not only for cosmetic reasons, but also to shield the eye against the sun and to treat many eye diseases, in consideration of the disinfectant qualities of Galena.

Unfortunately, the toxicity of lead affected the people.[32] In Cyprus the lead mineral used for cosmetic purposes is Cerusite[33] $PbCO_3$,[34] and Galena PbS (eye shadow) (Fig. 6 Ingot of lead found at Pyrgos, containing an high percentage of Arsenic).

Fig. 6: Lead ingot from Pyrgos, Inv.n.174

2.1.7 *Celadonite*.

Celadonite is a Hydrated iron, magnesium, potassium silicate containing small amounts of aluminium, calcium, sodium K (Mg, Fe) (Fe, Al) Si_4O_{10} $(OH)_2$.[35]

It is a greenish earth known as terre vert, highly prized by painters for its cool bright green. It was created by the interaction of seawater on lava at low temperature (<1500C).

The colour varies considerably from pale green, bright green, bluish-green, olive-green, and black-green, depending upon its constituent elements (Fig.7). To characterize these pigments and determine their origin, 76 samples dating from 1st to 3rd century AD and coming from 14 Roman sites in Switzerland and Pompeii were analysed. Celadonite was the most frequent pigment found among these samples, and its attribution was Cyprus.

---

[32]-http://www.healthyskinportal.com/articles/beauty-beware-historys-4-most-dangerous-cosmetics/370/#sthash.6OmOy0SQ.dpuf

[33] Name given by Wilhelm Karl von Haidinge in 1845 after the Latin word '*cerussa*' meaning white lead.

[34]- Taylor Cliff D., R.A. Zierenberg, Goldfarb R. J., Kilburn J.E., Seal II R.R., and M.D. Kleinkopf 1995: Volcanic-Associated Massive Sulphide Deposits (Models 24a-b, 28a; Singer, 1986 a, b; Cox, 1986) (https://pubs.usgs.gov/of/1995/ofr-95-0831/CHAP16.pdf)

[35]-Staudigel H., Gillis K. & Duncan R. 1986: K/Ar and Rb/Sr ages of celadonites from the Troodos ophiolite, *Cyprus. Geology*, 14, 72-75. Booij E., Gallahan W.E. & Staudigel H. 1995: Ion-exchange experiments and Rb/Sr dating on celadonites from the Troodos ophiolite, Cyprus. Chemical Geology, 126, 155-167.

Fig. 7: Celadonite from Pyrgos

This earth has reasonable tinting strength and covering power, and the pigment is easily ground. It is not toxic since it contains some clay, green earth absorbs oil at a moderate to high rate.

2.1.8 *Magnesium*

Magnesium carbonate (Magnesia Alba $MgCO_3$ or $CMgO_3$)) minerals (Magnesite; Carbonic acid, magnesium salt; Hydromagnesite) (Fig.8). Magnesite is a white, yellowish, greyish-white or a brown crystalline solid or crystalline powder, soluble in cold water, frequently occurs in nature mixed with calcite, forming dolomite or dolomitic limestone deposits. Today, it is a common cosmetic ingredient used in solid, cream and powder make up, deodorant preparation and as a perfume carrier. Its main properties are the absorbing capacity and the colouring (white) opacifying agent. Commonly it is melted with talc, natural starches, calcium carbonate (chalk), magnesium carbonate, limestone, kaolin, bismuth subchloride and subnitrate, zinc and magnesium stearate[36]. Hydrated magnesium silicate $H_2Mg_3 (SiO_3)_4$ or $Mg_3Si_4O_{10} (OH)_2$, (Talc)/Soap-stone Gypsum occurs extensively in Cyprus unfortunately often contaminated with asbestos material as chrysotile.[37]

---

[36] Barthoux J. 1925: Les fards, pomades et couleurs dans l'antiquitè, in *Congres International de geolologique. Le Caire*, Avril 1925, IV, 257-8. Found remains of Magnesium on some Egyptian palettes, probably late (interesting). He found Calcium carbonate, Magnesium carbonate, red ochre, red lead and "limoniteis" (a component of limestone in Cyprus).
-For Magnesium chloride and sulphates: Storrs R.& B. Justin O'Brien 1930: *The Handbook of Cyprus*, London. p. 105 mention Magnesium chloride and sulphates. Greensmith J.T. 1994: Southern Cyprus. Ed. 50 Geologist Association Guide.
[37]-Ronald F. Dodson & Samuel P. Hammar 2012: *Asbestos: Risk Assessment, Epidemiology, and Health Effects*.
"Talc has several unique chemical and physical properties (such as platyness, softness, hydrophobicity, organophilicity, inertness) that make it desirable for a wide range of industrial and commercial applications (e.g. paint, polymers, paper, ceramics, animal feed, rubber, roofing, fertilizers, and cosmetics). In these products, talc acts as an anti-sticking and anti-caking agent, lubricant, carrier, thickener, absorbent, and strengthening and smoothing filler (IMA, 2005)".

It is the principal ingredient of ancient and modern cipria, phard and cosmetic powder. It is realised in different colours, adding natural pigments as ochre often perfumed with different fragrances easily absorbed by the magnesium silicate.

Fig. 8: Magnesite mine Limassol district Cyprus

The *International Agency for Research on Cancer, IARC,* published a monograph on Cyprus Talc[38], *facing all the chemical properties, natural environmental occurrence, possible dangers in producing, processing, or using, its asbestiform habit, industry employ*[39], *cancer incidence among workers, geomorphology, history, use and trade of the Cypriot Talc.*

2.2 Organic ingredients

Organics in archaeological samples can be discriminated by Gas Chromatography and Mass Spectrometry. Most of them come from plants and some from insects and marine shells.

Organic dyes were used to paint housed walls, pottery, furnishing or dye textiles and different household materials. A number of them, sometimes mixed with inorganic ingredient have been used in making cosmetics and colours for body painting. Some, as suggested by Plynius

---

[38]*Monographs.iarc.fr/Eng/Monographs/vol100C/mono100C-11: Asbestos (Chrisotile, Amosite, Crocidolite, Tremolite, Actinolite and Anthophyllite).* Consumer products (e.g. cosmetics, pharmaceuticals) are the primary sources of exposure to talc for the general population. Information on the levels of exposure experienced by the general population using cosmetics is in the previous IARC Monograph (IARC, 2010). Blount (Blount AM (1991). Amphibole content of cosmetic and pharmaceutical talc. Environ Health Perspect, 94: 225–230. 10.2307/3431315 PMID: 165953) examined pharmaceutical- and cosmetic-grade talcs for asbestiform amphibole content using a density-optical method.

[39] 30%; ceramics manufacture, 28%; refractories, 11%; plastics, 6%; filler or pigment in paints, 5%; roofing applications, 5%; cement, 3%; cosmetics, 2%; and other miscellaneous uses, 10% (includes agriculture and food, art sculpture, asphalt filler, autobody filler, construction caulks, flooring, and joint compounds)

secundus, to give a better colour to the perfumed ointments[40].

We can divide the two categories of dyes and pigments according to the ingredient added to facilitate the application. Generally, the organic compounds need a short/long manufacture and the use of an extra component to obtain an amalgam.

Natural dyes can be extracted from flowers, fruits, leaves, shoots, roots and bark of different plants. These plants had probably great importance in the economy of Early-Middle Bronze age due the possibility to employ them in colouring textiles and in preparation of cosmetics and medicines, as most of them are of great medical properties. For example, Urtica dioica is used as medicine, food and dye (yellow-green) (Baytop, 1999)[41].

Dyes from pomegranate, lawsone from henna and juglone from walnut possess antibacterial and antifungal properties (Dogan et al., 2008)[42]. According to Zohary and Hopf (1994), dye plants were cultivated in southwest Asia prior to classical times[43] From Mohenjodaro the earliest evidence of a dyed textile comes dating back 5,000-year- (Rubia cordifolia: Mahanta & Tiwari, 2005)[44].

2.2.1 Purple

Murex

Mediterranean shellfish of the genera *Purpura: Murex brandaris*, *Murex trunculus* (Fig.9) and *Purpura haemastoma* produced by extraction of the secretions of the hypobranchial (6,60-dibromoindigotin indigo derivatives (6- and 60-bromoindigotin) brominated indirubin derivatives (6,60-dibromoindirubin, 6- and 60-bromoindirubins), indirubin and indigo.

Fig. 9: Murex trunculus, Pyrgos Inv.n. 1143

Pointing out that indigo is blue and the brominated derivatives are violet red, the shade of

---

[40] Plinius Secundus The thirteenth book of the Historiae of Natvre, chapter 2: *"There is a third thing between these, requisit also to the full making of these sweet oint|ments, namely, the colour: although many take no regard at all of it. And for this purpose, the perfumers put into their compositions Cinnabaris [i. Vermillionor Sanguis Draconis] and Or|canet. The salt moreouer that is strewed among, serueth to represse and correct the nature of the oile that vniteth all the ingredients besides. But those that haue the root of Orcanet (Alkanna tinctoria o Alkanet) in them, needno salt at all to be put in besides. As for Rosin and Gum, they are mingled with the rest to incorporate the drugs and spices, and to keep in the sweet odour thereof, which otherwise would evaporate and soon be lost.*

[41] Baytop, T. 1999: *Therapy with medicinal plants in Turkey, past and present*, 2nd ed. Nobel Tıp Kitabevi, Istanbul.

[42] Dogan,Y., S. Baslar, M. Ozturk and H. Mert. 2008: Plants used as dye sources. In: *Underutilized and Underexplored Horticultural Crops,* (Ed.): K.V. Peter. Vol. 3. New India Publishing Agency, New Delhi, India, 109-145.

[43] Zohary, D. & Hopf, M. 1994, Domestication of Plants in the Old World, Clarendon Press, Oxford.

[44] Mahanta D. & Tiwari S.C. 2005: Natural dye–yielding plants and indigenous knowledge on dye preparation in Arunachal Pradesh, northeast India, *Current science, vol. 88*, no. 9, 1474–1480.

purple depends on the species of mollusc, dye process and time.[45]

2.2.2 Blues: a-Indigofera *tinctoria (indaco)* and b-*Isatis tinctoria (Guado).*

In historical times, blue/indigo was obtained from different species of Indigofera (Ball S., Allan R. and Tomlinson P., 1990): *Indigofera tinctoria, argentea, intricata, spinosa* e *semitrijuga*. In plant communities/*phytocoenosis* of Cyprus (Zohary, 1973) they are associated with *Polygonum tinctorium (poligono tintorio)*[46], *Euphorbia, Amaranthus (Bosea cypria endemic), Hybiscus(indigenous)* and *Calotropis*.

In Cyprus, blue/indigo is also present in *Galega officinalis* (galactogogue plant of the family Fabaceae) and *Genista tinctoria* (native to meadows and pastures) (Tomlinson and Allan, 1984)[47].

2.2.2.1 *Indigo*: Indigo blue is one of the earliest and most popular dyestuffs in the world, largely employed in ancient times and still used. It seems that the plant native of the Near East spread in Mediterranean environment in subsequent periods (Belgiorno & Lentini 2008)[48].

It is a plant belonging to the leguminous family, including three hundred species. The raw material used in the production of blue is the leaves since they contain the greatest concentration of dye molecules. In the synthetic process, some passages and chemical reactions were employed, but the ancient process to extract colour never changed. The freshly cut leaves support three different passages of fermentation, which takes proximally 14-16 hours. The resultant mixture is filtered to remove impurities and dried to form a thick paste. Species of *Indigofera* produced a high-quality indigo, which is one of the most light-stable organic dyes, a characteristic that explains its longevity as a colorant.

2.2.2.2 *Isatis tinctoria*, woad: The plant belongs to the Brassicaceae (crucifer) family; a native to the Eastern Mediterranean, including Cyprus. It is the ancient *glastum;* Vitrum by Vitruvius I c. BC, glastum by Pliny 77 AD[49]. Today the plant is considered an aggressive, dry-land invader due to its prolific seed production. Blue woad was mainly used to dye textiles, but its dye also had other uses, as a tattoo ink and component for makeup. Woad contains high levels of glucobassincin, a chemical that has anti-cancer properties (Fig.10).

It is an astringent plant known for reducing fever and inflammation and is reported to have antiviral properties. In Europe, it was used as a poultice for pain in the spleen, for skin ulcers and as a treatment for syphilis and hepatitis.

Woad has also been used as a natural insecticide and to make soap. It was known by Egyptian

---

[45] Faber G.A. 1938: Dying and Tanning in Classical Antiquity, Vol. 9. Ciba Review. Society of Chemical Industry in Basle (Switzerland). Reese D.S. 1986: The Mediterranean Shell Purple-dye Industry; *American Journal of Archaeology*, 90 (2), 183. Clark R.J.H., Cooksey C.J., Daniels M.A.M, Withnall R. 1993: Indigo, woad and Tyrian purple. Important vat dyes from antiquity to the present in *Endeavour, New Series Vol. 17* (4), 191-199.

[46] Altay V., İbrahim İlker Özyiğit, Mustafa Keskin, Göksel Demir, İbrahim Ertuğrul Yalçın 2013: An ecological study of endemic plant *Polygonum istanbulicum* Keskin and its environs, Pak J. Bot., 45(S1), 455-459. For traditional use in medicine see: Zeb A, S.M. Khan, H. Ahmad, G. Jan, F.G. Jan, M. Ahmad and H. Ullah 2012: Ethnomedicinal Studies of Dughalgay Valley District Swat, Khyberpakhtoonkhwa, Province, Pakistan. *Proceedings (Special Issue of Pakistan Journal of Botany) of 12th National and 3rd International Conference of Botany (ICB-2012) arranged by Pakistan Botanical Society* (September 1 - 3, 2012) at Quaid-i-Azam University, Islamabad Pakistan.

[47] Tomlinson P., and A. Hall 1984: Progress in Palaeobotanical Studies of Dye Plants 1983/4. *Dyes on Historical and Archaeological Textiles* 3, *Meeting, York Archaeological Trust, September 1984*, edited by H.E. Dalrymple (Edinburgh, 1985).

[48] Lentini A. & M.R.Belgiorno 2008: Palaethnobotany investigations at the site of Pyrgos-Mavrorachi, Cyprus, in Kars H., Meyers P. and Wagner C.A. (ed) *International Symposium on Archaeometry*, 37, 296-297.

[49] Ball P.W. & Akeroyd J.R., 2010: Isatis L. In: Flora Europaea. Volume 1 Psilotaceae to Platanaceae [ed. by Tutin, T. G. \Burges, N. A. \Chater, A. O. \Edmondson, J. R. \Heywood, V. H. \Moore, D. M. \Valentine, D. H. \Walters, S. M. \Webb, D. A.]. Cambridge, UK: Cambridge University Press, 324-325.

(cloth of about 2500 BC), which probably used the plant also for medical purposes.

Fig. 10: Isatis tinctoria

The leaves were harvested in September, crushed and reduced to paste, put to ferment in balls for several weeks and then left to dry in the sunshine for four months becoming hard and brown-black. In this way the pigment persists unaltered for a long time.

2.2.2. 3 *Anchusa azurea* (indigenous)[50]: Anchusa azurea or Alkanet has been a source for red, pink, and blue dye since the time of the ancient Egyptians. It is possible to obtain a blue/violet dye only from the aboveground parts of the plant and red dye from the roots (see under RED).

Oil or fat is the best ingredient to solve the Anchusa dye: for this property, it has been largely employed in cosmetics and scented oils.

2.2.3 Violet

2.2.3.1 *Papaver rhoeas* subsp. *cyprium* (endemic)[51]. In Cyprus, there are six endemic species of poppy, all rich in alkaloids and narcotic substances, in addition to Papaver somniferous allegedly imported:
- *Papaver argemone* Meiklei[52];
- *Glaucium corniculatum*-(L) DC: called in Cyprus "*Anemochorton* or *Kollitsida*" with red petals tinged with black, largely used in Cyprus as a calming infusion of cough and tonic;
- *Glaucium flavum* Cr.: with yellow flowers,
- *Roemeria hybrida* (L) DC: with purple flowers,
Hypecoum-procubens (L): yellow flowers, very similar to *somniferous*;

---

[50] Chrtek J. & B. Slavík 2001: Contribution to the flora of Cyprus. 5 in *Acta Univ. Carol., Biol.* 45, 267-293; Meikle R.D. 1985: Flora of Cyprus 2; Chrtek J. & B. Slavík 1993: Contribution to the flora of Cyprus. 2 in Fl. Medit. 3, 239-259.

[51] Alziar G. 1985: Contribution a l'histoire naturelle de l'ile de Chypre – la flore. – Biocosme Mésogéen 2: 1-20; 1986: Contribution a l'histoire naturelle de l'ile de Chypre. La flore. 2e partie. – Biocosme Mésogéen 3: 49-57; 1995: Généralités sur la flore de l'île de Chypre. Quelques données quantitatives. – Ecol. Medit. 21: 47-52.

[52] Subspecies recognised by R.D. Meikle 1977. The Flora of Cyprus. Nicosia.

-*Papaver rhoeas* L.: said "*Pedinos or Paparouna*" with scarlet red flowers;
-*Papaver somniferous* L.: said "*Haskashi Paparouna*" (Fig.11) with purple petals shaded darker toward the centre (is the richest of narcotic substances).

Fig. 11: Papaver rhoas from Phafos forest

2.2.4 Green

2.2.4.1 Lavandula *stoechas* *(indigenous* Fig. 12*)*

Fig. 12: Lavandola stoechas, Limassol

2.2.4.2 *Chamomile Matricaria* *(indigenous)*

2.2.4.3 *Urtica Dioica* *(endemic)*

2.2.4.4 *Pistacia Lentiscus* (indigenous)

2.2.4.5 *Hedera pastuchovii* subsp. *cypria* (endemic)

2.2.5 Yellow:

This dye is present in plants containing flavonoids, widely known in medicine for their antioxidant properties. Among the Cyprus varieties the most useful are:

2.2.5.1 Anthemis *tinctoria*[53] dyer's chamomile (*indigenous*)[54]

2.2.5.2 Berberis *vulgaris* (*indigenous*)[55]

2.2.5.3 Crocus *veneris* (*endemic*)

2.2.5.4 Genista *fasselata* var. crudelis (*endemic*) [56]

2.2.5.5 Reseda *luteola* (*indigenous*)[57]

2.2.5.6 Rhamnus *alaternus* (*indigenous*)[58]

2.2.5.7 Rhus *Coriaria* (*indigenous*) [59]

2.2.5.8 Pomegranate (*mentioned 95 times in Plinii Naturalis Historiae*) **fruits**: the skin of fruit has 28% of tannic acid and may be used to prepare natural colour to dye fabric. The resulting dye paste is cured, pulverized to obtain a powdery natural dye.
The grounding comprises cleaning, drying, crushing and different passage in hot water. According to the material utilized (waste pomegranate rind) after the dying the fabric acquire a natural fragrance[60].

Thanks to the presence of tannins and flavonoids (red-blue and violet), the colours obtained by maceration of pomegranate peels are diverse: from pale yellow obtained from the skins of unripe pomegranate, with dark gold from mature skins, to orange using the complete fruit.

---

[53] Claude Delaval Cobham 1895: *Excerpta Cipria* p.342
[54] Meikle, Flora of Cyprus 1; Hadjikyriakou 2005; Alziar 2000; Oberprieler C. & Vogt R. 2000 ["1999"]: Notes on some species of Anthemis (Compositae, Anthemideae) in Cyprus. – Bocconea 11: 89-104.
[55] Hadjikyriakou 2005; Chrtek & Slavík. 2001; Meikle 1977.
[56] Hadjikyriakou 2009; Chrtek & Slavík 1981, Meikle 1977; Chrtek & Slavík 2001; Della A. 1992: Flora of a valley in the Pendakomo area in Agric. Res. Inst. Minist. Agric. Nat. Resources Cyprus Misc. Rep. 52; Alziar 2000; Coulot P. 2000: Approche de la flore de l'ile de Chypre in Monde Pl. 470. 2000
[57] Martín-Bravo S. & Jiménez-Mejías P. 2013: Reseda minoica (Resedaceae), a new species from the eastern Mediterranean region. – *Ann. Bot. Fennici* 50: 55-60.
[58] Hadjikyriakou 2009; Meikle 1977; Alziar 2000.
[59] Chrtek & Slavík. 2001; Meikle 1977; Hand R. 2006: Supplementary notes to the flora of Cyprus V. in Willdenowia 36.
[60] Plinius Secundus The thirteenth book of the Historiae of Nature, chapter 2: *Metopium an oile compounded, which the Ægyptians dos presse out first of bitter Almonds, but they added thereto for to incorporate the better, grape Verjuice: and the ingredients besides, were Cardamum, Squinanth, sweet Calamus, Honnie, Wine, Myrrhe, the graines or seeds of Baulme, Galbanum, Rosin, and Terpintine. One of the meanest and basest ointments now adaies, and therefore thought to be as aunctient as any other, is that which consisteth of the oile of Myrtles, sweet Calamus, Cypresse, and Cypros [Squinanth] Lentiske, and the rind of the Pomegranate.*

2.2.6 Red

2.2.6.1 *Anchusa Aegyptiaca Alkanet Alkanna tinctoria (indigenous)*[61]

Papyrus of Leyda reports many recipes to utilize this plant.[62] ***(Plinius orkanet** supra n. 27)*

2.2.6.2 *Papaver rhoeas* subsp. *cyprium (endemic)*[63]

2.2.6.3 **Robinia** *pseudoacacia* [64]

2.2.6.4 **Rubia** *tinctorum Madder* (*indigenous*)[65]

2.2.7 Caffè

2.2.7.1 *Alnus orientalis (indigenous)*[66]

2.2.7.2 *Iuglans regia (naturalized)*[67]

2.2.7.3 *Quercus Coccifera Galla (indigenous)* [68]

2.2.7.4 *Plantago Major (indigenous)* [69]

3. RESINS[70]

3.1 Resins are exudates of plants/trees formed as oxidation of various essential oils, and gums produced in response to wounding. The chemical composition is very complex consisting of gum sugary oligosaccharides, essential oils, and di/tri-terpenoid components. Most of resinous exudates are divided according to solubility of the main chemical components in organic solvents. Two groups can be distinguished, terpenoid and phenolic: Terpenoid resins contain mono/sesquiterpenes in their volatile fraction and di/triterpenes in non-volatile, while Phenolic

---

[61] Sánchez-Gómez G., J. F. Jiménez, J. B. Vera & C. Aedo 2008: Anchusa aegyptiaca (Boraginaceae), a new species for the Iberian flora in Fl. Medit. 18. Chrtek J. & B. Slavík 1993: Contribution to the flora of Cyprus. 2 in Fl. Medit. 3; Meikle R.D. 1985: Flora of Cyprus 2; Della A. 1992: Flora of a valley in the Pendakomo area in Agric. Res. Inst. Minist. Agric. Nat. Resources Cyprus Misc. Rep. 52; Alziar G. 2000: Compte rendu du 4ème Iter Mediterraneum in Bocconea 11, 5-83; Coulot P. 2000: Approche de la flore de l'île de Chypre in Monde Pl. 470, 16-20.

[62] Papyri de Leyde, recipes ns. 89, 90, 91,94, 95, 96, 97, 98, 99: Caffaro A. & G. Falanga 2004: Il Papiro di Leida un documento di técnica artística e artigianale del sec. IV, Salerno.

[63] Hadjikyriakou G. 2005: Symvoli sti meleti tis chloridas tis Kyprou 3. in Dasoponos 24; Chrtek J. & B. Slavík 1981: Contribution to the flora of Cyprus in Preslia 53; Kadereit J. W 1989: A revision of Papaver section Rhoeadium Spach in Notes Roy. Bot. Gard. Edinburgh 45, 225-286; Meikle R.D. 1977: *Flora of Cyprus* 1, Royal Botanic Gardens. London.

[64] Hadjikyriakou G. & E. Hadjisterkotis 2002: The adventive plants of Cyprus with new records of invasive species in *Z. Jagdwiss.* 48, Suppl.; Hand R. 2004: Supplementary notes to the flora of Cyprus IV. in Willdenowia 34.

[65] Meikle R.D. 1977: *Flora of Cyprus* 1, Royal Botanic Gardens. London.

[66] Meikle R.D. 1985: *Flora of Cyprus 2*, Royal Botanic Gardens. London; Hadjikyriakou G. 2013: Symvoli sti meleti tis chloridas tis Kyprou 16 in Dasoponos 54; Chrtek J. & B. Slavík 2001: Contribution to the flora of Cyprus. 5 in Acta Univ. Carol., Biol. 45; Alziar G. 2000: Compte rendu du 4ème Iter Mediterraneum in Bocconea 11.

[67] Hadjikyriakou G. 2013: Symvoli sti meleti tis chloridas tis Kyprou 16 in Dasoponos 54.

[68] Meikle R.D. 1985: *Flora of Cyprus 2*, Royal Botanic Gardens. London; Chrtek J. & B. Slavík 2001: Contribution to the flora of Cyprus. 5 in Acta Univ. Carol., Biol. 45; Alziar G. 2000: Compte rendu du 4ème Iter Mediterraneum in Bocconea 11.

[69] Meikle R.D. 1985: *Flora of Cyprus 2*, Royal Botanic Gardens. London;

[70] Langenheim J.H. 2003: *Plant Resins: Chemistry, Evolution, Ecology and Ethnobotany*. Timber Press, Portland, (Cambridge) Oregon.

resins contain phenylpropanoids and lipophilic flavonoids.

Their use probably came out as a sort of emulation after taking note of the fact that the lamp of plants produced the substance to repair and disinfect their wounds. In historical times, we find resins added to recipes of perfumes or cosmetics even if they do not retain any proper fragrance. They were an important component of any cosmetic stabilizing the composition and granting its efficacy.

In Egypt, most of the resins were odoriferous and employed both to make perfumes and ointments for embalming bodies[71]. However, from the evidence found at Pyrgos it seems that most of the resins used in Egypt (Frankincense/ Olibano, Myrrh and Galbanum) were completely unknown in Cyprus in the first half of the II millennium BC, while the resins from the local forest were widely used (Fig.13).

Fig. 13: Resin from Paphos Forest

In natural state, they appear as crystal amorphous lumps coming out from tree exhausting oleoresins from which the volatile essential oil has vapoured. Often a little odour will stay until oil removal has been completed. It is most probable that in Cyprus the greater proportions of the ancient resins were from Pinophyta trees including Pinaceae and Cupressus families. Meanwhile Stirax officinalis, Pistacia (Anacardiaceae family) and Ceratonia silique (Pea family) were considered a luxury and used for special purposes. Considering the Flora of Cyprus (endemic and indigenous) the resins (soluble

---

[71] Belgiorno M.R. The Perfume of Cyprus, Roma 2016.

in fat or alcohol) available for cosmetic preparations were those obtained from the trees of:

3.1 *Liquidanbar Orientalis* [72]

3.2 *Pistacia: Atlantica*[73], *Lentiscus*[74], *Therebintus* [75]

3.3 *Pinacea: Cedrus Brevifolia*[76], *Pinus Brutia*, *Pinus Nigra*

3.4 *Cupressus sempervirens* L.

3.5 *Juniperous Phoenicea* [77], ***Excelsa*[78], *Oxycedrus*** [79]

3.6 *Styrax officinalis* [80] *(resina vera storace)*

4. GUMS

4.1 Gums are formed after gummosis, a process consisting in the decomposition of cellulose of internal plant tissues. The product contains high amounts of sugar, is colloidal and soluble in water. They are odourless, tasteless flavouring and soluble and form a mucilaginous mass with the water. Gums are good adhesives, and this property favoured the use in association with colours, in painting, dyeing and finishing textiles. The gums themselves are often capable of resinification or hardening on exposure to air. As drugs, their employ is similar to the resins, included in recipes for internal and external diseases.

One of the most noticeable characteristic of the fruit gums is the difference in colour, ranging from the ivory white to the pinkish, reddish, light brown and almost black. The difference between resin and gum consist mainly in the solubility in various solvents. Excluding the use of embalming bodies, a ritual completely unknown in Cyprus, the use of these ingredients in Cyprus should be restricted (and addressed to produce) to cosmetics for beauty and medical purposes[81].

In Egypt, the gums were used also as an adhesive for painting on the walls, an employing

---

[72] Meikle R.D., Flora of Cyprus 1. 1977; The complicated history of Liquidambar in Cyprus has been discussed in detail by Hadjikyriakou G.N. 2007: *Aromatic and spicy plants in Cyprus. From Antiquity to the Present Day.* Nicosia.
[73] Hadjikyriakou G. 2009: Symvoli sti meleti tis chloridas tis Kyprou 12. in Dasoponos 38; Meikle 1977; Vogt R. & A. Aparicio 2000: Chromosome numbers of plants collected during Iter Mediterraneum IV in Cyprus in Bocconea 11, 117-169.
[74] Meikle R.D. 1977; Della A. 1992: Flora of a valley in the Pendakomo area in Agric. Res. Inst. Minist. Agric. Nat. Resources Cyprus Misc. Rep. 52; Alziar 2000; Hadjikyriakou 2009.
[75] Meikle 1977; Hadjikyriakou 2009; Chrtek & Slavík 2001.
[76] Farjon A. 2010: *A handbook of the world's conifers.* - Leiden & Boston; Qiao J.-Y., Ran J.-H., Li Y. & Wang X.-Q. 2007: Phylogeny and biogeography of *Cedrus* (*Pinaceae*) inferred from sequences of seven paternal chloroplast and maternal mitochondrial DNA regions. - Ann. Bot. 100: 573-580.
[77] Alziar 2000; Hadjikyriakou 2004; Chrtek & Slavík 2001; Meikle 1977; Farjon A. 2005: *A monograph of Cupressaceae and Sciadopitys.* Royal Botanic Gardens, Kew.
[78] Farjon A. 2005: *A monograph of Cupressaceae and Sciadopitys.* Royal Botanic Gardens, Kew; G. Hadjikyriakou G. 2004: Symvoli sti meleti tis chloridas tis Kyprou [1]. in Dasoponos 20; Meikle 1977; Hand R. 2003: Supplementary notes to the flora of Cyprus III. in Willdenowia 33.
[79] Supra n. 54; Chrtek & Slavík 2001.
[80] Meikle 1985; Della 1992; Alziar 2000.
[81] Dieterich K. 1920: *The Analysis of Resins and Gum Resins,* London 161.

completely ignored in Cyprus, where no wall painting has been found in Early Middle Bronze age. The finding of ancient recipes including gum components in the old Orthodox monastery manuscripts suggests a long cultural tradition in using gums for pharmaceutical compounds and remedies for skin. Ancient recipes for perfumes and cosmetics, including gums, can be found in the Egyptian Edwin Smith Surgical Papyrus (about 1600 BC) and the Ebers Papyrus (about1550 BC).

In Cyprus, the plants producing gums were:

4.1.1 Almond (*píssa tis athashiás tis pikrís – bitter almond gum*). Among the fruits the almond gum had a special distinction due to the numerous Almond trees that grow everywhere in Cyprus.

4.1.2 Prunus *(cherry gum)*[82]

4.1.3 Cistus *(Laubdanum)*

4.1.4 Ceratonia siliqua *(tragasol)*
The carob, *Ceratonia siliqua*, produces tragasol, a mucilaginous hemi cellulose occurring in the pods, which were crushed to make the mucilage.

4.1.5 Convolvulus scammonia *(scamonea)*

4.1.6 Olive

5. OLEORESINS

5.1 Oleoresin is a viscous liquid produced by the solvent extraction of gum and resins. Some oleoresins are much under-used, as they offer interesting odour qualities, but they may not be completely soluble in ethyl alcohol

In the present incomplete review of the Mycenaean oleaginous plants ki-ta-no is not considered. Ki-ta-no is probably a member of the Pistacia family, and Timaeus (de mir. ausc. 88) quotes the usage by the inhabitants of the Balearic Islands of an oil obtained from the turpentine tree. Both Xenophon (Anab. IV.4.13) and Theophrastus (HP 3.3.1) mention turpentine fruits as an ingredient in perfumes and unguents5.

While still used today in balsams, the products of the Pistacia family are to be strictly considered as oleoresins (P. Lentiscus, only 2 percent of essential oil; P. Terebinthus, 14 per cent).[83]

---

[82] The gums from different species of plum have been used in Cyprus for centuries, as they were commonly available. The cherry gum was the most cited, but similar gums as almond, apricot and pear were also used even if not distinguished clearly.
[83] Melena J.L. 1974: KI-TA-NO en las tablillas de Cnoso, *Durius 2:1*, 45-55; and 1975: La producción de plantas aromáticas en Cnoso, *Estudios Clásicos* 78, 180-183; Perrot Em. 1944: Matières premieres du règne vegetal, Paris 1943-1944 1309; Wylock M.: 1973: Les aromates dans les tablettes Ge de Mycènes, *SMEA* 15.

6. OILS[84]

6.1 Vegetable oils made probably the difference between the Egyptian and Cypro-Mediterranean Cosmetics. It was not intentional, due to the abundance of Olive (Fig.14), Almond and Lentiscus trees.

Fig. 14: Imprints of olive leaves on 2000BC ceramic and earth from Pyrgos

Their economic use in place of the animal fat could have played an important role in the quality and conservation of ointments, medicines and cosmetics, lowering the rancidity factor of the compounds. Many inscriptions report the high quantity of Cyprus olive oil imported from Egypt and from Eastern Mediterranean countries, sometimes partly scented as the famous Coriander olive oil mentioned in the Linear B tablets. According to the results of the Archaeometry investigation made by Alessandro Lentini in the ITABC-CNR laboratories, the oils used at Pyrgos in the Early-Middle Bronze age were: ***Olive*[85]*, Linum usitatissimum L.*[86]** (Fig.15), ***Almond and Lentiscus.***

Fig. 15: Linum fossilised seeds

---

[84] Honey and olive oil were the favored ingredients in cosmetics: Forbes R.J. 1955: *Studies in Ancient Technology* vol. III, 40; 1957: *Studies in Ancient Technology* I, 34; Lau J.Y. 1976: *Bees and Honey*, Dominion Press. Australia: 58; *Manniche* L. 1989: *An Ancient Egyptian Herbal*, British Museum; 1999: Sacred Luxuries: Fragrance, Aromatherapy, and Cosmetics in Ancient Egypt, Cornell Un. Press.
[85] Belgiorno M.R. 2016: The Production of Perfumes in *Antiquity in The Perfume of Cyprus*, Ch. 5, *Roma*
[86] Ramella R. 1944: *El lino oleaginoso*, Buenos Aires; Forbes R.J. 1955: *Studies in Ancient Technology* III, 7-17; Sacconi A. 1971: A proposito dell'epíteto omerico ΛΙΝΟΘΩΡΗΞ, *ZA* 21, 49-54. For a general survey see Legget W. F. 1949: *The Story of Linen*, New York Chemical Publ.

7. WINE[87]

7.1 Almost all Egyptian recipes report wine as the main ingredient with which to start making perfumes, ointments, and medications. The process began with the boiling of animal fat in wine to remove the smell of meat, and acquire that of wine.

The other ingredients, in specific proportions, were added in succession, depending on type, measure, and expected time for production. The process was interrupted several times, even for days, to give time for the amalgam to mature. In these phases of "rest" the alcohol contained in wine grew in intensity because of added sugars, stabilizing the perfume.

The composition should not boil, but only reach the correct temperature, which allowed the melting of resins, terpenes, and various fat components. Otherwise, the alcohol would evaporate. Wine was the osmotic agent of oil perfume composition, as it allowed the melting of ingredients[88].

Along with olive oil, it had an extraordinary importance in preparation of cosmetics, pharmaceutical remedies, and magic potions[89].

Considering cultural exchanges with Egypt and the importance given to production of wine at the beginning of the Bronze Age, it is hard not to speculate in Cyprus a targeted use of wine in making cosmetics, perfumes, and pharmaceutical compounds. Moreover, the industrial complex of Pyrgos has furnished several pots for wine with a characteristic pointed base (Fig.16), as well as seeds and pollen of *Vitis silvestris* and *sativa*.

It is hard then not to find a direct connection between wine production and the production of perfumes, considering that, per Theophrastus, Pliny the Elder and Dioscurides, two of the most famous perfumes of ancient Cyprus, the *Amarikinon* and *Ciprinum* need wine in their preparation. Although its use was probably linked to the production of medicines and pharmaceutical remedies.

However, we must not forget that per Pliny (Nat. Hist. Book XII) one of the most intoxicating

---

[87] McGovern P. E. 2003: *Ancient Wine. The Search for the Origins of Viniculture*: Princeton University Press; Belgiorno M.R. 2016: Notes on the use of wine in production of perfumes and pharmaceutical tinctures *in The Perfume of Cyprus* Ch. 8. Roma.

[88] On the walls of the Ptolemaic temple of Edfu, at Louxor, there is the recipe of a sacred ointment including wine as carrier, demanding 6 months to mature properly. Wilson P. 1997: *A Lexicographical Study of the Ptolemaic Texts in the Temple of Edfu*, Leuven.
-0,575 litre of carob sugar (*Ceratonia siliqua*)
-1010 grams of dry Frankincense
-600 grams of Styrax
-25 grams de aromatic Calamus (*Acorus calamus L.*)
-10 grams of Pistacia Lentisque (mastic) resin
-15 grams of Violet grains
-0,5 litre of mixed wine and water

[89] Plinius Secundus The thirteenth book of the Historiae of Natvre, chapter 1: *But I would thinke verily, that Oyntlments came to beeso divulged and common euery where abroad, by meanes of Roses most of all: considering, that nothing grows more rife in all places. Which was the cause, that the simple mixture of oile Rosate, without any sophistication besides, continued for a long time, hauing the addition of grape Verjuice, the floure of Roses, the Saffron, Cinnabaris, or Sang-Dragon, Calamus, Hony, Squinanth, the floure of salt called Sperma-ceti, or els in lieu therof the root of Orcanet, & Wine. The oile or ointment of Saffron was after the same sort made, by putting thereto Cinnabaris, Orcanet, & wine. Semblably is to be said of the oile of the sweet lesse Maioran, wherin was mixed grape verjuice and sweet Calamus. This composition was sin|gularly wel made in Cyprus & at Mitylene, where great store of sweet Majoran grows.* Idem chapter 2: *The Roiall Ointment therefore (which the Parthian kings vsed ordinarily, and of whome* [unspec B] *it took that name to be called Roiall) is tempered and composed in this manner: to wit, of Ben, Costus, Amonium, Cinamon, the Arbut or Comarus, Cadamonum, Spikenard, Marum, Myrrhe, Casia, Storax Calamita, Ladanum, Baulme liquor, sweet Calamus, Squinanth of Syria, the floure of the wild vine, Malabathrum, Serichatum, Cyperus, Aspalathus, Panace Saffron, Cypros, Marioram the greater, clarified, or purified Hony, and Wine.*

perfume was the essential oil extracted from the flowers of the grapevine, and the best processed from the flowers of wild grape of Cyprus.

Today, the "Zuccardi Family", who runs a winery in Argentina, near Mendoza, 1000 km from Buenos Aires, produces the "Malbec Cologne", a men's fragrance, based on Malbec, a renowned Argentine wine. Nevertheless, the attempt to bring together in an innovative product, the world of wine with the world of perfume was first experienced in France from renowned brands like Frapin, Ginestet and Courvoisier. The challenge is based on the belief that those who can make good wine (or Cognac) can also create a good perfume. In 2007 Courvoisier created a man fragrance "*Courvoisier L'edition Imperiale*".

Fig. 16: Wine jug, Pyrgos Inv.n. 238

Pierre Frapin, who belongs to a century-old family of producers of Champagne and Cognac (since 1270, mentioned by F. Rabelais in the 16th century) presented in 2008 "*Frapin 1270*". Then the brand continued to create new fragrances flavoured with wine and brandy. Among them, we include "*Terre de Sarment, Esprit de Fleurs, Caravelle Epicée* and *Passion Boisée*".

Ginestet in 2008 began production of three different fragrances, *Botrytis* and *Le Boise*, aged in oak barrels like wine, and *Sauvignonne* produced from the grapes of Bordeaux.

In Italy, the company Cesari (Umberto and Giuliana) has produced Tauleto since 2008, a fragrance made from special Sangiovese grapes.

And we must remember that researchers at the University of British Columbia, have recently confirmed that the smell of wine comes from the pollen grains stored in anthers of flowers, contrary to popular belief that it was the petals alone to produce the aroma.

While, studying the grapes of Cabernet Sauvignon from the Okanagan region (British Columbia), researchers at the UBC Wine Research Centre and Michael Smith Laboratories have identified a gene that produces and regulates the fragrance of wine in small bunches of flowers[90]

---

[90] Proceedings of the National Academy of Sciences Online Early Edition, April 2009

8. HONEY AND BEESWAX[91]

Use of Beeswax in cosmetics is associated with some of its peculiarities: it is an excellent emollient easily to be moisturized with other ingredients, mainly it is protective for the skin improving its elasticity and protects of sunscreens.

Honey is considered one of the most ancient ingredients of the world to make pharmaceutical/cosmetics compounds for its well-known anti-microbial, healing and antibacterial properties.

9. INSTRUMENTS

Actions	*Tools*
Mining minerals	hammers
Transport	Baskets sacks
Harvesting plants and seeds	baskets and perishable sacks
crushing	mortars, pestles, basins
extraction of oils	pressing, basins for collection
stocking of products	pots
Powdering of dry resins	Mortars pestles
composition and dosage	recipes, balances, bottles
maturation and conservation	storage, bottles
sale	platform, seats

9.1 The instruments in polished stone represent a very important repertoire that completes the picture of tools outfit of the Pyrgos workshop, making it resemble a proto cosmetic-pharmacy, like a medieval alchemical laboratory.

The presence, processing and number of these tools give an index of productive engagement and economic progress of Pyrgos society, because it is based on the ability to modify and use agriculture and mineral resources to produce health substances for the community and

---

[91] Serpico M. and R. White 2009: Oil, Fat and Wax, 390- 430; Resin, Amber and bitumen, 430-475, in Paul T. Nicholson, Ian Shaw (ed) *Ancient Egyptian Materials and Technology*. Cambridge Un. Press; Bagde A.B., Sawant R.S., Bingare S.D., Sawai R.V., Nikumbh M.B. 2013: Therapeutic and Nutritional Values of Honey (Madhu) in: *International Research Journal Pharmacy*, 4 (3), 19-22.

ephemeral goods. Otherwise, at a time when metal tools were a luxury for few, it would not have been possible to produce drugs, cosmetics, and ointments without the disposability of such quantity of stone instruments. The same kind of objects was also in use in the domestic environment and metallurgy, with substantial differences in shape and size, a number could be considered multi-purpose. Many specimens abandoned from the previous occupation have been reused in the Middle Bronze age and adapted to the task. An interesting phenomenon related to these tools is the progressive increment of number in relation to the growth and difference of the materials to be treated. This suggests that there was a great variety of organic and inorganic substances that needed to be worked differently.

DIVIDED IN FOUR GROUPS:

9.2 Mortars with pestles.

Mortars are made primarily of basalt and limestone. Generally, the dimensions of the mortars of basalt do not exceed 15 cm in diameter, the shape is rounded or oval. The specimens of limestone may be very large and different shaped, a rare example was carved with 14 cups, probably for preparing different substances together[92] (n°227 and n°228 original dimensions 54cm X 30cm, decreasing thicknesses from 14,2cm to 1cm; this volume Lentini 137). (Fig. 17).

Fig. 17: Multiple mortar, Pyrgos Inv.n. 227+228

This peculiar cosmetic mortar was found in a room, adjacent to the perfumery, devoted to the production of textiles. However, any remains of colours have been found in the cups of

---

[92] Belgiorno M.R. 2007: Catalogo n° 195; in M.R. Belgiorno (ed) *I Profumi di Afrodite e il segreto dell'Olio*, 151-247, Roma.

the mortar, meanwhile lumps of different colours, including Indigofera argentea (Lentini p. 126; Figs 23-24)have been found scattered in the room. The Archaeometry analyses reported only traces of rutina (Lentini p. 127)

The mortar, including two basalt pestles, has been found cut in two pieces, next to a large bowl encrusted with resin mixed with opium (Lentini 2009). Both parts show a worn side that seem to suggest that they have been used for a long time before abandon in the Middle Bronze age II. The cutting in two parts seems intentional, probably to modify an earlier too large instrument. The original multi cups mortar was obtained from a large limestone block, carefully worked to incline the surface towards the operator. On the countertop were originally carved 16 cups, of which only 11 survive. Two cups, one right and one left have an extra circle carved outside, perhaps to recover the surplus of a specific substance who could easily transfer from the cup during pulverization.

The fact that only two cups have an extra ring may indicate that the object was carefully created to mix and grind simultaneously several substances.

9.3 Pestles

Most of the pestles are basalt, chalcedony and quartz modified pebbles, the shape follows more or less the original of natural pebbles easy to find on the local beach or along the riversides and chosen for their ergonomic form. The shape may be conical, cylindrical, bell-shape, drop or spatula. Some of polished pink quartz pestles have been found together with palettes and it seems obvious that they were used for preparing cosmetics. Similar pebble pestles have been found associated with palettes in Predynastic Egyptian burials, confirming our suggestion (Petrie 1896:10)[93] (Fig.18).

Fig. 18: Pestles with their mortars from Pyrgos

The dimension is highly variable going from 2-3 centimetres for smaller palettes or shells to

---

[93] Petrie, W.M.F. 1896 Naqada and Ballas. Warminster: Aris and Philips Ltd.

more than 15 cm. for larger specimens.

9.4 Millstones.

The ground stone artefacts from Pyrgos are of common types of Cyprus Neolithic sites. The major materials utilized for the manufacture are basalt, Gabbro, andesite, sandstone and quartz. The millstones consist of slabs presenting an upper surface on which you grind organic and inorganic material to reduce it in powder. Most of them have been reused for different activities, which hides the primary use (Roux 1985)[94]. The shape is generally elongated or tongue shaped, others are flat, intended as a fixed spot on which rest objects for chopping, sanding and refinishing.

Generally, the thickness increases with overall length and width dimensions, and the surface is concave suggesting the use of heavy hand stones as upper, mobile tool used against the planar face of the querns. Most of them can be found on the beach which is 4 km far from the village.

9.5 Quartz Strikers

Quartz ball is a peculiar and common type of striker in Pyrgos tool assemblage. They are pebbles of chert collected on the graves used for pecking flint blades and smoothing basalt tools. The specimens found to have an internal structure composed of irregular layers of different colours, with a few small cavities that are outlined with tiny quartz crystals (Fig.19).

They are slightly translucent when the user has completely removed the cortex. The surface is rough with multiple bits of splintered crystals formed by using the object for hammering.

Fig. 19: Quartz ball striker, Pyrgos Inv.n. 4248

Most of them have been found half divided, reduced in two hemispherical parts.

---

[94] Roux, V. (1985) Le Materiel de broyage: etude ethnoarcheologique a Tichitt (R.I. Mauritanie). Paris: Editions Recherche sur les Civilisations, Memoire no. 5

9.5 *Palettes*[95] with their *pounders*

The tool named *cosmetic palette* is a slab of stone, or a modified squared fragment of a large vessel, varying in thickness from less of 1 to more than 3 centimetres, normally not exceeding the length of 20 cm. On its surface were generally mixed pulverized coloured earths or minerals, resins, spices, oils and organic ingredients. These objects appear in Mesopotamian and Egyptian horizons in the fourth millennium BC, spreading throughout the Mediterranean at the beginning of the third millennium BC

Sporadic examples of palettes, often fragmentary, come from various Mediterranean, Late Neolithic contexts, but it is the Neolithic Egypt that returned the most elaborate and artistic realizations in relevant number. They are characteristic funerary goods that will take a symbolic value of power and personal prestige with the advent of the first Pharaonic dynasties. On the contrary, the Cypriot palettes found in Pyrgos are simple tools found in an industrial context (Fig.20).

Fig. 20: Some examples of palettes with their pounders from Pyrgos

Their use seems closely related to workshops, and unlike the Egyptians, are not funerary objects or status symbol and do not identify the owner. Some were found with polished pestles of quartz and basalt, or spatulas made reshaping fragments of broken palettes. None of them shows signs of violent percussion or abrasion due to a possibly different use.

---

[95] For clay Palettes sherds which fit nicely into the hand with one or all eroded edges: Musawwarat Es Sufra: A meroitic pottery workshop at Musawwarat es Sufra David N. Edwards p. 13.; http://acrossborders.oeaw.ac.at/reuse-of-pottery-sherds-from-sav1e/Re-cut pot sherds as tools with multiple functions are frequently found at New Kingdom domestic sites as can be illustrated by material from Qantir (Raedler 2007; Prell 2011, 92) and Elephantine (Kopp 2005b; see also Budka 2010c). Such a reuse of ceramics is also attested in Nubian cultures, e.g. for cosmetic palettes (Williams 1993, 45 with note 49). Budka, J., Review of *Die Keramik des Grabungsplatzes Q1 – Teil 2; Schaber – Marken – Scherben*. Forschungen in der Ramses-Stadt, Die Grabungen des Pelizaeus-Museums Hildesheim in Qantir – Pi-Ramesse 5, ed. by E. B. Pusch & M. Bietak, Hildesheim 2007, *Orientalische Literaturzeitung* 105/6, 2010, 676–685.Peña, J. T. 2007: *Roman Pottery in the Archaeological Record*, Cambridge 2007.
Reused stone palettes Elżbieta Kołłosowska, Mahmoud el-Tayeb and Henryk Paner Sudan and Nubia 7, 21-26.
Plate 1. Classic Kerma pottery combs and palette. Plate 4. (Pyrgos type F.)

The large number of palettes found at Pyrgos, although justified by the presence of an industrial area, is a unique event and a rare example of instrumental destination for a possible commercial production of cosmetics. The presence of these objects and their pestles in different investigated rooms, suggests that some different workshops took turns between the Early and Middle Bronze age.

Although there is a wide chronological difference, the Cypriote types have a comparison with the simple undecorated Egyptians (first typological group) included in the Petrie's corpus[96].

Comparison of Pyrgos palettes with the Egyptian allowed us to identify some peculiarities of these objects facing their manageability.

We found that over the thickness and dimension, the shapes are characteristic. They are rounded (for those basalt) or rectangular (for those of quartzite) with bevelled edges, often with a sort of invitation or cutting from one side, so that you can grip with one hand while mixing something on with the other hand, holding a wooden spatula or a stone pestle.

The underside has a rough surface and the upper smooth, polished and worn in the centre with the use. Following the Petrie's corpus, we have identified 12 distinct types: eye, disc (round and oval), shift, lozenge, squared, rectangle and elongated rectangle... etc.

9.6 *Palette Typology*

The total palettes found at Pyrgos, reported on the map, are 130. They are roughly shaped slabs of schist, limestone, and basalt: 73, plus a *navette* of black steatite[97] have been found in the workshop excavated in 2012, 57 in other sectors. As the most ancient Egyptian (Petrie 1st group) they are not decorated.

We have divided them into 12 types, using the corpus of Petrìe[98] for comparisons (Fig. 22, 23). The thickness varies from 0,8 to 2,52 cm (Fig. 21).

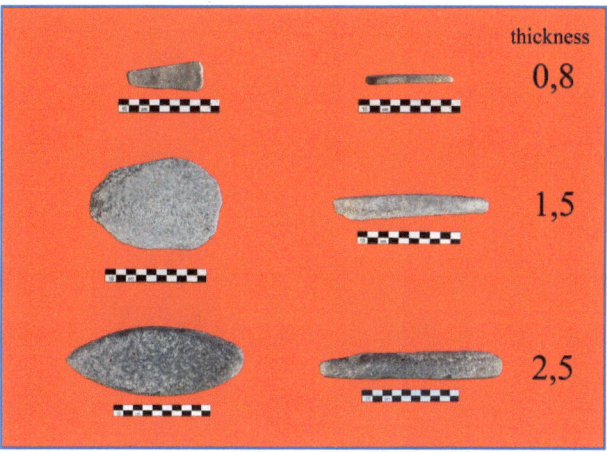

Fig. 21: Examples of palettes and their thickness from Pyrgos

---

[96] Sir William Matthew Flinders Petrie in 1910 drew up the corpus of the Egyptian palettes, a number of which is in the "Petrie Museum of Egyptian Archaeology of London: it provides a valid comparison instrument for similar objects found in the Mediterranean area.
[97] Belgiorno M.R. 2014. I Profumi di Venere in *Archeo* 347,1, fig. 135, 141.
[98] Flinders Petrie W.M. 1953: *Corpus of prehistoric pottery and palettes* (British School of Archaeology in Egypt 1921), London.

Type	Pyrgos	Petrie
A Eye-oval	5 items 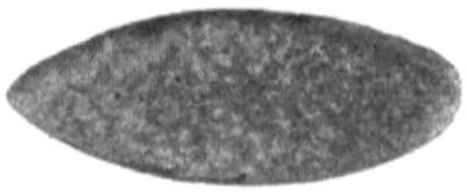	 9077
B Disk rounded	4 items 	
C Trapezium rectangle	23 items 	 4671
D Trapezium isosceles	12 items 	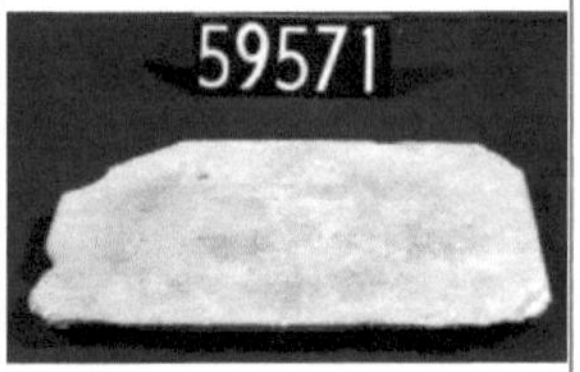 59571
E Rectangle	26 items 	
F Rectangle with rounded corner	34 items 	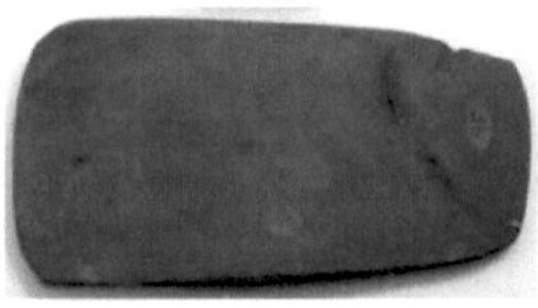

Fig. 22: Pyrgos palette typology table n.1

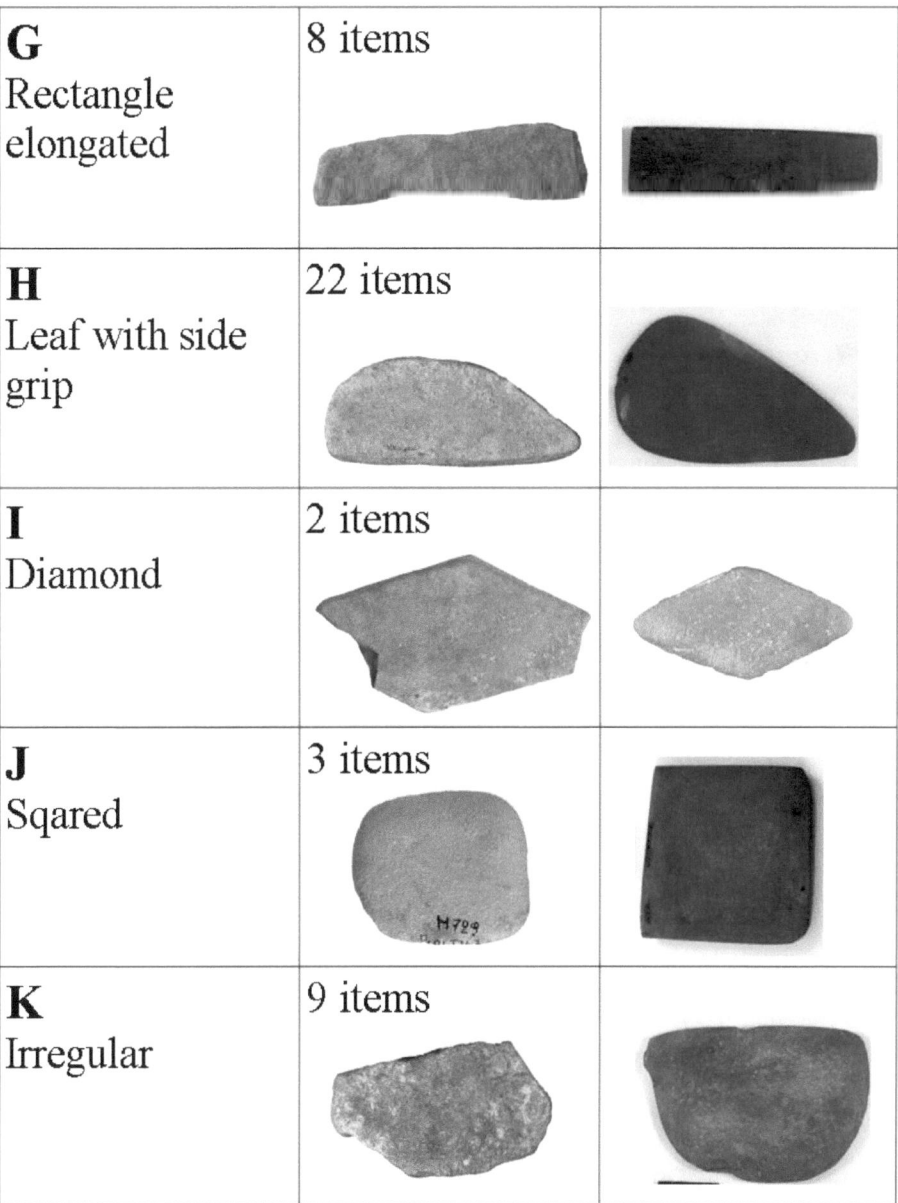

Fig. 23: Pyrgos palette typology table n.2

In the literature, these objects are considered tools to both pulverize and mix colours preparing cosmetics. The pulverize of colours is difficult to accept, either because the object does not have a raised edge to prevent the spread of dust, either because pulverizing of minerals, such as ochre, would leave deep marks on the object (comparison palette with mortar of Pyrgos). Instead, it is reasonably the second option, to prepare cosmetics, blending grounded substances with a vehiculant to get a homogeneous mixture[99].

Their proper definition should be the Matthäus', who in 1989 calls them "ointment palettes"[100] adding that: "*Although this is not a surgical instrument, it does have associations with pharmaceutical*

---

[99] Milne J. 1907: *Surgical Instruments in Greek and Roman Times*, 171.Oxford.
[100] Matthäus H. 1989: *Der Arzt in römischer Zeit. Medizinische Instrumente und Arzneien* (Limes Museum Aalen), Stuttgart.

procedures and is found frequently in the archaeological record. The palettes are of stone and often found with rubbing marks on the surface on one side. It is also possible that it was used to make-up and paints".

As mentioned before, there is a chronological and numerical discrepancy among the number of palettes found at Pyrgos and the number of examples from other Cypriot sites, Egypt and the Near East. Moreover, there is a high chronological gap between Cyprus (Early-Middle Bronze age) and Egypt (Neolithic: Predynastic and Protodynastic), something more than 1000 years. Instead, in the Middle East, we find parallels in the late Chalcolithic, but the number does not exceed ten specimens per site.

In Cyprus, we have eight palettes, four complete and four fragmented from the late Chalcolithic site of Kissonerga[101], two from Markì (Early Middle Bronze) and one from Sotira Kaminoudhia (Early-Middle Bronze). Then, in view of the number of palettes found at Pyrgos, we can deduce that the specimens found were instruments properly created to work specific substances.

To find these substances we have activated an Archaeometry protocol, which includes comparisons among historical sources, archaeological evidence and Archaeometry analyses.

First, to get an idea of the ingredients used, not having Cypriot literature on this subject, we took suggestions from Egypt, which had extensive trades and cultural relations with Cyprus.

I refer to the papyri, and more precisely to the "Medical papyri", some of which date back to the early 2nd millennium BC, as the papyri found at Fayyum by Petrie, the Ramesseum papyri (IV and V 1900 BC), the papyrus of Hearst and the papyrus of Eber (Bardinet translation 1995)[102]. In these texts, we find a detailed list of diseases and pharmaceutical remedies with recipes and a description of the procedure to make the composition. There is no distinction between beauty, diseases, or health diseases, as there is no distinction between cosmetics and pharmaceuticals.

9.7 Small containers of clay and shell

Among the characteristic objects there are small containers for pigments and cosmetics or precious ingredients: miniature ladles, bowls (Fig. 25), and valve of shells[103]. Containers of shell[104] consist mainly of valve of oysters (Fig. 24) and large back of Limpets.

Miniature bowls have been found in various Cypriot sites from the late Neolithic: some made of stone, some clay. Small bowls are often present as applied decoration on many vessels, positioned around the rim or body, sometimes, especially on pottery of the beginning of Middle Bronze age.

This fact suggests that they had a special value or a symbolic meaning possible related to cosmetics and pharmaceutical compounds or symbolize that content of the vase includes such ingredients. Often these vases have been identified as cult vases, even if there is any specific relation to rituals or religion.

---

[101] Pentelburg E. et al. 1998: *Excavations at Kissonerga-Mosphilia*, 1979-1992, Volume II.1B (Part 1), 211, 236, Edinburgh.
[102] Comp. note 152; Bardinet T. 1995: *Les Papirus mèdicaux de l'Egypte pharaonique*, Fayard, Paris.
[103] Often these miniature bowls found in tombs have been misunderstood as special goods for children.
[104] Stuart Moorey P. R. 1994: *Ancient Mesopotamian Materials and Industries: The Archaeological Evidence*. 134-138. Oxford University press.

Cosmetics

Fig. 24: n° 4301, 4558, oyster shell containers from the workshop of cosmetics.

At Pyrgos the smallest clay example was found in the workshop excavated in 2012, in a pit set against the southern wall, covered by small querns and pestles. In the same pit, there were some palettes, small pestles, large flints, picrolite comb pendants, shells worked or half processed and small bone tools. The pit was positioned in a corner full of hundreds of stone powders, flints, and shells, including an oyster valve with remains of green paint and lumps of ochre. In the same room, have been found two small mortars with pestles and more fragments of miniature bowls. Similar tiny bowls and mortars have been found in the sector of the olive press room identified as perfume workshop.

Fig. 25: Fragmentary miniature bowls, the first on the left is intact and shaped as a "Limpet" shell. n° 4444, 4816, 4917, 4818.

10. ARCHAEOMETRY

10.1 The preliminary results of the Archaeometry investigation mainly underline that the procedure to obtain a remedy for external or internal use is very similar of today, including the ingredients and the way of administering the "medication"[105] (below Alessandro Lentini).

When examining the recipes, we notice that these usually refer to a blend of creamy substances or semi-solid products obtained by mixing "therapeutic" ingredients with a vehiculant of common use[106].

The first elemental analysis and microscopic investigation executed at Pyrgos by Alessandro Lentini[107] on the patina of some palettes, revealed the presence of lead oxides, with values between 35 and 52% salt residues and remains of red and yellow ochre[108]. Interesting is the presence of Magnesium, Aluminium, Sodium, and Copper: *During the preliminary analysis to find readable elements, some samples dissolved in distilled water and dried on muffle, allowed observation by the digital stereo microscope of pseudo crystals of green, red, blue and white colour with diamond and cubic morphologies. The sediments show various degrees of over saturation of elements that crystallized, according to a process known for its sodium chloride and copper sulphate. The white crystals contain Magnesium ($MgCl_2$) and Sodium (Na Cl)* (Fig.26).

Fig. 26: Crystals Na Cl on palette n.4146

While the blue crystals contain copper sulphide ($CuSO_4$). The greenish and red belong to clay rich in silicates of Aluminium, Iron, and Magnesium ($Mg 2+ Fe2 + Fe3 + Al3 +$). Therefore, we have two different types of saline compositions: sodium chloride and magnesium chloride, present in water meadows and salt lakes of Cyprus. While copper salts $CuSO_4. 5H_2O$, are characteristic products of the extensive deposits of carbonates, sulphides,

---

[105] Two of our earliest extant treatises are by women. One is very obscure indeed although we know the authoress, Cleopatra (not the queen) sought to make gold: note the symbolism of the Ouroboros (tail-eating) snake.
[106] Lefevre G. 1999: *Essai sur la médecine égyptienne à l'époque pharaonique*, Paris.
[107] Lentini A. 2014: Cipro, Afrodite e la cosmesi", *Archeo, 347*, 1, 32 – 35.
[108] Among the often-mentioned ingredients, we found several times curative ochre. For instance, Cyprus is famous for exporting the best quality in the world, even today.

and sulphates of copper in Cyprus (Fig. 27).

Fig. 27: Crystals CuSO4 on palette n.4096

These salts were widely used and traded for their disinfectant properties (recognized by the World Health Organization), since unmemorable times and employed to make pharmaceutical compounds. Moreover, the analyses made with Bellier's reaction indicated the occurrence of olive oil, while the Lugol's reagent showed the presence of cereals starch (Fig. 28), which is a well-known ingredient of paediatric talc and cosmetic powders, today present in creams and beauty products.

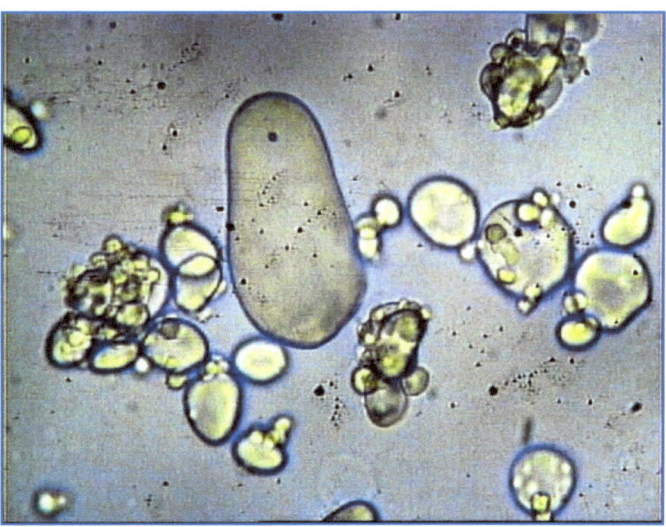

Fig. 28: Wheat starch on palette n. 4178

One interesting example is the use of *Trigonella Foenum Graecum* (Fig.29) containing 45% galactomannan polysaccharide, well known in Egyptian cosmetic, which is extensively employed today in curative creams against the wrinkles. Carbonized seeds of Trigonella have been found at Pyrgos/Mavroraki in the workshop of cosmetics in 2012 during the Organic Stratigraphic Investigations made by Alessandro Lentini (OSI. Py12 B10b/C10a), suggesting a specific use in producing beauty remedies.

Fig. 29: Trigonella foenum graecum, contain 45% galactomannan polysaccharide, well known ingredient against wrinkles. Seeds from Pyrgos/Mavroraki

Both olive oil and wheat starch are elements that integrate the Archaeobotanical evidence from Pyrgos, published on several occasions[109]. However, the most important ingredient, which is characteristic of Cyprus and has been and is a basic component of many cosmetics ("make up") is Magnesium, ever present in modern Cipria, coloured Phard, eye powder and lipstick[110]. This first data highlight a new aspect of Cypriot proto-cosmetics, the employ of no-toxic inorganic ingredients mixed with organic, to create not only a make-up but a healthy product to increase the skin beauty.

It is something that made the difference in comparison with the products at the time circulating as the Egyptians. Perhaps what create a legend about the origin of the female beauty in Cyprus, hundreds before Aphrodite, considering that the preliminary analysis has detected the presence of substances that prelude to simple forms of real cosmetics, still worldwide used.

11. THE WORKSHOP OF COSMETICS

11.1 Position. The excavation of 2012 brought to light a workshop for cosmetics, separated from the main complex by a wide road. The building consists of two interconnecting rooms, of which only one was fully excavated.

The shape is rectangular and has two separate entrances: one South and one on the Northwest corner (Fig. 30). A third opening led into the second room.

It was partly covered on three sides with a sort of the inner court (Fig. 31), which was lit from above. We find similar building solutions in Egypt, North Africa, and the Near East, with an internal staircase that goes up to the roof. In the centre, there was a double bench built with rubble and lime, over, a natural step of bedrock.

---

[109]Lentini A. & M.R. Belgiorno 2008: Palaethnobotany investigations at the site of Pyrgos-Mavrorachi, Cyprus, in Kars H., Meyers P. and Wagner C.A. (ed) *International Symposium on Archaeometry*, 37, 296-297.

[110] http://www.mineralepuro.it/ This site reports the components of makeup products, each containing Magnesium.

Cosmetics

Fig.30: View of cosmetic workshop

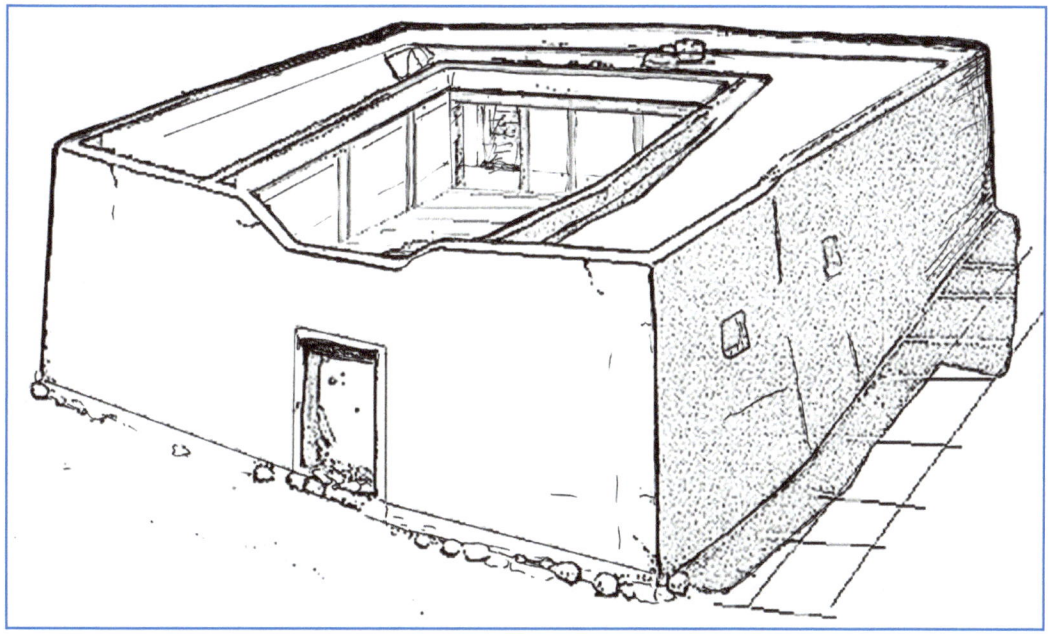

Fig. 31: A possible reconstruction of the first room

11.2 Implements. Some pits of convenience and a large slab of basalt stuck under the bench, with small pebbles and lime, and remains of a hearth near the entrance, form the immovable furnishing.

Scattered around the rich repertoire of mortars, millstones and hundreds of stone tools testified different activities, mainly concerning the production of jewellery and the processing of cosmetics and medicines.

Considering the number of finished and unfinished shells and picrolite items that illustrate the entire processing line to make the amulets[111], we have ascertained that the Pyrgos artisans were specialized in picrolite and shells working. Remains of picrolite-working also occurred at Pyrgos in previously excavated areas, moreover the sequence of the items found in 2012 suggests that a specialist workshop in processing picrolite was arranged there. It includes 2 complete "comb" pendants, 2 unfinished comb pendants, 1 complete ring, 1 large broken ring, 1 (4 cm) roundel, 1 spindle whorl, 4 large polished and processed plate lumps, 2 pieces with signs of process, 3 splinters of wasting processing, 3 raw nuggets. By the same laboratory should come other items found in 2009 outside the eastern wall, which consist in 2 broken comb pendants and 2 beads, for a total of 24 items.

Figure 246: the first four picrolite specimens from the workshop of Pyrgos show the working process of a pebble to become an amulet.

The repertoire includes 498 polished stone tools, including 71 pestles, 6 large millstones, 212 rubbing stones, 29 pebbles of burned basalt, 1axe, 5 mortars, 130 strikers, 1 hammer, 14 powders and 9 expedient tools, plus 374 flints, one flint axe, 23 quartz items.

Including 10 strikers, for 896 items, which adding up 73 cosmetic palettes gives a total of 969 stone tools.

Among the fragmentary pottery, which comprises some miniature bowls it is interesting to note the absence of Red Pol. IV, which instead represents the largest percentage of the vessels found in the perfume factory, suggesting a chronological difference.

12. CONSIDERATIONS

The discovery of Cosmetic workshops improves the industrial and commercial character of Pyrgos. A character that was probably common to many of the Cypriot sites, whose existence is known for the necropolises found in the territory. However, it is probable that this peculiar character turned Cyprus into a competitive trading country during the second millennium BC, as the merchandise found in wreck ships and records on the Mycenaean and Egyptian tablets show.

As regards to the pattern of cosmetic workshop, archaeological evidence and division of space, we can imagine that the production process was quite complex and laborious. Starting from the setting of the workplace, designed and built ad hoc, we must consider the preparation of instruments and the supply of ingredients, before you begin the real production.

More or less, they follow the steps listed below:

1- Construction of the working place

2- Sourcing of organic and inorganic materials

---

[111] Belgiorno M.R. 2014: I Profumi di Venere in *Archeo* 347,1, 27-38.

3- Supply of stone tools

4- Ceramic containers

5- Processing of picrolite and shells

6- Crumbling and mixing ochre and minerals

7- Dough organic materials

8 -Composition and storage

9- Commerce

An important aspect of the discovery of a workshop for cosmetics at Pyrgos is the presence of a rich instrumental outfit of polished stone tools including palettes. The availability of such many tools reveals that the workshop was active for a long period and that many people worked there.

This peculiar layout for the production of compounds for personal use is an unprecedented reality that calls for a parallel with Pre-dynastic Egypt, considering the fact that this civilization is the only one to have returned a vast repertoire of recipes and cosmetic tools for the processing and production of cosmetics.

I would like to emphasize the findings in the Neolithic tombs of Naqada I and II of objects of personal beauty as palettes, pestles and ointments because they are an important social evolution in human history. These tombs do not belong to special élite people, furthermore, we find cosmetic material among the funeral goods.

This material testifies that something of extraordinary was happening. It was something that would change the story of science and technology, giving birth to cosmetics and medical science in Egypt. Everything started around 4200 BC at the end of the Badarian period with few unshaped palettes and went hand in hand with the emergence of the great Nilotic civilization.

The constant evolution that accompanies the first millennia of the Egyptian culture until the early dynasties is a period in which the cornerstone of technology and science expressed in 360 degrees in all arenas of human knowledge, from medicine to architecture, from writing to religious beliefs appear.

It seems that some objects assumed a prestige character deserved to identify the cultural level more than wealth. The Egyptian palettes had an important role, underlined by their typology evolution that covers a period of about 2000 years.

The first specimens simply slab shaped are in fact dating back to the period of Naqada 1. The second group, characterized by zoomorphic forms, lies instead in the periods of the Naqada II and III A-B. While the third group, consisting of commemorative and parade palettes reserved for nobles and Pharaohs, dates to the Naqada III B C and the 1st Dynastic period. By then, the palettes disappear from the funeral outfits of all lifestyles, but the level of knowledge in medicine and cosmetic compounds reached the top as documented by the famous Egyptian medical papyri.

In the first Dynastic Period, a special spiritual power was recognized to the owners of palettes, pointing to exclude the feminine environment from the elite depository of the stones and ores to produce makeups[112].

---

[112] Baduel N. 2008: Tegumentary paint and cosmetic palettes in Predynastic Egypt: Impact of those artefacts on

On the contrary, the palettes of Pyrgos seem to have had a functional significance, without any second scope of power expression. Any of them is personalized or decorated. The only approach we can do with the most ancient Egyptians concern the exclusive feminine control of their use.

Something that was completely erased by the Pharaoh himself, who excludes everybody by their use and claims being the sole repository of the scientific knowledge related to the well-being of the body.

It seems clear that in Cyprus the magical, religious expression and healing support linked to these objects was managed by women who effectively control the entire production of elite goods, tied to the new social need for beauty.

A phenomenon that distinguishes the final Early /Middle Bronze Cyprus, a period during which largest importance is given to the personal appearance, as widely demonstrated by the richness of the clothes of the female figurines, production of perfumes, replica of clay of the Egyptian stone containers for ointments, cosmetics, and new jewellery solutions.

But there is another aspect that we must consider, it regards the different destination of most of the Egyptian and Cypriot cosmetic products. Comparing the funerary ritual of Egypt and Cyprus of Bronze age, the difference regards mainly the treatment and conservation of bodies. In the first situation, we have mummification, in the second normal inhumation. However, in both we find pots containing food, ointments, and fragrances for a possible awakening or for the journey to the Hereafter, goods belonging to the world of the living.

It seems obvious that both the cultures believed in an afterlife, but Cyprus, unlike Egypt, had any interest in preserving the dead bodies and in producing a line of products for mummification.

It is possible that this different rituality greatly influenced the choice of cosmetic ingredients and Cyprus started to produce cosmetics for "living" using the natural resources of the island. In fact, in Egypt we find since the first appearing of cosmetic use, a massive use of resins with a very aggressive smell such as Pine, Frachincense and Myrrh, in the composition of the seven sacred ointments[113], and natural asphalt (of a consistency similar to resin), blended with fragrant seeds (of conifers and other plants) and *Peresh oil* (probably Moringa).

1. **Seti heb** 'the scent of the feast': *Sefy* (Dead Sea Bitumen or Gebel Zeit), 77 seeds of *Tekhu*, white *Frankincense* resin, white *Frankincense*, *Pine* seeds, fresh *Incense*.
2. **Hekenu** *Menen* (pitch of wood obtained cooking resin). *Fresh Frankincense*, dry *Frankincense*, white *Acacia* flowers.
3. **Sefet** 'fir oil': (pitch wood), white (*Frankincense*) *Gesfeck*, *degem* of [.?.].
4. **Nesmen:** *Menen* (pitch pine), *Sefy* (bitumen)

---

the birth of the monarchy, in: *Egypt at its origins 2: Proceedings of the international conference "Origin of the State, Predynastic and Early Dynastic Egypt," Toulouse (France), 5th - 8th September 2005.* Orientalia Lovaniensia Analecta 172, ed. Béatrix Midant-Reynes, and Yann Tristant 1057- 1090.

[113] The first seven sacred ointments are all based on resins dissolved in scented Moringa oil. The same resins were already used during religious rituals, and so it is assumed that their first use was linked to religion. Archaeological findings also show that the resins have been used for different purposes: as a sealant to secure the tool handles, glue, waterproofing, adhesives, wound healing, and skin disinfectant. Their texture and aroma, along with the fact that ooze from the wounds of tree bark of plants, were considered like human blood, and regarded as expression of lifeblood in which essence of life flows.

5. **Tua**: *Menen* (pitch wood), *Frankincense*, *Pine* (seeds) White [*Frankincense*].
6. **Hat-en-ash** 'The best Pine' *Menen* (pitch wood), *Sefy* bitumen, oil *Peresh* (?), its flowers.
7. **Hat-en-tjehenu** "the best Libyan": *Menen* (pitch wood) oil of *Peresh* [?], its flowers.

Whereas in Cyprus we find together with minerals, resins with a different light smell, such as those produced by the Pistacia, Cupressus, Pine and Styrax trees, Laubdanum, gum of Almond and Cherry, melt into green oil of olive, almond or Pistacia, with the fragrant plants of the forest such as Myrtle, Rosemarie, Laurel, Marjoram, and Lavender. It is a total different manner to think about the use of cosmetics.

Of course, the Egyptians had an extensive knowledge about the pharmaceutical compounds, remedies for remaining younger and makeups, however, for the other countries with different religion (and when the Egyptian religion passed away) they remained famous for the ability of embalming the corpses and produce cosmetics for dead.

We can presume that the people of the time considered the difference, looking at the products addressed to embellish the living with more interest.

The fact of the matter is that, the island will be recognised by the Aegean culture as the country of Aphrodite, trading the ideology to the centuries after. Something that justifies the Cyprus cosmetic canons are still valid and used by modern industries that, especially in recent years, have aimed to produce natural cosmetics using the same organic and inorganic ingredients that might have made Cyprus, home of female beauty and Aphrodite.

REFERENCES

- Altay V., İbrahim İlker Özyiğit, Mustafa Keskin, Göksel Demir, İbrahim Ertuğrul Yalçın 2013: An ecological study of endemic plant *Polygonum istanbulicum* Keskin and its environs, Pak J. Bot., 45(S1), 455-459.

- Alziar G. 1985: Contribution a l'histoire naturelle de l'ile de Chypre – La flore. – *Biocosme Mésogéen* 2: 1-20.

- Alziar G. 1986: Contribution a l'histoire naturelle de l'ile de Chypre. La flore. 2e partie. – *Biocosme Mésogéen 3*: 49-57.

- Alziar G. 1995: Généralités sur la flore de l'île de Chypre. Quelques données quantitatives. – *Ecol. Medit. 21:* 47-52.

- Alziar G. 2000. Compte rendu du 4ème Iter Mediterraneum in *Bocconea 11*, 5-83.

- Baduel N. 2008: Tegumentary paint and cosmetic palettes in Predynastic Egypt: Impact of those artefacts on the birth of the monarchy. in *Egypt at its origins 2: Proceedings of the international conference "Origin of the State, Predynastic and Early Dynastic Egypt," Toulouse (France), 5th - 8th September 2005.* Orientalia Lovaniensia Analecta 172, ed. Béatrix Midant-Reynes, and Yann Tristant 1057- 1090.

- Bagde A.B., Sawant R.S., Bingare S.D., Sawai R.V., Nikumbh M.B. 2013: Therapeutic and Nutritional Values of Honey (Madhu) in: *International Research Journal Pharmacy*, 4 (3), 19-22.

- Ball P.W. & Akeroyd J.R. 2010: Isatis L. in: *Flora Europaea. Volume 1 Psilotaceae to Platanaceae* (ed. Tutin T.G., Burges N.A., Chater A.O., Edmondson J.R., Heywood V.H., Moore D.M., Valentine D.H., Walters S.M., Webb D.A.) Cambridge University Press, 324-325.

- Bardinet T. 1995: *Les Papirus mèdicaux de l'Egypte pharaonique*, Fayard, Paris.

- Barthoux J. 1925: Les fards, pomades et couleurs dans l'antiquitè, *Congres International de geolologique. Le Caire, Avril, IV* pp. 257-8.

- Baytop, T. 1999. Therapy with medicinal plants in Turkey past and present, 2nd ed. Nobel Tıp Kitabevi, Istanbul.

- Belgiorno M.R. 2007: Catalogo; in M.R. Belgiorno (ed) *I Profumi di Afrodite e il segreto dell'Olio*, 151-247, Gangemi. Roma.

- Belgiorno M.R. 2014: I Profumi di Venere in *Archeo* 347,1.

- Belgiorno M.R. 2016: *The Perfume of Cyprus*. Roma Ermes ed.

- Blount A.M. 1991: Amphibole content of cosmetic and pharmaceutical talc. *Environ Health Perspect*, 94: 225–230.

- Booij E., Gallahan W.E. & Staudigel H. 1995: Ion-exchange experiments and Rb/Sr dating on celadonites from the Troodos ophiolite, Cyprus. *Chemical Geology, 126*, 155-167.

- Brock S., 2000: Aristotele.

- Brooks W.E. 2012: Industrial Use of Mercury in the Ancient World, in *Mercury in the Environment: Pattern and Process*, edited by Bank Michael S., 19-24. University of California Press, 2012

- Bourghouts J. 1973: The evil eye of Apopis, *JEA 59*, p. 114-150.

- Budka J. 2010: The New Kingdom-Pottery from Elephantine, in D. Raue, C. von Pilgrim, P. Kopp, F. Arnold, M. Bommas, J. Budka, M. Schultz, J. Gresky, A. Kozak and St. J. Seidlmayer, *Report on the 37th season of excavation and restoration on the island of Elephantine*, Annales du Service des Antiquités de l'Égypte 84, 350-352.

- Caffaro A. & G. Falanga 2004: *Il Papiro di Leida un documento di técnica artística e artgianile del sec. IV*, Salerno

- Chrtek J. & B. Slavík 1981: Contribution to the flora of Cyprus in *Preslia* 53: 45-65.

- Chrtek J. & B. Slavík 1993: Contribution to the flora of Cyprus. 2 in *Flora Mediterranea* 3: 239-259.

-Chrtek J. & B. Slavík. 1994. Contribution to the flora of Cyprus. 3. Flora Medit. 4: 9-20.

-Chrtek J. & B. Slavík. 2000. Contribution to the flora of Cyprus. 4. Flora Medit. 10: 235-259.

- Chrtek J. & B. Slavík 2001: Contribution to the flora of Cyprus. 5 in *Acta Univ. Carol., Biol.* 45: 267-293.

- Cobham C. Delaval 1908 ed.: *Excerpta Cipria* : Materials for a History of Cyprus. Cambridge Un. Press.

- Cohen Ragas M. & K. Kozlowski 1998. *Read my lips: a cultural history of lipstick*, San Francisco Ca.

- Clark R.J.H., Cooksey C.J., Daniels M.A.M, Withnall R. **1993:** Indigo, woad and Tyrian purple. Important vat dyes from antiquity to the present in *Endeavour, New Series Vol. 17* (4), 191-199.

- Constantinou G. & Govett G.J.S. 1972: Genesis of sulphide deposits, ochre and umber of Cyprus, *Transactions of the Institution of Mining and Metallurgy* 81: 34–46.

- Consuegra S., Díaz-del-Río P., Hunt Ortiz M.A., Hurtado V., and Montero Ruiz I. 2011: Neolithic and Chalcolithic--VI to III millennia BC--use of cinnabar (HgS) in the Iberian Peninsula: analytical identification and lead isotope data for an early mineral exploitation of the Almadén (Ciudad Real, Spain) mining district, in J. E. Ortiz, O. Puche, I. Rábano and L. F. Mazadiego (eds.) *History of Research in Mineral Resources. Cuadernos del Museo Geominero, 13.* Instituto Geológico y Minero de España, Madrid.

- Corson R., 2005: *Fashions in Makeup from ancient to modern times*, Peter Owen ed.

- Coulot P. 2000: Approche de la flore de l'ile de Chypre in *Monde* Pl. 470, 16-20.

- Crosland M.P. 1962: *Historical Studies in the Language of Chemistry*, Heinemann, London.

- Della A. 1992: Flora of a valley in the Pendakomo area in *Agric. Res. Inst. Minist. Agric. Nat. Resources Cyprus Misc. Rep.* 52.

- Diels H. 1965: *Antike Technik 3*. (Leipzig 1924 repr. Osnabrück 1965).

- Dieterich K. 1920: *The Analysis of Resins balsams and Gum Resins*. London

- Dodson R.F. & S.P. Hammar 2012: *Asbestos: Risk Assessment, Epidemiology, and Health Effects.* CRC Press.

-Dogan Y., Baslar S., Ozturk M. and H. Mert. 2008: Plants used as dye sources. In: Underutilized and Underexplored Horticultural Crops, (Ed.): K.V. Peter. Vol. 3. New India Publishing Agency, New Delhi, India, 109-145.

- Durman A. 2002: The Neolithic settlement in Vina, *IAMS Newsletter*, Institute for Archaeometallurgical Studies, London.

- Edwards D.N. 1999: Musawwarat Es Sufra: A meroitic pottery workshop at Musawwarat es Sufra, *Meroitica 17*, 2. Harrassovitz Verlag

- Faber, G.A. 1938: *Dyeing and Tanning in Classical Antiquity*. Vol. 9. Ciba Review. Basle, Switzerland: Society of Chemical Industry in Basle (Switzerland).

- Farjon A. 2005: *A monograph of Cupressaceae and Sciadopitys*. Royal Botanic Gardens, Kew.

- Farjon A. 2010: *A handbook of the world's conifers*. Leiden & Boston.

- Ferber J.J. 1774: Beschreibung des Quecksilberbergwerk zu Idria in *Mittel-Krayn Ch. F.* Himburg, Berlin.

- Forbes R.J. 1965: *Studies in Ancient Technology III*, Brill ed. Leiden

- Gajic-Kvaščev M., Stojanovic M.M., Šmit Ž., Kantarelou V., Karydas A.G., Šljivar D., Milovanovic D., and Andric V. 2012: New evidence for the use of cinnabar as a colouring pigment in the Vinca culture. *Journal of Archaeological Science* 39(4): 1025-1033.

- Greensmith J.T. 1994: *Southern Cyprus*. Geologist' Association Guide n° 50. London.

-Haddow S.D., Boz B. and B. Glencross 2013: The Human Remains I: Interpreting Community Structure, Health and Diet in Neolithic Çatalhöyük in I. Hodder, *Humans and Landscapes of Catalhoyuk, Reports from 2000- 2008 seasons, The Humans and Their Lifestyles*, 2013 Monumenta Archeologica 30, 339- 396.

- Hadjikyriakou G. 2004: Symvoli sti meleti tis chloridas tis Kyprou 1, in Quarterly Magazine Forester *Dasoponos 20*. Nicosia.

- Hadjikyriakou G. 2005: Symvoli sti meleti tis chloridas tis Kyprou 4, in Quarterly Magazine Forester *Dasoponos 25*. Nicosia.

- Hadjikyriakou G. 2007: *Aromatic and spicy plants in Cyprus. From Antiquity to the Present Day*, Nicosia.

- Hadjikyriakou G. 2009: Symvoli sti meleti tis chloridas tis Kyprou 13, in Quarterly Magazine Forester, *Dasoponos 39*, Nicosia.

- Hadjikyriakou G. 2013: Symvoli sti meleti tis chloridas tis Kyprou 16, in Quarterly Magazine Forester, *Dasoponos 54*. Nicosia.

- Hadjikyriakou G. & E. Hadjisterkotis 2002: The adventive plants of Cyprus with new records of invasive species in *Z. Jagdwiss. 48*, Suppl.

- Hand R. 2003: Supplementary notes to the flora of Cyprus III. in *Willdenowia 33:* 305-325

- Hand R. 2004: Supplementary notes to the flora of Cyprus IV. in *Willdenowia 34:* 427-456.

- Hand R. 2006: Supplementary notes to the flora of Cyprus V. in *Willdenowia 36*. 761-809.

- Jonckheere F. 1952: La 'Mesdemet', cosmétique et médicament égyptien, dans *Histoire de la Médecine, 2° année, no 7*, Paris.

- Kadereit J.W. 1989: A revision of Papaver section Rhoeadium Spach in *Notes Roy. Bot. Gard. Edinburgh* 45, 225-286;

- Kołosowska E., Mahmoud el-Tayeb and H. Paner 2003: Old Kush in the Fourth Cataract Region" in *Sudan and Nubia 7*, 21-26.

- Kopp, P. 2005: Small finds from the settlement of the 3rd and 2nd millenium BC, 17, in: D. Raue et al., *Report on the 34th Season of Excavation and Restoration on the Island of Elephantine*.

- Kroll W. 1934: Bolos und Demokritos in *Hermes* 69, 228-32.

- Langenheim J.H. 2003: *Plant Resins: Chemistry, Evolution, Ecology and Ethnobotany*. Timber Press, Portland, Oregon.

- Lau J.Y. 1976: *Bees and Honey*, Dominion Press. Australia.

- Legget W.F. 1949: *The Story of Linen*, New York.

- G. Lefevre 1999. *Essai sur la médecine égyptienne à l'époque pharaonique*, Paris.

- Lentini A. & M.R. Belgiorno 2008: Palaethnobotany investigations at the site of Pyrgos-Mavrorachi, Cyprus, in Kars H., Meyers P. and Wagner C.A. (ed) *International Symposium on Archaeometry*, 37, 296-297.

- Lentini A. 2009: Archeologia e paesaggio naturale: indagini archeobotaniche e fisico chimiche, in: M.R. Belgorno (ed), *Cipro all'inizio dell'Età del Bronzo. Realtà sconosciute della comunità industriale dy Pyrgos/Mavroraki*, Gangemi Editore, Roma, 128-187.

- Lentini A. 2014: Cipro, Afrodite e la cosmesi, *Archeo 347* (1) 32 – 35.

- McGovern P.E. 2003: *Ancient Wine*. The Search for the Origins of Viniculture Princeton: Princeton University Press;

- Mahanta D. & Tiwari S.C. 2005: Natural dye–yielding plants and indigenous knowledge on dye preparation in Arunachal Pradesh, northeast India', *Current science, vol. 88*, no. 9, 1474–1480.

- *Manniche* L. 1989: *An Ancient Egyptian Herbal*, British Museum.

- *Manniche* L. 1999: Sacred Luxuries: Fragrance, Aromatherapy, and Cosmetics in Ancient Egypt, Cornell Un. Press.

- Martín-Bravo S. & Jiménez-Mejías P. 2013: Reseda minoica (Resedaceae), a new species from the eastern Mediterranean region. – *Ann. Bot. Fennici 50*: 55-60.

- Matthäus H. 1989: *Der Arzt in römischer Zeit. Medizinische Instrumente und Arzneien* (Limes museum Aalen), Stuttgart.

- Meikle R.D. 1977: *Flora of Cyprus 1*. Royal Botanic Gardens. B-M, London.

- Meikle R.D. 1985: *Flora of Cyprus 2*. Royal Botanic Gardens. B-M, London.

- Melena J.L. 1974: «KI-TA-NO en las tablillas de Cnoso», *Durius 2:1*, 45-55.

- Melena J.L. 1975: La producción de plantas aromáticas en Cnoso, *Estudios Clásicos 78*, 180-183.

- Milne J. 1907: *Surgical Instruments in Greek and Roman Times*. Oxford.

- Miloi V. 1943: Das vorgeschichtliche Bergwerk, Šuplja Stena am Avalaberg beiBelgrad in Serbien, *Wiener Prähistorische Zeitschrift XXX*, 41-54.

- Moorey P.R. Stuart 1994: *Ancient Mesopotamian Materials and Industries: The Archaeological Evidence*. 134-138. Oxford UP.

- Nunn J.F. 1996: *Ancient Egyptian Medicine*, London.

- Oberprieler C. & Vogt R. 2000: Notes on some species of Anthemis (Compositae, Anthemideae) in Cyprus. – *Bocconea 11*: 89-104.

- Peña, J.T. 2007: *Roman Pottery in the Archaeological Record*, Cambridge.

- Pentelburg E. et al. 1998. *Excavations at Kissonerga-Mosphilia*, 1979-1992, Volume II.1B (Part 1), 211- 236, Edinburgh.

- Perrot Em. 1944: Ma*tières premieres usuelles du Règne Végétal*, Paris ed. Masson.

- Petrie W.M.F. 1896: *Naqada and Ballas*. Warminster: Aris and Philips Ltd.

- Petrie W.M.F. 1953: *Corpus of prehistoric pottery and palettes. British School of Archaeology in Egypt 1921*. London.

- Pointer S. 2005: *The artifice of beauty: a history and practical guide to perfumes and cosmetics*, Stroud.

- Prell S. 2011: Einblicke in die Werkstätten der Residenz – Die Stein- und Metallwerkzeuge des Grabungsplatzes Q I, *FoRa vol. 8*, Hildesheim.

- Qiao J.Y., Ran J.H., Li Y. & Wang X.Q. 2007: Phylogeny and biogeography of Cedrus (Pinaceae) inferred from sequences of seven paternal chloroplast and maternal mitochondrial DNA regions. - *Ann. Bot. 100:* 573-580.

- Raedler, C. 2007: Die Schaber der Werkstätten des Grabungsplatzes Q I, in: Pusch, E.B. (Hg.), Die Keramik des Grabungsplatzes Q I – Teil 2, Schaber – Marken – Scherben, *FoRa Bd. 5*, 11-266, Hildesheim.

- Ramella R. 1944: *El lino oleaginoso*, Buenos Aires.

- Reese D.S. 1986: The Mediterranean Shell Purple-dye Industry; *American Journal of Archaeology*, 90 (2), 183.

- Roux V. 1985*: Le Materiel de broyage: etude ethnoarcheologique a Tichitt* (R.I. Mauritanie). Paris: Editions Recherche sur les Civilisations, Memoire no. 5.

- Sacconi A. 1971: A proposito dell'epíteto omerico ΛΙΝΟΘΩΡΗΞ, *ZA 21*, 49-54.

- Sánchez-Gómez G., Jiménez J.F., Vera J.B. & Aedo C. 2008: Anchusa aegyptiaca (Boraginaceae), a new species for the Iberian flora in *Fl. Medit. 18*.

- Sauneron S. 1958: Une recette égyptienne de collyre, *BIFAO 57*, 157-61.

- Serpico M. and R. White 2009: Oil, Fat and Wax, 390- 430; Resin, Amber and bitumen, 430-475, in Paul T. Nicholson, Ian Shaw (ed) *Ancient Egyptian Materials and Technology*. Cambridge University Press.

- Shujaul Mulk Khan, Habib Ahmad, Gul Jan, Farzana Gul Jan Mushtaq Ahmad and Hayat Ullah, Ethnomedicinal studies of Dughalgay valley district swat, in *12th National and 3rd International Conference of Botany* Septemebr 1st to 3rd 2012 Quaid- e- Azam Islamabad University.

- Stevenson A. 2009: Palettes. In *Willeke Wendrich (ed.), UCLA Encyclopedia of Egyptology*, Los Angeles.

    http://digital2.library.ucla.edu/viewItem.do?ark=21198/zz001nf6c0

- Storrs R.& B. Justin O'Brien 1930: *The Handbook of Cyprus*, London.

- Vasi M. 1932: *Preistorijska Vina I, Industrija cinabarita i kosmetika u Vini*, Beograd.

- Staudigel H., Gillis K. & Duncan R. 1986: K/Ar and Rb/Sr ages of celadonites from the Troodos ophiolite, Cyprus. *Geology, 14,* 72-75.

- Taylor Cliff D., R.A. Zierenberg, Goldfarb R.J., Kilburn J.E., Seal II R.R., and M.D. Kleinkopf 1995: Volcanic-Associated Massive Sulphide Deposits online: (https://pubs.usgs.gov/of/1995/ofr-95-0831/CHAP16.pdf).

- Tapsoba I., Arbault S., Walter P. and C. Amatore 2010: Finding Out Egyptian Gods' Secret Using Analytical Chemistry: Biomedical Properties of Egyptian Black Makeup Revealed by Amperometry at Single Cells. *Anal. Chem., 82* (2), 457–460.

- Tomlinson P., and A. Hall 1984: Progress in Palaeobotanical Studies of Dye Plants 1983/4. *Dyes on Historical and Archaeological Textiles* 3, *Meeting, York Archaeological Trust, September 1984*, edited by H.E. Dalrymple (Edinburgh, 1985).

- Vogt R. & A. Aparicio 2000: Chromosome numbers of plants collected during Iter Mediterraneum IV in Cyprus, in *Bocconea* 11, 117-169.

- Walter P. 1995: La peinture des femmes préhistoriques, in *La Dame de Brassempouy*, (*Études et Recherches Archéologiques de l'Université de Liège*), 74, 259.

- Walter P., Martinetto P., Tsoucaris G., Bréniaux R., Lefebvre M.A., Richard G., Talabot J. & E. Dooryhee 1999: Making make-up in Ancient Egypt, *Nature*, vol. 397; 483-484.

- Williams B.B. 1993: Excavations at Serra East. A-Group, C-Group, Pan Grave, New Kingsom, and X-Group Remains from Cemeteries A-G and Rock Shelters, *OINE X*, Chicago.

- Wilson P. 1997: *A Lexicographical Study of the Ptolemaic Texts in the Temple of Edfu*, Leuven.

- Wylock M. 1973: Les aromates dans les tablettes Ge de Mycènes, *SMEA* 15: 105-146.

- Zeb A., S.M. Khan, H. Ahmad, G. Jan, F.G. Jan, M. Ahmad and H. Ullah 2012: Ethnomedicinal Studies of Dughalgay Valley District Swat, Khyberpakhtoonkhwa, Province, Pakistan. *Proceedings (Special Issue of Pakistan Journal of Botany) of 12th National and 3rd International Conference of Botany (ICB-2012) arranged by Pakistan Botanical Society* (September 1 - 3, 2012) at Quaid-i-Azam University, Islamabad Pakistan.

- Zohary, D. & Hopf, M. 1994: *Domestication of Plants in the Old World*, Clarendon Press, Oxford.

4. ARCHAEOMETRY

Alessandro Lentini

Abstract

Archaeobotanical, paleopalinological and sedimentological investigations plus exploration in the areas adjacent to the Pyrgos site have evidenced a series of environmental discontinuities that make Cyprus's natural landscape a highly varied one, thereby confirming indirectly the preliminary analytic results of the first investigations of stratigraphic sections (PY04G7 – 8) dating from between 1950 and 2000 B.C. For the purposes of an initial comparison of the archaeobotanical data, we updated a map of rainfall distribution on Cyprus, with temperature and rainfall data for the period from 1973 to 2007, to produce an updated view of possible microclimates on the island. These data were collected at 25 weather stations located irregularly across the island, some concentrated in the central part (the Mesaoria plain, from Nicosia to Famagosta), others on the West coast (from Morocampos to Episcopi) and still others near the heights of the Trodos mountains (from Platania to Trimiklini), with significant absences in the North East, the North West and on the southern coast. The weather data were processed with the aid of the Köppen formula. The updated climate data processed on the basis of contour lines obtained from cartographic elements reported in the past show a distribution in eight microclimates that reflects the island's geological and altimetric features. In fact, some areas are marked off by geographic barriers (the Trodos and Pemtadattilo mountains) and their characteristics of their plant populations are allopatric, while others are marked off by abiotic factors that operate in the same geographic area with various sympatric plant species.

The aspects considered in this investigations to remains of food plants related to the history of agriculture and cultivated plant processing technologies. We also found drupes and berries of various spontaneous species, most likely officinal. We have used terms such as paleocarpology and paleoseeds to define the paleobotanical aspects of ecology and ethnography, and morpho-biometric as regards the dimensions of the seeds and drupes in archaeological contexts. In parallel, the ecological approach entailed analyzing the paleocarpological finds in order to define the environments in which prehistoric agriculture was able to develop. The economy of Pyrgos in 1850 B.C. appears to have been characterized by diversified cereal farming (with various species of wheat and barley), and supported by the cultivation of legumes, olive trees and grapevines, and by the early stages of the cultivation and selection of species that prefigure the start of industrial farming

The chemical-toxicology investigations effect through varied methods (Halphen-Grimaldi methods, Blor's mixture, Liebermann reaction, Marquis, Chen, Vitali, Bellier, Bechi e McNally reactions and toxicology methods), they are begun during the archaeological excavations in 2003. Different organic residues have been analyzed withdrawn interior various pottery of different typology, find the presence of varied substances, obtain from officinalis vegetation species of the Mediterranean area. The active principles characterized, were probably known since antiquity and the most usual they were employed for elementary pharmacological preparations and for perfumed essences.

During the 2004 some of the recovered loom weights had sealed sediments inside their perforations. We floated these sediments in small quantities of glycerinated water. After soaking, some fibers became bloated with to the surface of solutions. We initially examined 932 morphologies, of which 150 of cotton (Gossypium ssp.), that it turns out to be the most represented with fibers of Asclepias ssp. (62) and Hibiscus ssp. (45) for the vegetables fibers, while for the animals prevails wool with 297 filaments. Analytic investigations carried out with different methods (colorimetry, plasma emission spectroscopy, X-ray fluorescence [XRF], chromatography and electrospray) started during archaeological excavations in 2004-5. Samples of residues of different colours were taken inside different types of pottery, and samples of sediments were taken from holes in loom weights. Analyses showed that dyes had been obtained from official plants and molluscs native to the Mediterranean area. The dyes, Purple of Tyre, Indigo Blue and Rutin Yellow had been mixed to obtain a wide range of secondary colours. The 2004-2008 archeological excavations turned up 41 whole seeds of different varieties of grapes and a number of pedicel fragments, in Stratigraphic Units (SUs) PY04F8L1, PY05GH9L4/5, PY05L4 and PY06L5/2. All these seeds were found near pottery vessels (classified typologically as wine containers). Our morphological characterization of the whole seeds was keyed to a number of distinctive ampelographic features. We sought to distinguish the wild subspecies from the cultivated one, based on the morphological descriptions and biometric measurements reported in the literature The sediments on the bottom of a vase, coming from the US Py04 FG8 border 7, have been extracted (elutriation) with H_2SO_4 to 20 %,. Subsequently to the super floating it has been added 0,02 gr. of β, β' – binaphtol. The obtained solution submitted to irradiation with UV lamp of 240-250 nanometres, assumed a green colour under the fluorescent rays. The green coloration of the solution reveals that it contains high rate of tartaric acid, typical of the wine produced in the Mediterranean area.

The set of results obtained from the micro samples selected from the bull's head discovered in SL PY 09D.10B was characterized by the significant presence, in the palynological record, of grassy and bushy floral species native to the island of Cyprus and associated with the presence of phytoliths, textile fibres and epithelial plant structures that point in this SL to an activity of selection of very particular plant species.

The sediments on the surface of the 34 archaeological artifacts (cosmetic tablets) were selected and picked up. The residues were divided chromatically with the Munsell system. The results of the colorimetric observations essentially divide the sediments into four groups, nine whites, fifteen light gray, brown nine type terra di Siena, four yellow and one red. The analysis of ICP - AES performed on selected residues from these artifacts have noted a significant amount of Pb, with values ranging between 35 and 52%. The percentages of lead recorded in these sediments seem to refer to an attempt to preparing a compound similar to the white lead

They identified two types of ocher relating to yellow (limonite) and red (hematite). Moreover During the first phase of investigation of drying in a muffle hygroscopic water present in the sediment selected, were observed some color change to green, red, blue and white.

The sediments flocculation in crystal were brought into solution by different methods and then analyzed carry out by ICP-AES. The crystals of white color have different compositions, one is present in the magnesium, in the second sodium. The blue crystals are characterized by the presence of copper. In parallel with the methodologies. Toxicological the solution extracted from these sediments are colored in red, for the presence of certain fatty acids found in olive oil. The presence of olive oil and sodium salts and magnesium refer to something similar to the known and similar dermatological solution "scrub" or "gommage". The red and green clays purified silicates come from the Lefkara formation, an area particularly rich in clays originated in sedimentary deposits of deep water during the Cretaceous. The characteristics of the clays on the various properties antitoxic, antiseptic, absorbent and healing are well documented in the literature.

Recent archaeometric investigations conducted by the ITABC archaeological mission at Pyrgos-Mavroraki and Erimi

1. Our nine years of archaeometric investigations at Pyrgos Mavroraki began in 2004 with the excavation of two areas (SU G7L5) devoted to textile manufacture. Several spindle whorls (Philia - Phase MC II) preserved sealed archaeological sediments inside their biconical-lenticular sections. Small quantities of these sediments were extracted and floated in a glycerinated water solution (Belgiorno and Lentini 2005). Several mineralized fibres imbibed the water, swelled and rose to the surface. A total of 932 morphologies was examined. Most of the plant fibres were found to be cotton (*Gossypium* ssp., 150 specimens), followed by *Asclepias* ssp (62) and *Hibiscus* ssp (45). Wool, with 297 filaments, predominated among the animal fibres (Belgiorno and Lentini 2010).

In parallel, we analysed of coloured matter that had been found near dyeing vats (USJ6L5). These tests (colourimetry, XRF fluorescence, plasma spectrometry and various microanalytic techniques) showed the presence of several colouring substances obtained from plants and molluscs native to the Mediterranean basin.

The three components we identified – Tyrian purple, indigo and rutin (Belgiorno and Lentini 2008) were probably already known in the Early Bronze Age, and were used in mixtures to produce a wide range of colours. In April of 2005, an archaeometric research project was started on the Erimi Copper Age jars, to determine how they were used.

These analyses, sponsored by the Italian Embassy in Nicosia, were performed on samples taken from inside the bases of 18 jars found during the excavations carried out by Porphyrios Dikaios, which were stored at the Limassol museum and had never been cleaned (and to date unpublished). In fact, 80% of the Erimi / Bamboula materials are still in the same packing crates where they have been stored since the excavation. They comprise some 300 cases numbered according to the excavation stratigraphy, which corresponds to about eleven different levels. Ovoid jars with pointed bases are present in all the levels, and are all more or less the same size.

The analyses were performed in the restoration laboratory of the Nicosia and Limassol Archaeological Museum, in collaboration with the Antiquities Department's staff. Twelve of the jar bases contained large amounts of tartaric acid in its natural form (the dextrorotatory stereoisomer D-(-)-tartaric acid**)**, characteristic of wine, while six contained only traces of this substance (Lentini 2005).

The archaeometric investigation was then extended to other types of Middle Bronze Age pottery vessels that were likewise characterized by pointed bases; some had been found in the industrial complex at Pyrgos and others in a tomb at Anoyira. The tests performed on all these objects confirmed the residual presence of tartaric acid that had remained in the containers after they were used to transport or store wine (Belgiorno and Lentini 2012).

The archaeometric investigations that began in the 2006 season were subsequently directed toward dry assays of certain archaeological sediments that appeared to be made up of organic substances. These sediments pointed to preservation conditions within sealed levels consisting mainly of silt containing low percentages of sand. Our study focused on archaeological sediments and organic residues (some of them retrieved from artefacts) selected in different areas of the excavated structures.

The analyses presented here were made with the remains of edible and officinal plants, and thus contribute to the study of the history of cultivated plants and related technologies. Some specific terms used to define paleoethnobotanical features (such as paleo carpology and paleo seeds) are proper to ecology and ethnography, while the term morpho biometric refers to the dimensions of seeds found in archaeological contexts. In parallel, the ecological approach involved interpreting the paleo carpological elements to define the environments in which prehistoric agriculture could develop.

The economy of Pyrgos in the Middle Bronze Age seems to have been characterized by diversified cereal cultivation (Lentini and Belgiorno 2008) in which multiple species of grain (*Triticum dicoccum*, *T. monococcum*, *T. durum* and *Hordeum distichum*) were present. The cereal crops were flanked by the cultivation of various leguminous crops (*Cicer arietinum*, *Lens culinaris* MEDIK, *Lens culinaris* ssp. *orientalis* and *Pisum sativum* L.), olive trees, grapevines, and by a nascent cultivation and selection of industrial crops (*Linum usitatissimum* L.).

Moreover, the presence of *Vicia ervilia* L. and of officinal species (*Laurus*, *Myrtus* and *Coriandrum*) typical of the natural Mediterranean landscape constituted another element of technological evolution in livestock raising and in the production of therapeutic substances (Lentini and Belgiorno 2012a). These developments have been documented by the presence of particular types of pottery vessels and by chemical and toxicological analyses that indirectly confirm widespread knowledge and management of the natural landscape and high technological capacity for growing and transforming crops.

The archaeometric investigations that began in the 2005-2006 seasons were aimed at separating certain sediments that appeared to be organic (resinous). These sediments (SUs G7L5, J5L8, J7L2, J7L6, F8L4, G7, G7L3, G7L8, G9, G9L4, Samples H1044) pointed to preservation conditions.

The sediments and residues we analysed were found in two workshops, two metalworks to produce copper and of bronze objects, an olive-oil press connected to a jar-storage area, and a facility to produce aromatic and therapeutic essences (this latter area was in the north-eastern corner of the large olive-oil-press room). The chemical and toxicological tests were performed according to several different methods (Halphen, Grimaldi, Bloor mix, Liebermann, reaction Marquis, Chen, Vitali, Bellier, Bechi and McNally reactions, toxicological tests and HPLC methods).

We analysed residues containing organic matter retrieved from inside pottery vessels of various types. These analyses revealed the presence of various substances (Lentini 2008) obtained from officinal plant species growing in the Mediterranean region (Lentini and Nelli 2008). The active principles we identified most frequently (turpentine, colchicine, sylvestrene, pinene, coriander oil, narcotine, cotarnine, ephedrine alkaloids and sulphates, quinoline, isoquinoline, olive oil, almond oil and animal sterols) were probably already known in this historical context and were used to produce elementary pharmacological preparations and perfume essences.

Moreover, the micro-remains of *Vitis*, *Triticum*, *Hordeum*, *Lens*, *Vicia*, *Linum*, *Pisum*, *Cicer*, *Laurus*, *Myrtus* and *Coriandrum* (already reported in other Cypriot contexts dating from different periods) raise questions about the geographic distribution of these species (biogeography) on Cyprus, about biodiversity in the island's natural landscape (Lentini 2009a), and about species that entered Cyprus in various ways or were partially domesticated by humans. In this context, the oldest vegetal macro-remains probably indicate levels where biodiversity was less defined.

In fact, evaluating biodiversity in archaeological contexts is a very complex task, due above all to the fact that there are still no certified methods for classifying these paleo-environmental structures, because the main recognizable units represent different sectors of a highly variable anthropized environment.

The archaeobotanical, paleopalynological and sedimentological investigations, and the surveys carried out in areas adjacent to the Pyrgos site identified a series of environmental discontinuities that make Cyprus's natural landscape very irregular and varied, thereby confirming indirectly the preliminary findings from the first analyses of stratigraphic units (PY04 G7-8) dated to between 1950 and 2000 BCE.

Several stratigraphic units of archaeological interest, such as those found during the 2009 excavation campaign, were investigated in detail with multiple analytic methods.

For instance, the lithified head of a bull (*Bos Taurus primigenius*) was found in SU PY04 D.10 B near the religious building that had been discovered during the 2008 season. The head is 28 cm long and 10 cm wide; the maximum height of the poll to the base of the cheek is 11 cm. A fragment of clay horn (7 cm long, 3 cm wide and 4 cm thick) was also found. This find, considered as a microenvironment, is especially interesting for its archaeological, archaeometric and paleo environmental characteristics.

We therefore decided to investigate the organic residues present in the head with different archaeobotanical, paleopalynological, physical and chemical methods to obtain useful evidence about the seasons, the natural landscape, and the various levels of human activity in this part of the archaeological area (Lentini and Belgiorno 2012b).

The results obtained from the micro-samples randomly selected from the bull's head point essentially to two phases. The first one occurred during a hot and humid climate period characterized by components of the Mediterranean and streamside bioma (as reported in our study of the SU PY04 H6 stratigraphic section).

The significant presence characterized the second phase, in the palynological record, of grassy and bushy floral species native to the island of Cyprus and associated with phytoliths, textile fibres and epithelial plant structures. Their presence in this SU is evidence of a human activity aimed at selecting plant species. The high percentages of floral species (*Papaver* sp., *Lilium* sp., *Tulipa* sp., *Iris* sp., *Hedysarum* sp., *Gagea* sp., *Narcissus* sp. and *Rosa* sp.), and the presence of various phytoliths of *Triticum* sp., *Hordeum* sp., *Bromus* sp. and Juncaceae, seem to be associated with intentional dynamics aimed at selecting and producing floral compositions, decorations, ornaments, and garlands.

In our most recent study, we used multiple methods and devices to analyse 39 apparently organic residues (sediments) retrieved from inside various types of pottery vessels found in different contexts and dating from different periods. Seven of the samples came from the necropolis of Erimi (Table 2), eight from the necropolis of Pyrgos (Table 3), five from the Pierides collection in the Larnaca Museum (Table 4) and nineteen from the Pyrgos archaeological area (Table 5). The purpose of this investigation was to make and report a more extensive analysis of certain trace elements contained in the organic substances, and thereby add to the data already published on the Pyrgos Mavroraki site.

Materials and methods

2. The samples were characterized chromatically, using the Munsell system in transmitted light (placing each sample between the light source and the observer, who can thus see the sample's true colour). For each sample, we recorded the hues, the chromatic values and the RGB coordinates, and we also referred to the CIELAB ranges and standards (Table 1, Hanbury and Serra, 2001). These standards were set by the International Commission on Illumination (CIE) to define colours independently from the devices used (to this end, the CIE has defined criteria based on the colour perceived by the human eye through a triple stimulus) and used in colorimetric practice for analysing non-self-luminous coloured surfaces.

The CIELAB standard contains two kinds of information, one regarding luminance (the quantity of white or black present in the perceived colour, i.e. the distance of a given colour from the black and white extremes), represented by the Y component, and the other regarding chromaticity (which defines the contrast of light, hence carries all the information essential for understanding the observed scene or object), defined by the direction of the triple-stimulus vector (each colour is represented by three numbers – X, Y and Z – positioned in a three-dimensional space and called triple-stimulus values).

The archaeometric investigation

3. In performing the first part of the study, we took account of the texture of the sediments and the presence of organic matter, which was found in all the samples we examined, through calcining tests run in a muffle furnace for one hour at 650°C (Fejgi M. 1989). The next set of tests was run according to three different methods. One type, a toxicological test, uses essentially wet analytic procedures. The other two tests are HPLC (High Performance Liquid Chromatography) and ICP-AES (Inductively coupled plasma atomic emission spectroscopy).
It should be noted that the findings of archaeometric studies conducted with several different types of tests performed on archaeological sediments from areas not subjected to human activities may contain over-representations or under-representations caused by variables present in the processes of burial in nitrophilous sites, and can be hard to interpret.

Toxicological methods

4. The chemical analyses were performed according to the methods of analytic and environmental toxicology, which prescribe chemical and biochemical colour test procedures. Because of their high identification capability, several of these colour tests (the Halphen-Grimaldi method, the Bloor mixture, the Liebermann, Marquis, Molish, Bellier, Chen, Vitali, Bechi and McNally reactions) are also commonly used in chemical-forensic and commercial analyses (Wayne et al. 2004), while others (the Froehde, Vasicky and Mandelin tests) are typically pharmacological (Villavecchia and Eigenmann 1973). In some cases, we used Benedict, Dragendorff, Fehling, Geiess and Lugol reagents, normally used in toxicology (Hodgson, 2004). These methods are based on solubilizing the residues extracted from the archaeological sediments with acidified or alkalified solvents, then using an appropriate reagent to obtain a specific colour that gradually delimits the analytic field, until the reaction that identifies the unknown substance occurs. Circumstances, we used chloroform acidified with HCl to extract alkaloids that had been salified in the chloroform phase; alcohol + HCl to identify essential oils; alcohol + H_2SO_4 to identify essences from officinal plants; and $NaOH + CuSO_4$ (Villavecchia & Eigenmann, 1973) to identify vasoconstrictor alkaloids present in some Ephedraceae. Because the resulting reactions are extremely sensitive, these methods can be used with very small quantities of archaeological sediments.

ID	SU	Hue	Chroma	R	G	B	Range	CIELAB standard
Erimi necropolis								
Tomb 92	3	5	Y 6/2	232	205	170	2.7	B5 Light reddish-brown
Tomb 119	1	2.5	YR 3/3	221	207	186	2.6	A+5 Very dark grey
Tomb 115	14	7.5	YR 6/8	218	244	180	2.7	Light brown
Tomb 115	2	2.5	YR 3/4	232	205	170	2.7	B-5 Dusky red
Tomb 118	1	5	R 6/6	232	205	170	2.7	B-5 Light red
Tomb 115	11	2.5	YR 3/4					Dusky red
Tomb 121	1	5	Y 6/6	216	248	185	2.3	Olive yellow
Pyrgos necropolis								
Tomb 47	PY6	10	Y5 5/2					Greyish-brown
Tomb 47	PY6	10	YR 4/1	232	205	170	2.6	Pale brown
Tomb 47	PY3	7.5	YR 6/8	218	244	180	2.7	Light brown
Tomb 47	PY2	7.5	YR 7/2	219	204	118	2.4	B-3 Pinkish grey
Tomb 47	PY6	10	YR 7/3	218	244	180	2.7	Very pale brown
Tomb 47	PY 4 II	10	YR 5/2	233	207	173	2.8	Greyish brown
Tomb 46	PY6	10	YR 7/2	216	200	176	2.1	L+3 Light grey
Pierides Museum								
Palestinian perfume bottle	-	10	YR 8/1	0	0	0	0	White
Mycenaean perfume bottle	-	10	YR 8/4	218	244	180	2.7	Very pale brown
Bronze measuring spoon	-	5	Y 7/4	220	256	183	2.5	Pale yellow
MIT 1102 AL	-	5	YR 8/1	0	0	0	0	White
MIT 353	-	5.2	YR 5/2	218	244	180	2.7	Very pale brown

Table 1. Colorimetric characterization (Munsell colour system) performed under transmitted light. For each sample, the table lists hue, chroma, RGB coordinates, range and CIELAB standard.

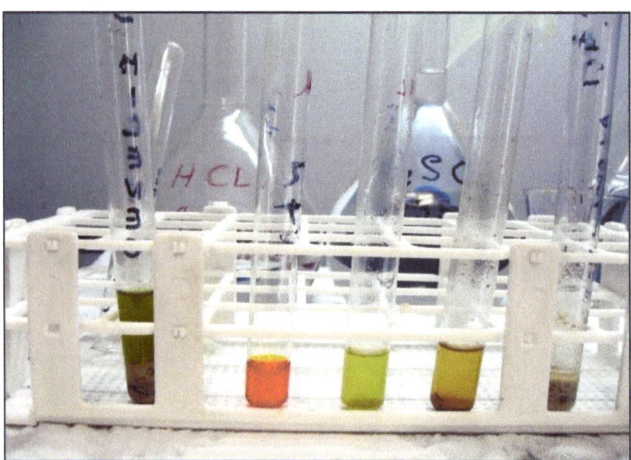

Fig. 1. Tomb 119: n° 1; Tomb 115: n° 2; Tomb 115: n°11. Specific reaction in which the colour changes to green, indicating that the substance is azulene.

The Erimi necropolis

5. Erimi is a village situated partly in the district of Limassol and partly in the British overseas territory of Akrotiri and Dhekelia. In several tombs dated to 1800 BCE, seven residues were taken from pottery vessels found among the grave goods.

Tomb 119, n° 1; tomb 115, n° 1; tomb 115, n° 11

The sediments were treated with chloroform and methyl alcohol, the standard method used for complex extractions. The first test was performed with HCl in increasingly higher concentrations, but all the results were negative. Next, H_2SO_4 at 20% was added to another part of the material treated with methyl alcohol; the result was positive, with a colour change to green (Fig. 1), indicating azulene (present in *Anthemis nobilis*, *Anthemis cotula*, *Anthemis tinctoria* and *Matricaria Chamomilla*). The chromatographic investigation later confirmed this result.

Tomb 92, n° 3; Tomb 121, n° 1

The extraction was made with the Bloor mixture (2 parts alcohol and 1 part ether), and the material was subjected to a series of colour tests with chloroform + HCl and methyl alcohol + H_2SO_4. A few drops of formaldehyde were then added to the extract (Marquis reaction). A bright sky-blue colour developed; this colour is specific to the aromatic compound γ-terpinene, the active principle characteristic of oregano (*Origanum vulgare* L.) and marjoram (*Origanum Majorana* L.).

These two species – both typical of the Mediterranean region and well known for their aromatic properties – are rich in an essential oil (Figueredo et al. 2005) that in classical times was added to the myrtle-and-laurel ointment (Donato 1984).

In Roman times, winemakers also used it, to suffumigate their casks before removing the mast (Columella, XII, 25:4). In antiquity, it was known to grow on the islands of Cyprus and Mytilene (Donato et al. 1986). Marjoram oil obtained by maceration or pressing was a constituent of many perfumes (Pliny the Elder, XIII.1, XV 7). Marjoram perfume from Cyzicus (the capital of

Mysia, in Asia Minor) was widely used.

Tomb 115, n° 14

The sediment samples were treated with Dragendorff's reagent, the standard method for detecting alkaloids. After mixing for a few minutes, they were briefly transferred to an ultrasonic bath. The mixture then became cloudy and its colour veered to orange, which indicated the presence of alkaloids (*Papaver* sp.). Further confirmation was sought with the Vitali reaction (concentrated HNO_3), which likewise indicated the presence of these alkaloid groups. The chromatographic investigation eventually confirmed these results too.

Tomb 118, n° 1

With the Liebermann reaction (H_2SO_4 + KNO_2) the meniscus in the test tube turned bright yellow; this colour corresponds to polyphenols or flavonoids and their esters, with aromatic nuclei deriving from quercetin. In nature, they are commonly found in propolis, in some seeds and in the peel of fruit and vegetables.

PROVENANCE (ERIMI)	COMPOUNDS
Tomb 119, n° 1	Azulene (*Compositae*)
Tomb 115, n° 2	Azulene (*Compositae*)
Tomb 115, n° 11	Azulene (*Compositae*)
Tomb 92, n° 3	γ-terpinene (*Origanum vulgare* L. and *Origanum majorana* L.)
Tomb 121, n° 1	γ-terpinene (*Origanum vulgare* L. and *Origanum majorana* L.)
Tomb 115, n° 14	Alkaloids (*Papaver* sp.)
Tomb 118, n° 1	Quercetin (propolis and fruit)

Table 2: Compounds identified by chemical-toxicological tests.

Pyrgos necropolis (2350-1750 BC).

6. Located East of the archaeological area and older than the Erimi necropolis.

PY Tomb 47, n° 6

The concretions were extracted with ethyl alcohol; after a few minutes, the supernatant was removed. The solution was treated with HCl (first diluted, then gradually increasingly concentrated) and turned brown, indicating the essence of lavender (*Lavandula* sp.). Moreover, the McNally reaction revealed the presence of polyphenols (quercetin).

PY Tomb 47, n° 6 III; PY Tomb 47, n° 3

The sediments were subjected to the Molisch test (1 ml of water with a few drops of β-naphtol dissolved in ethanol, after which 1 ml of concentrated H_2SO_4 is added and forms a layer on the bottom of the test tube). A red ring formed at the interface between the two liquids, thus revealing the presence of glutamic acid (Fig. 3). Since this acid is the ultimate product of the breakdown of the organic matter, its presence may indicate that the vessel contained food (derivatives of milk or meat).

Fig. 3. PY Tomb 47, n° 6 III, and Tomb 47 n° 3. The reddish metamere that formed in the middle of the test tube indicates the presence of glutamic acid.

PY Tomb 47, n° 6

The sediments were initially diluted with the Bloor mixture (2 parts alcohol + 1 part ether), then with iron (III) chloride in concentrated H_2SO_4. This treatment revealed the presence of coriander (*Coriandrum sativum* L.). Further testing (using the Liebermann and Lugol reactions) revealed that the sediments also contained quercetin and wheat-flour starches.

PY Tomb 47/4

The test performed with phenol + H_2SO_4 showed the presence of conifer resin (*Pinus* sp., *Alies* sp.), as the colour veered from green to purple. This result was later confirmed by the chromatographic analyses, which showed that the resin was (1S)-(-)-β-pinene (Mills and White 1989).

PY Tomb 46, n° 6

In a colorimetric test based on chloroform + HCl (Fejgi 1989), the solution turned transparent yellow in the upper layer, while the lower layer remained colourless. This result pointed to the presence of Cyprus turpentine (*Pistacia terebinthus* L.), also known as Chios turpentine.

PROVENANCE (PYRGOS)	*COMPOUNDS*
Tomb 47, n° 6	Lavender essence (*Lavandula* sp.)
Tomb 47, n° 6 III	Glutamic acid (milk and meat products)
Tomb 47, n° 3	Glutamic acid (milk and meat products)
Tomb 47, n° 6	Coriander (*Coriandrum sativum*) Starches (wheat flour)
Tomb 47/4	(1S)-(-)-β-pinene (resin)
Tomb 46, n° 6	Turpentine (*Pistacia terebinthus* L, known as Cyprus or Chios turpentine)

Table 3. Compounds identified by toxicological-chemical tests

Grave goods

7. The results of the chemical-toxicological tests performed on residues taken from tombs in the two necropolises indicate the presence of substances obtained from plant species native to the Mediterranean area, and in some cases (*Papaver* and *Lavandula*) from species native to the island of Cyprus.

They seem to point to different funerary contexts. The residues of the offerings in the Pyrgos tombs contain glutamic acid, coriander, and resins, which can be easily attributed to food.

Conversely, the offerings in the Erimi necropolis seem unusual for the Middle Bronze Age, because besides products – Propolis, fruit and oregano – common in funerary offerings, we also identified azulene (present in many species of the Compositae family) and alkaloids (Papaveraceae). The earliest morphological references to Compositae are to be found in Theophrastos, who calls these plants *Anthemis* (*Hist. Plant.*, I:13.1 and VII:8,3).

The officinal and therapeutic properties of Compositae plants were described by Pliny the Elder (XXII, 53-54), who likewise calls them *Anthemís*. Later, Dioscorides (*Mat. Med.*, III, 137) gave precise therapeutic indications and directions for using this botanical species. The preparation obtained from the whole plant and mixed with wine or honey was used as a diuretic, to expel bladder stones and to treat liver ailments, while the balm (chamomile dried, powdered and mixed with olive oil) was used to treat "periodic fevers."

In conclusion, we can say that the investigation of the samples from the two necropolises (dating from the Early and Middle Bronze Age) present in the same territory of Limassol, east and west of the port, provided interesting information about certain aspects of the funerary ritual, of the natural landscape and of the seasonal transitions, and a useful base for comparison with the species found in the archaeometric, palinological and archaeobotanical tests performed on materials from the Pyrgos-Mavroraki site.

8- Pierides Museum, Larnaca

Palestinian perfume bottle. The residues taken from the bottom (Fig. 4) contain small dark organic lumps and a large triangular lump of purple dye (Fig. 5). The first test was performed with ammonium molybdate and H_2SO_4 at 20%. The reaction produced a yellow colour on the top and a dirty yellow on the bottom. The dirty yellow reveals the presence of the anti-oxidants typical of rosmarinic acid, a polyphenolic acid present in many plants belonging to the Lamiaceae (Labiatae) family, including rosemary, sage and oregano. This sample was probably the residue of a more complex mixture whose base was oil extracted from one of these plants. It is interesting to note that Palestinian rosemary is still used today in the production of essences, and has originated genetic experiments to obtain prized varieties.

Fig. 4. Palestinian perfume bottle.

Fig. 5. Lump of purple dye.

Mycenaean perfume bottle. The residues sampled from the bottom of this pottery bottle (Fig. 6) have very fine granulometry (< 2mm) and include elements whose morphology ranges from rounded to sub-globulous. For colour testing, the residues were treated with a solution of iodine in petroleum ether. The reaction produced an orange colour that revealed the presence of a complex containing anethole, which is present in significant quantities in fennel (*Foeniculum vulgare* Mill.), whence its aroma.

Fennel, a component of the Mediterranean bioma that is found today in all temperate areas, has both aromatic and officinal properties (Lentini 2009b). The essential oil extracted from fennel seeds is classified as an "isolate," and can have hallucinogenic effects (Greig 1989).

Furthermore, when the residues inside the bottle were examined for sampling, they were found to include a fragment of copper (Fig. 7) which displays several micro-areas of oxidation and corrosion. The copper fragment may have been a rudimental catalyst that would have polarized the original compound and facilitated its fluidization.

Fig. 6. Mycenaean perfume bottle.

Fig. 7. Fragment of copper catalyst.

Bronze measuring spoon. After the fragments of copper oxides and crystals were removed from the artefact, the residues it contained looked like small brown quadrangular lumps that fit the concave shape of the spoon (Fig. 8). The only positive result found in the toxicological tests was that when fluoroglucin and HCl were added to the part of the sediments that had been extracted with chloroform, the colour of the solutions turned to the reddish hue that is typical of resinous substances (Lentini 2009c).

Fig. 8. Bronze measuring spoon Pierides Museum, Larnaca.

MIT 1102 AL. Residues consisting of substances with crystalline symmetry (Fig. 9). The crystals' morphology ranges from cubic to rhombohedral (trigonal). The chemical-toxicological tests yielded no positive results. The sample seems to be a formation of insoluble compounds that were probably associated with a detergent liquid used to dissolve them.

Fig. 9. Insoluble substances with crystalline symmetry.

MIT 353. Sediments consisting of small roundish homogeneous lumps. An insect wing (elytra) was also found (Fig. 10). The sample was subjected to extraction with HNO_3; the supernatant was then removed and phluoroglucin dissolved in petroleum ether was added (Bellier reaction). The solution turned red, due to the presence of fatty acids typical of olive oil (*Olea europea* L., var. *europea*; *Olea europea* L., var. *sylvestris*).

Fig.10 Elytra insect

ID	COMPOUNDS
Palestinian perfume bottle	Rosmarinic acird (*Labiatae*)
Mycenean perfume bottle	Anethole (*Foeniculun vulgare* Mill.)
Bronze measuring spoon	Resinous substances
MIT 1102 Al	Insoluble compounds
MIT 353	Olive oil (*Olea europaea* L.)

Table 4. Officinal substances identified by chemical-toxicological tests.

High Performance Liquid Chromatography (HPLC)

9. The second phase of the archaeometric investigation used HPLC methods. These techniques are based on the differential distribution of the components between two phases: a mobile phase (containing the sample) that flows continuously through a stationary phase (adsorbent). This technique is widely used in archaeometric investigations to analyze complex mixtures, as are most archaeological samples. Its main advantages are the small size of the chromatographic column, which avoids unknowns produced by changes of direction (movements of the longitudinal mobile phase) or alternative paths; constant and adjustable elution speed (flow of the mobile phase through the column); and the fact that HPLC analyses can be performed on small samples (micro-liters).

HPLC is used in archaeology to determine the presence of ionic substances. The degradation products that form on the surfaces of archaeological remains are saline (therefore ionic) compounds: sulphates, chlorides, nitrates, oxalates, and so on. HPLC makes it possible to separate two or more compounds present in an unknown sample after extracting them with a solvent (methyl alcohol, chloroform, or ether), exploiting the affinities between the stationary phase and the mobile phase that flows through it (Snyder and Kirkland 1982).

A substance that has a greater affinity for the stationary phase than for the mobile phase takes more time to flow through the chromatography column (retention time) than a substance that has a greater affinity for the mobile phase than for the stationary one. In HPLC, the energy that enables the vector to flow through the column is supplied by the pressure (applied by a pump in the upper part of the column) which drives the mobile phase through the stationary phase.

This not only speeds up the process; it also makes it possible to obtain a larger number of theoretical plates for better resolution. The theoretical plate of a chromatography column is the segment in which a chemical substance is in equilibrium between the two phases (stationary and mobile) before the vector pulls it into a subsequent stage. The specific number of a column's theoretical plates (N) is given by the equation:

$$N = 16 \cdot \left(\frac{T_r}{W}\right)^2$$

where W is the amplitude of the peak and T_r is the retention time, i.e. the amount of time between the moment when the unknown sample is put in and the moment when the peak is reached (Jonsson 1987).

10. Description of the device

The HPLC system comprises an aspirating module (Solvent Module 125S) and two micro-pumps (Beckman Gold System) interfaced with a spectrophotometer (RF 10 AXL Schimadzu fluorescence detector) and an ultra-sphere column dp 5μ 4.6 mm x 25 crt (Beckman Counter) placed in an HPLC oven (Beer 1000 P). The analytic system is managed with Nouveau Gold Beckman software. In our investigation, the results obtained with the HPLC system were compared with standards certified by Extra syntheses, at Lyon.

Preparation

The sediments we analysed were extracted with methanol, or in some specific cases with isopropyl alcohol. The solutions thus obtained were treated in an ultrasound bath, then centrifuged after the supernatant liquid was removed.

PY5J7L2 - Aryballos

The chromatogram shows essentially three peaks (Fig. 11). The first one pertains to almond oil (*Amigdalis communis* L.); its similarity index can be juxtaposed with that of the standard curve.

The subsequent dips and modes indicate the presence of linalool and linalyle acetate, which are present in the essential oil of lavender (*Lavandula* sp.). Pliny (XIII: 2, XV: 7) said that the main ingredient of the perfume called *metopium* was oil of bitter almonds. This oil was obtained by boiling minced almonds in water. As the liquid cooled, the oil separated out. Then, to eliminate the presence of hydrogen cyanide – present on average in percentages ranging from 2% to 4.5% (Villavecchia and Eigenmann 1973) – the liquid was passed through limestone filters that cause hydrogen cyanide to precipitate in the form of calcium ferrocyanide.

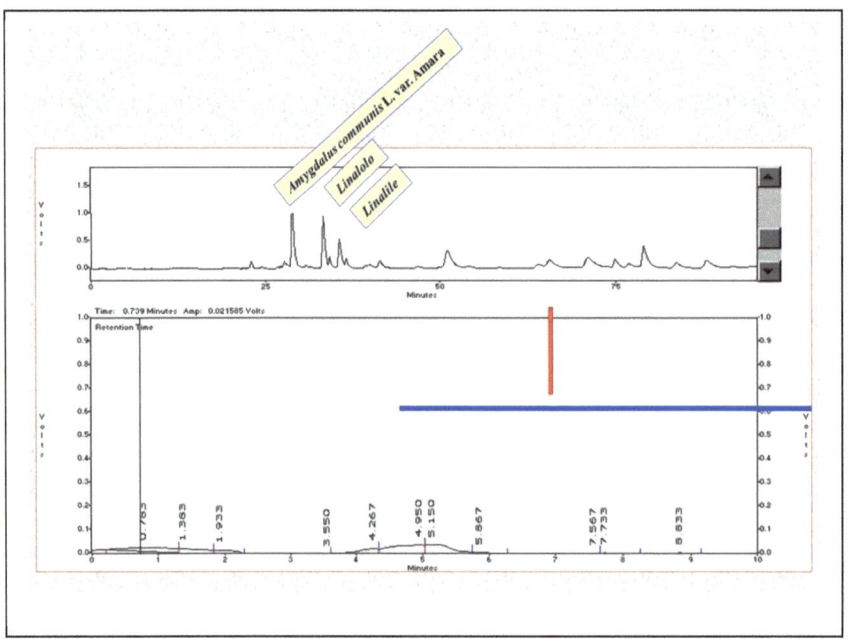

Fig. 11. PY5J7L2 - Aryballos. Chromatogram of the trimodal distribution of the sample.

PY05 G9L4 - Zoomorphic askos; PY05 J7L3 - Interior, section 2

The azulene present in this sample was characterized by means of the addition method. The presence of juniperine falls within the area of similarity of the certified standard (Fig. 12). Juniperine is a very bitter dark yellow substance (Lehninger 1989) found in the berries of *Juniperus phoenicea* L., which grows in Mediterranean coastal areas where the soil consists mostly of highly saline dolomitic limestone (Lentini 2009).

Popular medicine ascribes very high therapeutic value to cade oil (i.e., the oil obtained from juniper berries); it is used to treat digestive disorders, respiratory diseases and rheumatic complaints (Della Loggia 1993). Today oil and essences extracted from juniper berries are used in distilling liqueurs. Today, juniper berries are exploited for their oils and essences and to produced distilled alcoholic beverages. Pliny (XXIV: 36) compares the fragrance of juniper oil (*oleum juniperi*) to that of citron.

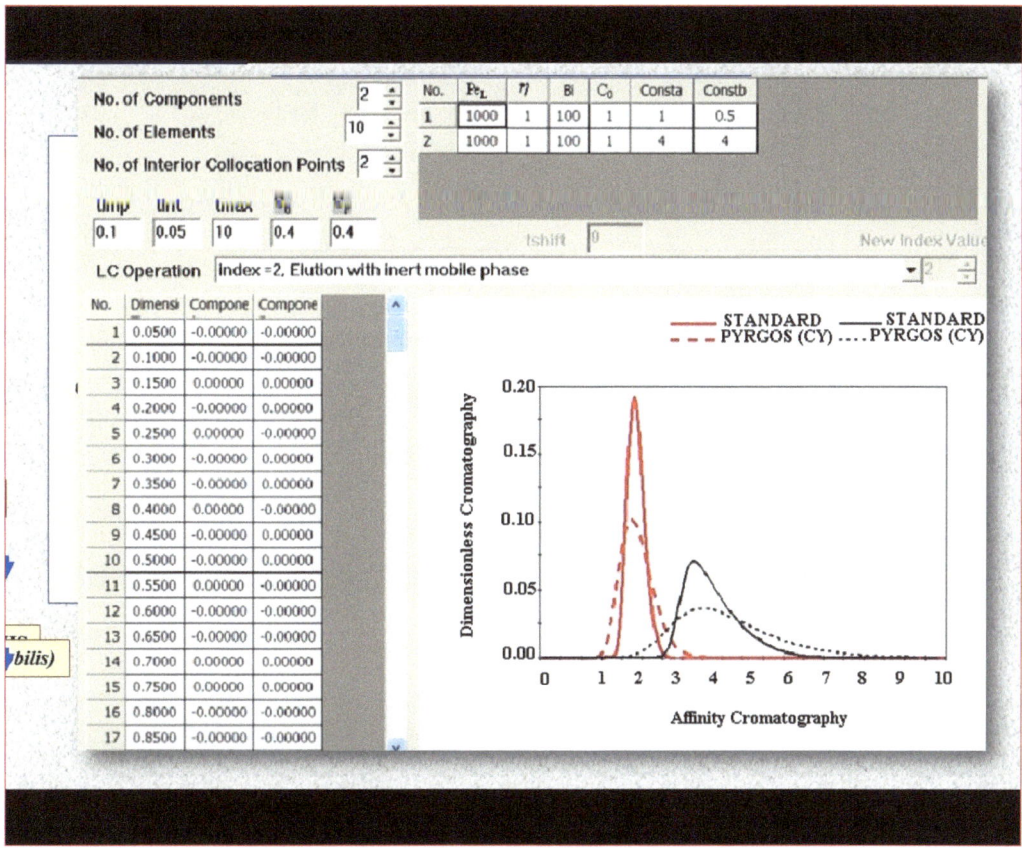

Fig. 12. NIH-EPA database used in searching through comparison libraries; to the right, the area of similarity between the certified standard and an archaeological sample.

PY02 J616 - Juglet

The sample contains significant quantities of beeswax, which can be recognized by the presence of typical indicators, those related to the n-alkane series in the C21-C33 interval, which appear in the chromatogram of the neutral fraction. The presence of beeswax is confirmed by the acid fractions resulting from the presence of palmitic acid and of lignoceric acid in the C22-C34 interval. Moreover, the acid fraction is dominated by the series of saturated monocarboxylic fatty acids in the interval from C10 to C32.

Indicators of oleic acid (a component of olive oil - *Olea europea* L., var. *europea*) also appear (Regeret, Colinart, Degrand and Decavallas 2001). Today this compound is used to make soothing and moisturizing creams (Donato 1984). The olive tree is one of the first plants to have been cultivated in the Mediterranean region. According to De Candolle (1883), the domestication of the olive tree goes so far back that today it is impossible to identify the area where this tree originated.

The biogeographic distribution of *Olea* is generally distributed in temperate and hot paleotropical zones. The olive tree played a primary role in the circum-Mediterranean flora during the Oligocene and Miocene eras. In the Mediterranean region, it is represented by both cultivated and wild varieties that are classified, respectively, as *Olea europaea* var. *sativa*, and *Olea europea* L. var. *sylvestris*.

PY09 19B13 - Basin

The composition of less complex fatty acids with a prevalence of stearic acid points to the presence of animal fats. Moreover, the presence of pinene in the form of (1S)-(-)-β-pinene could indicate a heat-treatment applied to create an organic binder.

PY105 J5-6 - Spout

The presence of absinthin, anabsinthin and artabsin in the standard's area of similarity shows the presence of worm wood oil (*Artemisia* sp.), which probably seeped into the pores of this artefact. This essential oil (*oleum absinthii*, Plinio XIII:2) was known for its fresh fragrance, and was one of the components of the perfumes called *Melinon* and *Kyprinon* (Donato, Branca and Rallo 1975). It has various pharmacological properties that are useful for the digestive system, but it is also highly toxic and dangerous.

PY04 G8, bordering 7L4 - Amphora

The sample contained salvin acid, which points to the presence of sage (*Salvia* sp.). This perennial shrub, found throughout the Mediterranean region, prefers areas with temperate-hot climates, resists in dry conditions but does not survive easily in places where the winters are long and cold.

Sage leaves and flowers are used both fresh and dried, and their essential oil is extracted by steam distillation. Hippocrates recommended its use to treat sores and for its cooling effect. In ancient Egypt, sage oil was the main fixative used in preparing various types of perfume (Donato, Branca and Rallo 1975). In ancient Rome, sage had to be harvested according to a special ritual, without using any metal objects (Pliny, XIX: 62); the Romans used sage mainly to preserve meat.

Ancient herbals attributed many therapeutic properties to combinations of sage and other officinal plants (e.g., Bartolomeo Sacchi, *De honesta voluptate et valetudine*): sage and lavender (probably a balsamic essence), sage and gentian, sage and absinth, and Cyprus sage (probably a balsamic essence containing *Salvia willeana* and *Salvia veneris*, which are native to Cyprus).

Because of the effectiveness of its active principles (Perfumi, Arnold and Tacconi 1991), sage is used in popular medicine as an antiseptic and in the treatment of infections of the upper respiratory tract.

PY04 G8 - Bowl

Valerenic acid – characteristic of *Valeriana officinalis* L. and of the species *Valantia eburnea*, which is endemic to Cyprus – was reported in the past in SU PYO3 G7L3. The identification of this acid in this sample further confirms the presence of valerian at Pyrgos. This perennial herbaceous plant, a part of the Mediterranean bioma, can grow up to two metres high.

The part used for medicinal purposes is the rhizome with its roots, which is preferably harvested gathered during the so-called "balsamic period" (autumn or spring) from plants that are at least two or three years old. The extract used is generally the dry concentrate (Pedretti 1986), which provides high quantities and qualities of the active principles. Its essential oil contains monoterpenes: borneol, bornyl acetate and bornyl isovalerate.

PY09 D10 DL2 - Jug (from the Philia facies)

The fact that only naringenin-7-0-glucoside appears in the chromatogram attests to the presence of organic substances that came from some fruit-tree species belonging to the sub-family of the Maloideae (*Malus* sp., *Pyrus* sp., *Cydonia* sp., *Sorbus* sp.).

PY06 Unit 3 M5L3 - Jug

The chromatographic investigation revealed only the presence of rosmarinic acid (*Rosmarinus officinalis* L.). Rosemary oil has many chemical variants, depending on the characteristics of the soil and the environment the plant grows in. The many different essential oils that rosemary can produce are called chemotypes; that is, though distinct from each other, they are generated by the same species (Evans, 1991).

Rosemary oil is used in making perfume; it is obtained from the petals of the flowers, is highly aromatic and contains camphor. Pliny (XIX: 62) calls it *oleum rosmarini* and describes its scent as like that of incense.

PY06 Unit 2L5 - Jug

Lauric acid ($CH_3(CH_2)10COOH$) was detected after a lengthy retention time (21 minutes), and with the spectrophotometer set at 232-270 UV IR. Laurel oil (*Laurus* sp.), like many other essences, does not have any scent when it is concentrated, but when diluted with other solvents it acquires particular enduring fragrances (Lentini, 2009). It was used in oil-making, and was mixed with myrtle oil (Pliny, XIII:2) to produce inexpensive perfumes.

PY04L3/4 - Bowl

The characterization of DL-aspartic acid ($C_4H_7NO_4$) revealed the presence of amino acids (contained in vegetables and meat).

PY01J6 - Neck of a vessel

After a very long retention time (23 or 24 minutes) and with the detector (spectrophotometer) set at 230 UV IR, we found that the sample's area of similarity corresponded to apiole ($C_{12}H_{14}O_4$). Apiole is a phenylpropene present in the essential oil of parsley (*Petroselinum sativum*), which had already been identified at Pyrgos when the sediments of SU PY03 were analysed.

PY08 E11-b12, PY03 L3, PY05 I8L2, PY02 (2 handle pithos-jar), PY04 J4L3, PY04 (phitoi area) and PY04 (pit)

These samples did not yield any positive result despite the presence of organic matter in the sediments we analysed.

STRATIGRAPHIC UNIT	SUBSTANCES
PY5J7L2 - Aryballos	Almond oil (*Amigdalis communis* L.), linalool and linalyle acetate (*Lavandula* sp.)
PY05 G9L4 - Zoomorphic askos	Juniperine (*Juniperus phoenicea* L.)
PY05 J7L3 - Interior, section 2	Juniperine (*Juniperus phoenicea* L.)
PY02 J616 - Small pitcher	Beeswax and olive oil (*Olea europea* L., var. *europea*)
PY09 19B13 - Basin	Stearic acid (animal fat) and (1S)-(-)-β-pinene (*Coniferae*)
PY105 J5-6 - Spout	Absinthin, anabsinthin and artabsin: wormwood oil (*Artemisia* sp.)
PY04 G8, bordering 7L4 - Amphora	Salvin acid (*Salvia willeana, Salvia veneris*)
PY04 G8 - Bowl	Valerenic acid (*Valeriana officinalis* L., *Valantia eburnea*)
PY09 D10 DL2 - Pitcher (Philia)	Naringenin-7-0-glucoside (*Maloideae* fruit trees)
PY06 Unit 3 M5L3 - Pitcher	Rosmarinic acid (*Rosmarinus officinalis* L.).
PY06 Unit 2L5 - Pitcher	Lauric acid (*Laurus* sp.)
PY04L3/4 – Bowl	DL-aspartic acid (vegetables and meat)
PY01J6 - Neck of a vessel	Apiole (*Petroselinum sativum*)
PY08 E11B12	Negative
PY03L3	Negative
PY05I8L2	Negative
PY02 (phytos 2 - handle)	Negative
PY04J4L3	Negative
PY04 (phitoi area)	Negative
PY04 (pit)	Negative

Table 5. Officinal substances identified by HPLC.

Presence of copper in the Pyrgos environment

11. Recent studies (Johasson et al. 2005; Gücel 2009) of the traces that certain heavy metals release into the soil and on the vegetation near the mining districts of Cyprus encouraged us to try a similar experiment in the archaeological area of Pyrgos, a site well known for the metallurgical facilities and the large number of copper objects, slag, minerals, crucibles and sundry metal-working tools found there.

Some samples that had been selected for the previous tests were analysed with a plasma spectrometer (Inductively Coupled Plasma Atomic Emission Spectroscopy, or ICP-AES) to record the amount of copper present in the archaeological sediments.

Inductively Coupled Plasma (ICP)

12. In archaeometric analyses of the chemical constituents of the organic and inorganic fractions of archaeological materials, the major elements are usually not considered significant because they merely define the material, whereas minor and trace elements are especially important because they point to the provenance of materials (mines, quarries, etc.) and to the intentional use of certain natural substances in the productions of artefacts. When the presence of impurities in solutions is very small – in concentrations on the order of percentages (10^{-2}), parts per million (10^{-6}) or even smaller (parts per billion) – it is best to use methods and technologies that can analyse trace elements quantitatively (Hatcher et al. 1995). The diagnosis of a single element does not specifically characterize a sample, whereas a multi-element analysis made with instruments based on physical-chemical methods can reveal its essential characteristics.

The use of ICP analysis makes it possible to acquire qualitative and quantitative data on the samples, because it identifies the presence of emissions at the characteristic wavelength of the elements one is seeking. This technique is still one of the most effective in studying the different categories of organic and inorganic archaeological materials, especially when only small amounts of material are available for analysis.

Preparation of standard solutions

13. 100 mg of archaeological sediments of the 2-mm fraction were weighed on an analytical balance, then transferred to teflon crucibles. The samples were then dissolved in 8 ml of concentrated HF + 2 ml of concentrated $HClO_4$. The crucibles were then placed in a sand bath set at 200°C and heated until they had dried out. The residue thus obtained was left to cool at room temperature, after which 2 ml of concentrated HNO were added. Lastly, deionized water was added to the preparation to increased it to a known volume. For each element, the chemical standards we used for comparison had been made with solutions containing 1000 ppm. These standards – ISO 9001:2000 series, at concentrations of 997±3 mg/ml (Fig. 13) – were certified by Inorganic Ventures Inc.

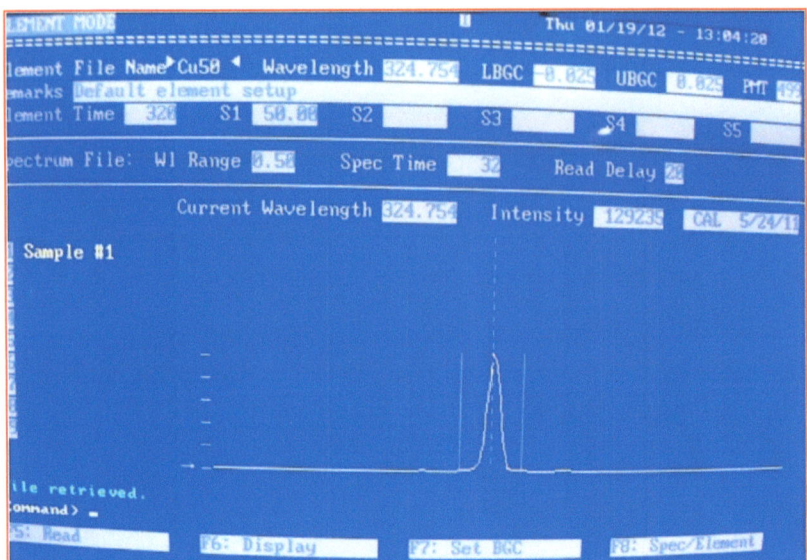

Fig. 13. ICP-AES analysis. The sample (white line) falls within the area defined by the certified standard for copper.

Copper in the officinal residues

14. The presence of copper in the earth's crust averages around 70 parts per million (ppm). Copper is present naturally in the environment in the form of sulphides or, more rarely, oxides, carbonates and silicates, and as native copper. Traces of it can be found in almost all rocks and soils, at different concentrations. In Mediterranean areas, concentrations vary from 2 to 375 ppm (Townsens et al. 2003), depending on factors such as geological origin, soil texture, and presence or absence of mines. It is not easy to establish at what point copper concentration in the soil exceeds the toxicity threshold.

According to the LARN (Nutrients Intake Reference Levels) published in 1996, the attention threshold is thought to be a copper content higher than 100 ppm. Toxicity is due more to the portion readily available for organisms (exchangeable copper) than to the total copper content. This portion depends in turn on the soil's physical, chemical and biological characteristics. In fact, once copper enters the ground it undergoes immobilization reactions on the part of various components (carbonates, iron oxides), or it can be adsorbed by colloids (clayey minerals, organic fraction, humid substances).

The values found in the analyses are expressed in ppm (Table 6). Overall, in the analysed sediments the major elements are not distributed in a Gaussian pattern. In every sample, we observe a bimodal distribution: Ca and Cu, the two elements that most influence the levels analysed. Copper, a transition element associated with carbonates and clay, balances other elements with similar atomic radius contained in carbonates (Bonifacio and Falsone 2005). This is a characteristic of ancillary minerals in carbonate depositional environments.

In conditions where the pH is higher than 7, copper precipitates in the form of hydroxide ($Cu(OH)_2$), which is practically insoluble in water. If the soil's pH falls lower, its sensitivity to copper is greater, especially if organic substances and clayey minerals are scarce. Given copper's affinity for humid molecules, the smaller the organic content, the more the clayey minerals retain the copper. This circumstance might explain the high copper content in the residual fraction found in the site's lower levels.

Stratigraphic Unit	TRACE ELEMENTS (ppm)											
	Cu	As	Ca	Pb	Fe	Sn	Ni	Zn	Bi	Sb	Co	Ag
PY05 J7L3 - Interior, section 2	287	10	210	29	86	52	65	58	32	11	35	31
PY09 19B13 - Basin	290	8	198	25	88	48	58	50	34	9	30	28
PY04 G8, bordering 7L4 - Amphora	270	8	204	21	90	49	60	52	30	9	28	29
PY08 E11B12	275	6	200	23	91	45	57	50	31	10	28	27
PY05I8L2	270	7	198	21	88	48	58	51	30	10	26	28
PY04 (phitoi area)	256	6	195	20	85	48	56	50	29	9	21	24
PY04 (pit)	251	8	200	21	88	45	57	48	30	10	21	24

Table 6. Results of the ICP-AES analysis of the most significant major and trace elements

Bioarchaeology of the primary production

15. The substances we characterized, which were obtained from officinal plant species growing in the Mediterranean area, are numerically significant. Many of the officinal principles identified by chemical tests come from species documented on the site through archaeobotanical investigations that began during the 2004 excavation season. These investigations are still in progress. Various plant macroremains were found through dry sieving in SUs G7L3, H5L6, J6L5, J6L6, J5L8, G9L4, J7L5, G9L7 and F8L4.

Four *Coriandrum sativum* seeds with sub-globulous morphology were recovered. (Fig. 14); four of them show accidental fractures. Twelve semi-globulous *Laurus* sp. drupes were found still in their calyxes (the thickening of their exocarps is a clear sign of violent carbonization), and eight *Myrtus* sp. berries, whose morphology ranges from globulous to ovoidal, with reticular exocarp on which large cavitation areas can be seen. Moreover, some olive pits (from *Olea europea* L.) were identified, and the imprint of a leaf (Fig. 15).

We also characterized 40 grape seeds with different morphologies and biometries. For the time being, the significant presence of *Vitis* species among the archaeobotanical components at Pyrgos cannot be compared with their presence in neighbouring sites, due to the particular features of the materials we examined.

Fig. 14. G9L7 - Carbonized *Coriandrum sativum* seeds viewed under an optical video stereomicroscope (5X).

Fig. 15. J5L8 - Imprint of elliptical-lanceolate leaf. Note the primary vein and the secondary ones, viewed under an optical video stereo microscope (5X).

Finds of *Myrtus* berries and leaves have been reported at Mediterranean archaeological sites, among them Mount Carmel (Israel), in the levels dating from the beginning of the Neolithic (Yadun and Evron 1994). *Laurus* drupes were found in room 227 of the Iron Age palace of Ashkelon, likewise in Israel (Weiss and Kislev 2004).

Although *Coriandrum sativum* remains dating from 700 BCE have been found at Egyptian sites near the huge Fayyum area (Schultze-Motel 1992), this species is considered endemic to Cyprus, one of the Mediterranean islands whose orographic characteristics furthered the phylogenetic evolution of many plant species in the past. Thus, Cyprus is still especially rich in native species (Pantelas, Papachristophorou and Christodoulou 1993).

The vegetation on Cyprus includes elements from different phytogeographical regions.

Conifers (Irano-Turanian element) are among the most typical traits of Cyprus's ancient vegetation (Zohary 1973). On the slopes of the Troodos mountains at altitudes ranging from 500 to 1000 metres above sea level, on soils with outcropping rocks and in general in places where other tree species would find it harder to survive, vestiges of the ancient vegetation still persist near Paphos, in the valley of the cedars (*Stavros Tis Psokas*), along the middle stretch of the Pyrgos River, and near the old asbestos mines (Dimmata). *Juniperus phoenicea* (Syrian element) grows in the mountainous areas that slope towards the sea, with soils consisting mostly of highly saline dolomitic limestone.

Typical Mediterranean species (Di Castri and Mooney 1973), such as *Pistacia*, *Olea*, *Amygdalis*, *Vitis*, *Laurus*, *Rosmarinus*, *Coriandrum*, *Salvia*, *Petroselinum*, *Valeriana*, *Lavandula*, *Origanum*, *Artemisia*, *Myrtus* and various Compositae, Asteraceae and Maloidae, abound in the area studied (Meikle 1985). In 1998, many of these species – some of them native to Cyprus – were included in the official list (Pandeli 1998) of the island's medicinal plants (Georgiades 1992).

Especially interesting is the presence of *Papaver*. Poppies, often an anthropocore species (that is, introduced by man), grow wild in the Mediterranean area, and are generally found in anthropized areas, such as the edges of cultivated fields. The island has five native species (Meikle 1985): *Papaver argemone* ssp. [Kadereit – Syn.: *P. minus*, Meikle], *Papaver rhoeas* ssp. *cyprius*, *Papaver rhoeas* var. *oblongatum* and *Papaver orientale* var. *bracteatum*. They can be found from the Troodos and Pentadactyl mountain ranges to Stavrovouni, and sometimes even near the sea (at Paphos and Limassol).

Conclusions of the archaeobotanical study

16. The presence of many officinal species growing wild in the natural Mediterranean landscape, many of them native to Cyprus, may have fostered technological evolution in the selection and domestication of these species and in the production of fragrant or therapeutic substances, already documented in the past by various specific types of pottery vessels (Belgiorno 2007) and by chemical-toxicological analyses (Lentini 2007) that indirectly confirm widespread knowledge and management of the natural landscape and high technological capability in semi-industrial processes.

Olive oil was used in the wool-spinning process (Belgiorno and Lentini 2005), as a base to produce officinal and medicinal substances, and as fuel for metallurgical furnaces. Together with the selection and cultivation of grapevines for the production of beverages – attested to in the past by archaeobotanical, chemical, physical and archaeological evidence (Flourentzos, Belgiorno and Lentini 2005) – it points to an agricultural context of highly complex nitrophilous environments in which were present all the synanthropic elements that make up the essential variables in a sophisticated production system characterized by a certain degree of seasonality in continuous production processes in which the distribution of labour was very diversified.

The officinal species we characterized presage varieties that came to be used in the classical period, and were described in detail by Pliny, Dioscurides and Theophrastus, and sometimes by the agronomist Columella as well.

Organic colours at Pyrgos

1. A large number (280) of whole shells of *Murex trunculus*, a marine prosobranch gastropod mollusc of the Muricidae family (suborder Stenoglossa), was found near the tubs located in SU G7L5 (Belgiorno 2004). Many sea snails belonging to this family have large shells with long spines (Hovart 2001). *Murex trunculus* has a conical shell and a gland that secretes a mucus that was used to make a purple-blue dye much prized in antiquity.

Biometric measurements of the polar and equatorial axes (Figs. 16 and 17) of the holes opened into the shells to reach the purpurigeneous gland differed by only 0.1 mm. We therefore concluded that the shells had probably been perforated with a dedicated tool. Variously sized fragments of iron and copper minerals (Fig. 18) and of aluminium and chrome alums were found near the SUs we were studying; these substances were probably used to make colour-fixing solutions (mordants) (Timar-Balaszsy and Eastop 1999).

Fig. 16. *Murex* ssp: opening a hole into the shell to reach the purpurigeneous gland was the first step in extracting and producing *ostrum* (royal purple dye).

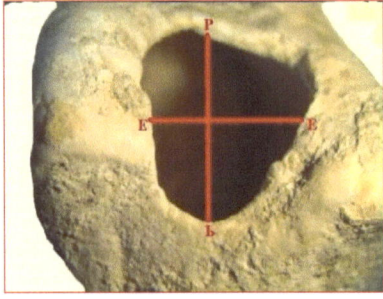

Fig. 17. Biometric measurements of the polar and equatorial axes of the holes opened in the shell.

Fig. 18. These iron (left) and copper (right) minerals found in SU G7L5 were probably used to make colour-fixing solutions.

In this same context, we found and analysed several coloured residues (fragments, globules and small lumps that appeared to consist of organic matter) removed from inside the tubs and from different types of pottery artefacts and spindle whorls. Chemical investigations made with different methods (colorimetric analysis, XRF, ICP analysis and various microanalytic techniques) began during the 2003 and 2004 excavation seasons.

Materials and methods

2. The samples from US G7-L5 and G/-L8 we studied were characterized chromatically using the Munsell system in transmitted light (Macbeth Division 1999). For each sample, we recorded

(Wyble and Fairchild 2000) the hues, the chromatic values and the RGB coordinates (Table 7).

Colour of sample	Hue	Chroma	R	G	B	Range	CIELAB standard
Red	5	R 3/60	216	200	176	2.02	A+5 Red
Pink	5	R 6/5	213	164	100	2.02	B+6 Pink
Indigo	5	YR 0/29	150	120	184	2.02	L+5 Light Blue
Yellow	5	Y 8/60	198	210	100	2.02	Yellow

Table 7. Results of the colorimetric observations (Munsell color system) made under transmitted light. For each sample, the table lists the hues, chrome values, RGB coordinates range and CIELAB standard.

We referred to the CIELAB ranges and standards (Hanbury and Serra 2001) used in colorimetric practice to analyse non-self-luminous coloured surfaces. This standard provides contains information on luminance, represented by the letter Y, and on chromaticity, defined by the direction of the triple-stimulus vector (Berns, 1999). The archaeometric investigation continued with analytic techniques using colorimeters, X-ray fluorescence (XRF), plasma analysis (ICP), microanalytic techniques and (for the colour yellow) electrospray techniques; because of the nature of the materials examined, these analyses were performed at the Italian National Research Council's Chemical Methodologies Institute.

Colorimetric analysis

3. The dye matrices were treated (leached) with a one molar solution of NaOH + 20% H_2SO_4 for the yellow, indigo, and red-pink matrixes (Lentini and Scala 2002). They were then diluted in various solutions and subjected to colorimetric readings (UV photoelectron spectroscopy) at 400 to 650 nanometres in the visible range.

The optoelectronic device used to measure UV light contains several sensors, three of which consist of a photodiode fitted with a red, green, or blue filter. All the readings (expressed in

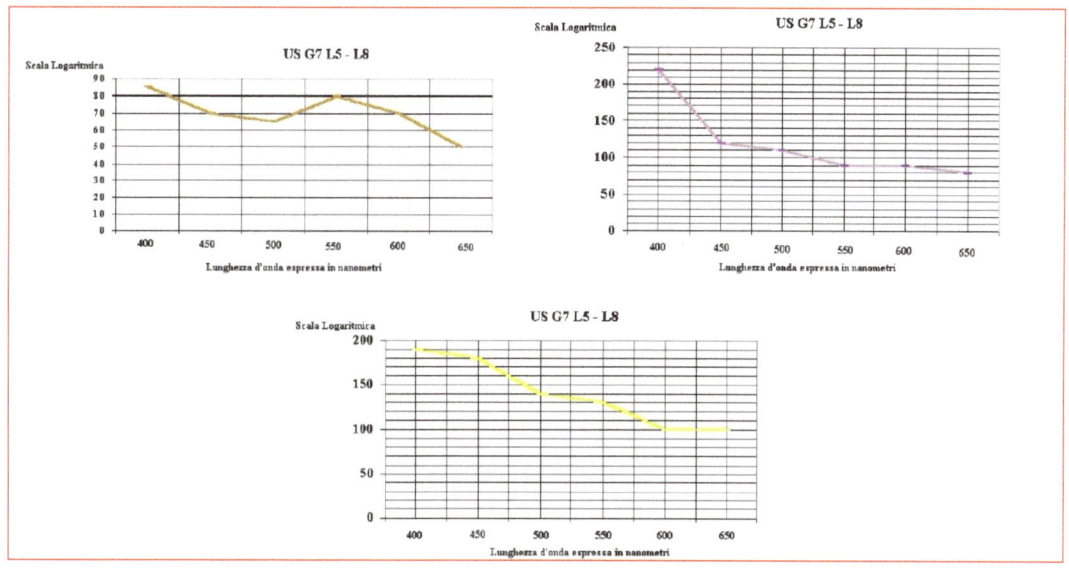

logarithms) were positive, and enabled us to create a scale of analytic values (diagrams 1, 2 and 3) that shows how the intensities of the colours differ, depending on the concentrations (in logarithmic form) of red-pink, indigo, and yellow. Diagrams 1, 2 and 3, showing the colorimetric readings.

4. Analytic investigations: XRF and ICP spectrometry

Red/pink

The first characterization of red/pink colours was made with a portable XRF spectrometer (60 kV 1.5 mA). This test showed the presence of bromine (Tables 8 and 9, Diagram 4), an element specific to Tyrian purple, associated with a significant presence of certain trace elements (Fe, Mn, Cu, Zn, and Sr).

ID	Fe	Mn	Cu	Zn	Sr	Br
I L	1	0.5	0.7	0.5	4	8
II L	1.3	0.4	0.7	0.6	4.1	8.8
III I	1	9.5	0.7	0.5	4.1	8.15

Table 8. Average spectrum of the red/pink matrix (sediments <2mm).

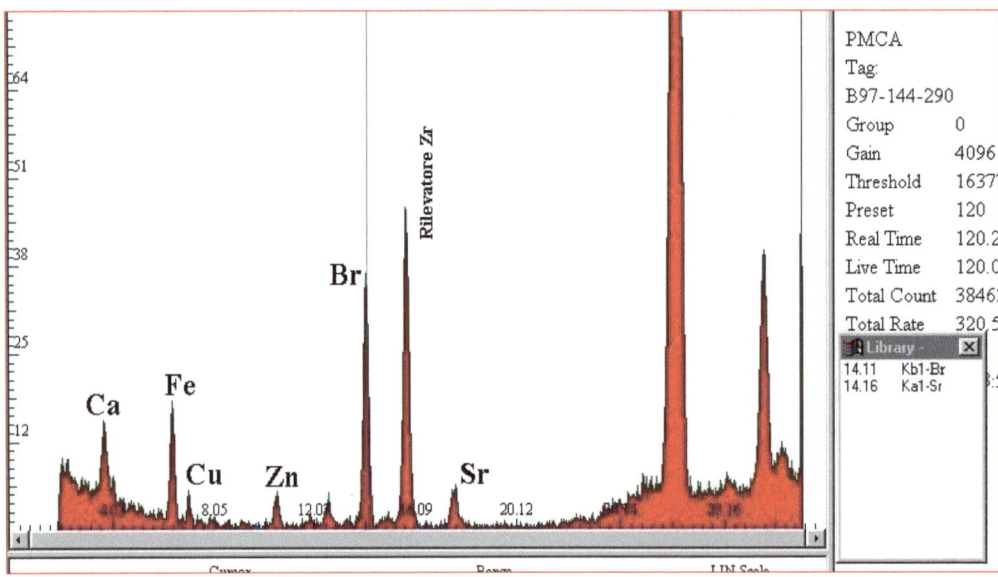

Diagram 4. Diffractogram obtained with XRF. Spectrum of the red-pink matrix (globular drops).

ID	Ca	Fe	Mn	Zn	Sr	Cu	Br
I G	1	1.51	0.52	0.32	2.21	0.45	8.15
II G	1.01	2.13	0.46	0.51	1.84	0.51	8.21
III G	1.62	1.94	0.57	0.45	1.86	0.52	8.18

Table 9. Average spectrum of the red-pink matrix (sediments <2mm).

The ICP analysis confirmed the quantitative presence of these elements (Table 10). At present, there are no certified standards for the overall chemical makeup of colours analysed with this method. The values we found were compared element by element with certified ISO 9001 international standards (British Chemical Standard - Inorganic Ventures, Inc.).

The results obtained with the different analytical methods do not allow any leeway for hypotheses concerning the degree to which the Tyrian purple was preserved in the archaeological sediments or the possible seasonal nature of its.

ID	Ca	Fe	Mn	Cu	Zn	Sr
I - Round drops	1	1.5	0.5	0.4	0.4	2
II - Round drops	1.8	2.1	0.4	0.5	0.5	1.8
III - Round drops	1.6	1.9	0.5	0.5	0.5	1.8
WAVELENGTH	396.847	417.206	259.373	224.700	202.548	421.552
I - Powder	1	0.5	0.7	0.5	4	8
II - Powder	1.3	0.4	0.7	0.6	4.1	8.8
III - Powder	1	0.5	0.7	0.5	4.1	8.15

Table 10. US G7L5 Tyrian purple samples. Percentages of the most significant elements found by ICP analysis, with a Plasma 40 Emission Spectrometer.

In this analysis, we noted the minimum detectable concentration, the concentration of the analysed elements, the gross count of observed peaks, the base count of observed peaks, the count time adjusted for unused time, the diffusion and the total absorption.

The different forms (earths, round drops) of Tyrian purple that we examined probably came from different types of production. The earths, finely powdered and mixed with other powders form new hues ((Figs. 19 and 20; Schutzemberger 1958). The blood-red globular morphologies (Fig. 21) are probably due to the dye precipitating after having been steeped in solid salt (Schweppe 1988).

Fig. 19. Finely powdered Tyrian purple.

Fig. 20. Powdered Tyrian purple mixed with other powdered substances to obtain new hues.

Fig. 21. After steeping in solid salt, Tyrian purple dye usually precipitates in the form of globular drops.

Tyrian purple is a dense and viscous substance, and has an unpleasant smell. The pigment was used mainly to dye textiles, to tint parchments and, mixed with powdered limestone, to colour pottery artefacts (Mastrocinque 1928). It is insoluble in alcohol, ether and chloroform, but is soluble in phenol and aniline. In the presence of yeast, urine, bran or natron, it is transformed by reduction into a chemical solution in the form of a leukoderivative (Tazzetti and Bonci 1963).

SU G7L5	Ca	Fe	Mn	Cu	Zn	Sr
Drops I	1	1.5	0.5	0.4	0.4	2
Drops II	1.6	19	0.5	0.5	0.5	1.9
Earth I	2.1	2.2	0.3	0.5	0.5	1.0
Earth II	1.8	2.1	0.4	0.6	0.5	1.1

Table 11. Tyrian purple: percentage contents of the most significant trace elements, found by ICP analysis (Plasma 40 Emission Spectrometer).

Indigo blue

As reported in the literature (Ball 2002), this colour contains all the same trace chemical constituents as Tyrian purple, except bromine. We performed the same analytic procedures used for Tyrian purple and found that in indigo the principal trace elements were present in different percentages (Table 11). At the same time, we performed a series of microanalytic tests aimed at characterizing the indigo molecule, $C_{16}H_{10}N_2O_2$ (Fig. 22). In the presence of the colour blue, adding NaOH (in a watery concentrate) and then slightly warming the solution turns the blue into reddish brown.

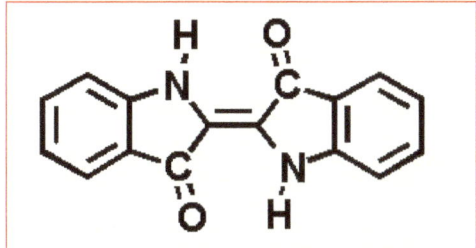

Fig. 22. Chemical structure of indigo

To verify this result, we added a few drops of HCl to the same sample; the acid produced no reaction, thereby confirming the validity of the previous analytic assay. Indigo dye (Figs. 23 and 24) is obtained from the leaves of *Indigofera* ssp. (Fabaceae), which are left to ferment in tanks full of water, whereupon indican, a glucoside naturally present in the plant (Tomlinson and Allan 1984) turns into an azure dye called indigotine (Rinaldi et al. 1986).

This grassy and/or bushy plant originated in the Near East and spread through the Mediterranean region in successive periods (Belgiorno and Lentini 2008). In later times indigo was also extracted from other ornamental species (Ball et al. 1990), of which the best known are *Indigofera tinctoria, argentea, intricata, spinosa* and *semitrijuga*. In the Cyprus phytocoenosis, these plants are associated with *Polygonum, Euphorbia, Amaranthus, Hybiscus* and *Calotropis* (Zohary 1973).

ID	Ca	Fe	Mn	Cu	Zn
Indigo 1 L	2	2	1	0.9	0.8
Indigo 2 L	2.4	2.1	0.9	1.2	0.8
Indigo 3 L	2.3	2.2	1.2	1	1

Table 12. Indigo: percentage contents of the most significant trace elements, found by ICP analysis (Plasma 40 Emission Spectrometer).

Later, this blue colour was also found in *Asclepias tingens, Eupatorium puerperum* (red aquatic hemp), *Galega officinalis, Genista tintoria, Isatis tinctoria* (woad) and in some Orchidacee (Tomlinson and Allan 1984). In the presence of an iron-based colour fixing solution (mordant), it dyes all kinds of cloth (Celoria 1971).

Figs. 23 and 24. Fragments of indigo dye.

Yellow

Microanalysis directly identified the colour yellow, using the spectrophotometric assay of the total phenols extracted (Folin-Ciocalteu reagent) and the calibration curve obtained with a certified commercial standard for rutin (Fejgi 1989). The considerable presence of rutin ($C_{27}H_{30}O_{16}$ - Molecular weight 610.51; Figs. 25 and 26) in the sample was confirmed by the electrospray technique – currently the most reliable one for defining not only individual constituents but also mixtures containing many different components (e.g., plant extracts).

This technique, associated with mass spectrometry, enables sure identification of the constituents based on their mass/charge ratio. Regarding the presence of rutin, the literature consists mostly of papers on the textile industry and on the various emulsions that can be obtained. No reports were found on very ancient contexts, probably because so few artefacts have been found.

Rutin is a dye obtained from the leaves of various Brassicaeae and Polygonacee (Hall et al. 1990), and from those of *Ruta graveolens*. Rutin, a flavonoid insoluble in any solvent, is a dispersion-type dye, meaning that a colloidal emulsion of the powder is fixed to the surface of textile fibres with the aid of an aluminium alum mordant. Rutin dyes all kinds of cloth yellow.

Fig. 25. Sample containing a considerable amount of rutin.

Fig. 26. Constituents and chemical Structure of rutin

Quercetin-3-rutinoxide, 3, 4, 5, 7 Tetraoxyflavonol-3-Rutinoxide

Conclusions of the study of organic colours

5. The substances described above, extracted from various plants and molluscs from the Mediterranean area (Lentini and Scala 2004; Zohary 1973; Cecalupo and Quadri 1996) are among the ones best known today. The analytical procedures we used (XRF, ICP and various microanalytic techniques) turned out to be complementary to each other for the identification of some of the chemical components that are specific to these substances.

The characterization of these components shows how advanced was the ancients' knowledge of the properties of these plant and shellfish species. We partly overcame the difficulties we encountered in seeking specific ICP standards applicable to the materials we were studying by adapting multi-element commercial standards and comparing the quantitative intervals element by element. About XRF, we made the initial calibration with a sample of Tyrian purple that had been produced in the 1960s in Taranto and belonged to a private collection.

The evidence found in samples from archaeological levels carbon-dated to 2000-1950 BCE raises questions about the need to revise the currently accepted chronology regarding the origin and spread of these substances and the technological procedures followed in making the basic colour matrixes, for until now no evidence had been found that natural dyes were used before 1200 BCE

Archaeoenvironmental investigations in the archaeological area of Pyrgos.

Introduction

1. During the 2009 and 2012 excavation seasons, two stratigraphic walls were chosen for sedimentological and paleopalynological investigations. The purpose was to document the changes that may have occurred in the natural landscape, and the probable impact of human activities in the Pyrgos Mavrorachi area. The first stratigraphic section, comprising nine levels, was selected in SU PY09H9, near the building devoted to religious practices that had been found in 2008.

The second stratigraphic section, comprising eight levels, was obtained from the untouched balk strata pertaining to SUs PY12 C10A, PY12 C9C, PY12 B9D and PY12 B10C, near the excavation grid squares in which cosmetic tablets were found. The deepest levels of the two stratigraphic columns contain fragments of artefacts from the Philia period, thus placing this phase of human occupation between the end of the third millennium and the second or first, since four C14 dates of this period coincide. Moreover, the aero-biological monitoring implemented during the 2008 and 2009 excavation campaigns (Belgiorno and Lentini 2010) showed that the archaeological area is free of air pollutants. Air-particulate elements are present (*Alternaria*, *Epicoccum*, *Stemphyllum*, *Drachslera*, *Fusarium* and *Didymella*), but are harmless for the people who frequent the dig and for the materials and standing structures in the archaeological area.

Materials and methods

2. The archaeo-palynological study took account of the texture of the sediments and the presence of abundant organic matter, which was found in all the samples we examined. Paleopalynological extraction was performed according to the methods developed by the University of Amsterdam's Department of Earth Sciences. Essentially, these methods envisage the following steps: sieving through a nylon filter (granulometry 2 mm; Gurley and Bendtsen standard), HCl 10%, acetolithic mixture, heavy liquid (density between 1.9 and 2.1) and HF 40%. To calculate the absolute pollen frequencies (APF), we added a tablet of *Lycopodium* to each sample and counted the number of pollen grains and spores per gram of sediment. The pollen spectrums are based on the total number of pollen grains counted.

The diagrams were constructed with Tilia and Tilia Graph software, which provided further indications for identifying the palynological areas. It should be noted that paleopalynological research conducted in archaeological sediments that have incorporated pollens and spores can be much more complex than in more traditional studies (e.g., of undisturbed geological formations, of areas unaffected by human activities, of cores extracted from ancient forests or lakes), and the results they provide can contain over-representation or under-representations that are due to human impacts and are hard to interpret.

The morpho biometric study of certain pollen types, such as Conifers, Graminaceae, *Cerealia*-type, Rosaceae (specifically *Rosa* ssp. and *Potentilla* ssp.) and Liliaceae (specifically *Narcissus* ssp., *Lilium* ssp., *Crocus* ssp. and *Iris* ssp.) was conducted through an image analyser that uses a camera mounted on an optical microscope connected to a computer (fitted with an image-acquisition board) which in turn is connected to another high-resolution monitor (for characterizing the acquired images).

Moreover, after a new software program was fine-tuned we could acquire RGB or B/W images. The images seen with the optical video microscope were acquired as RASTER images (binary matrix with an x-y origin) whose maximum size is 800 x 600 pixels. The pollen grain biometric features we recorded were:

- in vesiculate morphologies (*Pinus* and *Cedrus*), in equatorial view, the length of the polar axis, the diameter of the air-vesicles, and how much they protrude;
- the length of the polar and equatorial axes, and the diameter of the annulus (in Graminaceae and *Cerealia* type);
- in Rosaceae pollens (specifically *Rosa* sp. and *Potentilla* sp), the presence or absence of perforations;
- in monocolpate pollens of the Liliaceae family (specifically *Iris* ssp., *Narcissus* ssp., *Crocus* ssp. and *Lilium* ssp.), the length of the trough, the presence or absence of the pore vestibule recorded, and the arrangement of the columellae in the exine.

We compared the diagnostic features with pollen grains of the same species, provided by the CNR-ITABC'S pollen collection. We also added to the names of some taxa the indication "sp." to include any hidden biodiversity.

Sedimentological test:

3. Before the paleopalynological analysis, we performed various sedimentological tests to identify the granulometric composition of the two stratigraphic walls we had selected. We analysed the section levels with the Mériaux method, and found their texture to be very silty. The deepest levels (SU PY09 H9, from -54 to -63 cm, and SU PY12 C10A I, from -74 to -91 cm) contain a limited amount of sand (Figs. 31, right, and 32, right) resulting from the breakdown of the bedrocks; clay is nearly absent.

The <2mm fraction contains fragments of chalk (Fig. 27) and muscovite (Fig. 28), quartz crystals with sub-rounded to round habit (Fig. 29), and particles of variously hued ochre. Shells of *Alvinaria* sp. were also found, as were shells of the sweet-water gastropod molluscs *Gyraulus* sp. (Fig. 30).

The silty texture of all the levels, which could be interpreted as due to migration of finer sediment particles that were washed away during a lengthy humid phase, probably helped preserve the paleo pollens (Traverse 2007).

Fig.27: SU PY12C10A: Fragment of laminar chalk

Fig. 28: SU PY12 C10A: Fragment of muscovite.

Fig. 29: SU PY09 H9: Round quartz crystals.

Fig. 30: SU PY12 C10A: Shell of *Gyraulus* sp.

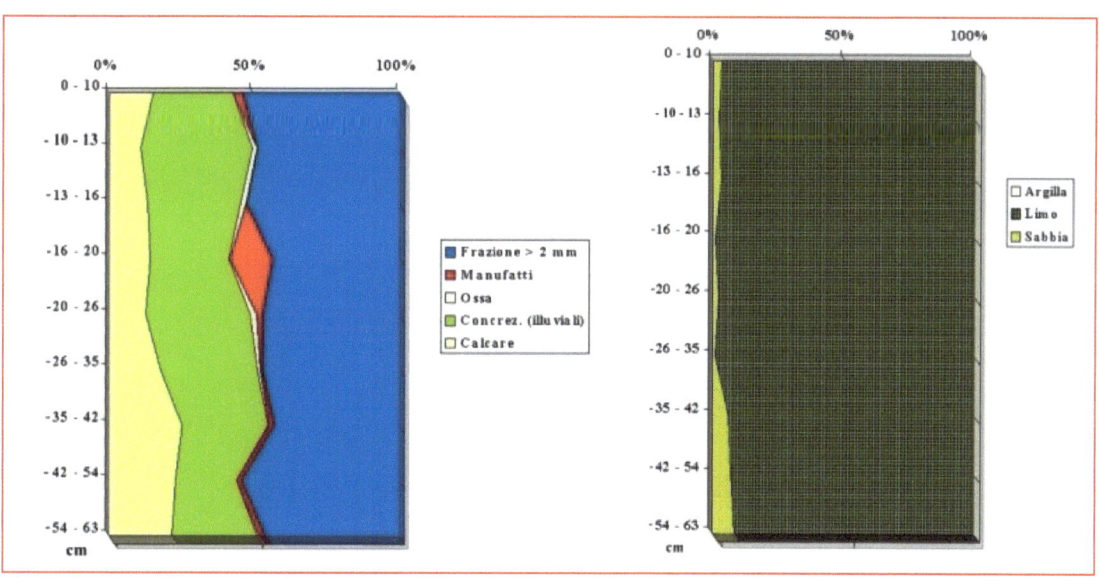

Fig. 31: SU PY09 H9: Stratigraphic diagram (left) and granulometric diagram (right).

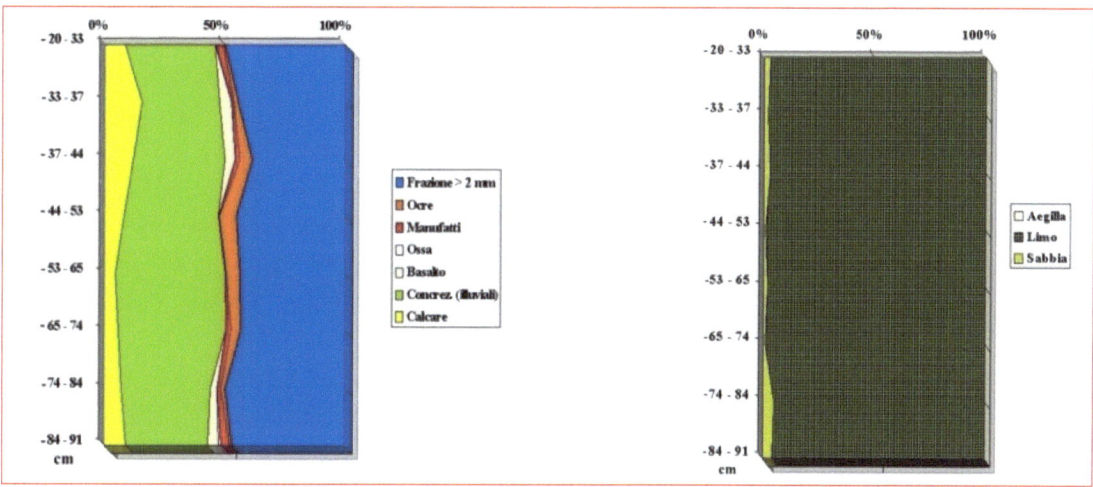

Fig. 32: SU PY12C10A: Stratigraphic diagram (left) and granulometric diagram (right)

In SU PY09 H9, the fraction ranging from 1.25 to 0.80 mm contains several fragments of copper. The granulometric diagrams (Figs. 31, left, and 32, left) of these two stratigraphies show the presence of anthropic elements resulting from continued occupation of the site.
Two main components essentially define its continuity – one natural and the other anthropic – that were associated with each other and helped build up the deposit.

The archaeo-palynological investigation

4. The preliminary results of the paleopalynological analyses are displayed in eight diagrams. The first two (Figs. 43 and 44) show the AP/NAP ratio (arboreal pollen to non-arboreal pollen). The third diagram and the fourth (Figs. 45 and 46) refer to the groups of phytogeographic elements (biomes). In Figs. 33 and 38, the individual paleopalynological zones are shown next to the stratigraphic column. Taken together, the results show four subsequent phases in the evolution of the vegetation and the climate, during which the natural landscape underwent significant changes.

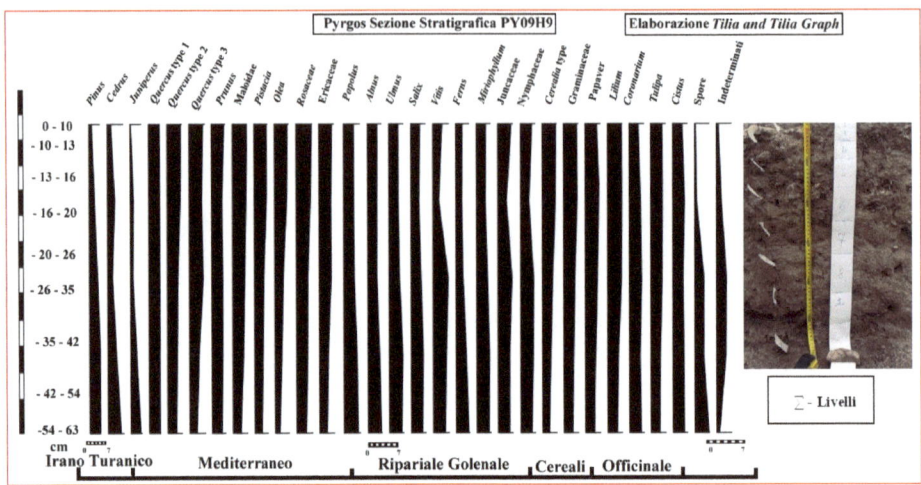

Fig. 33: SU PY09H9: Pollen diagram.

The stratigraphic series investigated at Pyrgos seems to be characterized by four major phases in the development of the vegetation: (a) the sizable presence of the streamside element; (b) constant percentages of native taxa; (c) the continuous presence of the Mediterranean element; and (d) increasing percentages of cereal crops.

The constant and significant presence of streamside species such as *Popolus*, *Salix*, *Alnus*, *Ulmus*, *Vitis* and *Myriophyllum*, Juncaceae, ferns and Nymphaceae throughout the palynological record suggests that the original river system was enlarged by creating a canal system near Pyrgos, possibly to increase the amount of arable land. Moreover, the streamside element seems to confirm indirectly the archaeological and archaeometric documentation on the production of olive oil, on textile dyeing and on metal-working activities, all of which require vast amounts of water.

The constant percentages, throughout the paleopalynological record, of species typical of the Mediterranean biome – *Quercus*, *Pistacia*, *Olea*, *Prunus*, *Maloidae*, Ericaceae (Fig. 34) and Rosaceae – point to a stable thermophilic phytocoenosis.

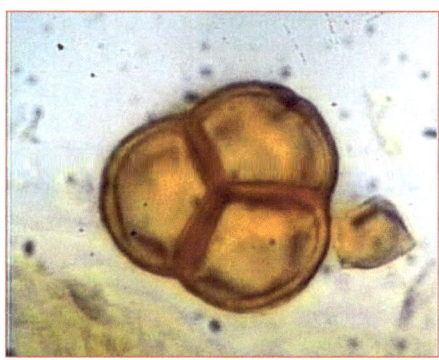

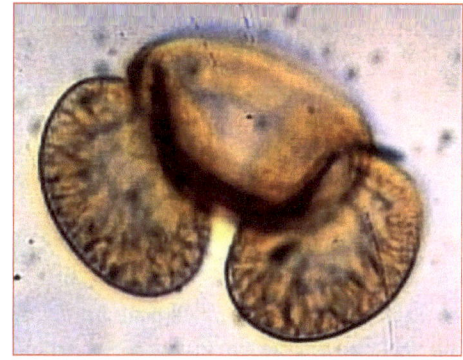

Fig. 34: SU PY09H9: Tetrad morphology, *Erica* sp. pollen grain (40x).

Fig. 35: SU PY09H9: Vesicular morphology, *Pinus* sp. pollen grain (40x).

Pinus (Fig. 35), *Cedrus* and *Juniperus*, associated with the herbaceous species *Papaver*, *Lilium* (Fig. 36), *Coronarium*, *Tulipa* and *Cistus* (Fig. 37) – all of them endemic plants – represent the most characteristic autochthonous biome (Lentini 2013) of the island of Cyprus.

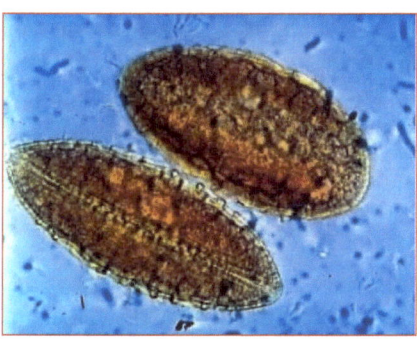

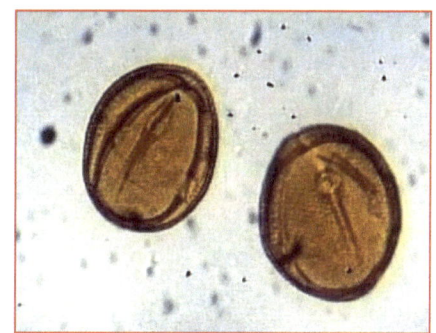

Fig. 36: SU PY09H9: Monocolpate morphology, *Lilium* sp. pollen grain (40x).

Fig.37. SU PY09H9: Tricolpate morphology, *Cistus* sp. pollen grain (40x).

Pine woods were the island's original biome, and in the past, they probably occupied a large part of the territory (Quezel 1979).

At present this biome spreads over the parts of the Troodos mountains that rise more than 1000 meters above sea level, covering them with vast conifer woods made up mostly of *Pinus brutia* and the endemic species *Cedrus brevifolia*.

At the higher altitudes, near Mount Olympus, are *Pinus palladiana* woods, with *Juniperus foetidissima* present in the clearings. Conifers are also present in some residual areas near Paphos, at sea level, and along the middle stretch of the Pyrgos River.

Most likely, in the past human activities and climate changes (Belgiorno and Lentini 2007) drastically impoverished the original biome in this area.

Native herbaceous plants such as *Papaver, Lilium, Coronarium, Tulipa* and *Cistus*, all of them present in low percentages, may be further evidence of Cyprus's autochthonous species. The analysis of a lithified bull's head found during the excavation of SU PY09 D10b, indirectly confirmed the presence at the site of a specific area where only selected floral species were brought and kept (Lentini and Belgiorno 2012).

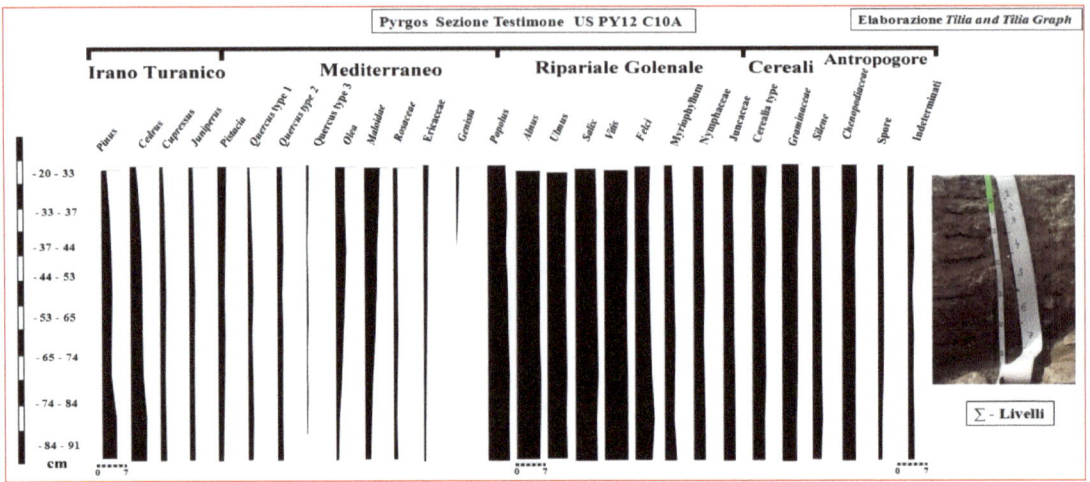

Fig. 38. SU PY12C10A: Pollen diagram.

In the stratigraphic levels of this section (Fig. 38) we noted a significant decrease in the species related to the Irano Turanic and Mediterranean elements, due to an initial presence of *Quercus coccifera* L. and of anthropochore species (Chenopodiacea, Graminaceae, *Genista* sp., Fig. 41; and *Lotus* sp.) found in arid Mediterranean garigues, associated with a significant presence of cultivated species (*Cerealia* type, *Vitis* sp. and Maloidae) that might attest to an increase in human activities in the Pyrgos area.

The species included in the streamside element (*Popolus* sp., *Salix* sp., *Ulmus* sp., Fig 40; *Alnus* sp., *Vitis* sp., *Myriophylum* sp., *Nymphaea* sp., Fig. 42; ferns and Juncaceae) seem to confirm the findings from SU PY09H9, though with a significant percentage increase in *Vitis* sp., *Alnus* sp. and *Salix* sp. The increase in pollen from *Vitis* sp. jibes with the large number of grape seeds recovered during the 2004 to 2008 excavation seasons in SUs PY05GH9L4/5, PY05L4 and PY06L5/2.

The main crops – documented in the past by paleo seeds (Lentini and Belgiorno 2012) for the periods investigated – and the percentages of pollen from *Cerealia* type, *Vitis* sp., *Olea* sp. and Maloidae remain constant throughout the paleopalynological record.

All the components present in the paleopalynological profile indicate that the climate was humid during the chronological phases represented.

The most significant elements of the Mediterranean and streamside biomes characterize this profile. Moreover, *Pinus* sp., *Cedrus* sp. (Fig 39) and *Cupressus* sp. are continuously present in these stratigraphic levels; these species are endemic, and are likewise found on the medium-to-high zones of the Troodos mountains, of the Paphos forest, in the Valley of Cedars and along the steep cliffs bordering the Yialias and Pedieios rivers.

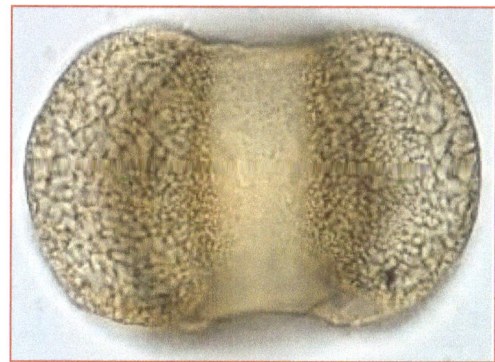

Fig.39. SU PY12 C10A: Vesicular morphology, *Cedrus* sp. pollen grain (40X).

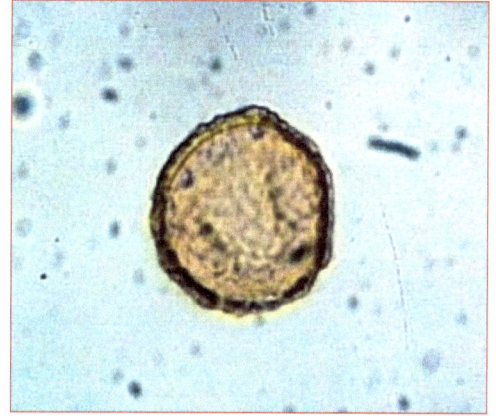

Fig. 40. SU PY12 C10A: Zonoporate morphology, *Ulmus* sp. pollen grain (40X).

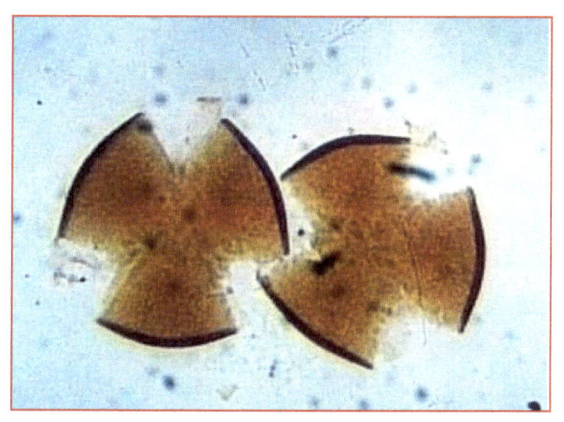

Fig. 41. SU PY12 C10A: 3-colporate morphology, *Genista* sp pollen grain (40X).

Fig. 42. SU PY12 C10A: Monoporate and anaporate morphology, *Nymphaea* sp. pollen grain (40X).

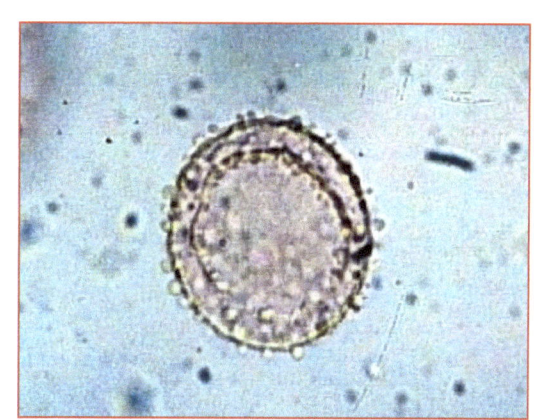

Conclusions

5. The two stratigraphy we examined show differences in the distribution of the phytogeographic elements found in the paleopalynological investigations. These differences are probably due to human activities at the site.

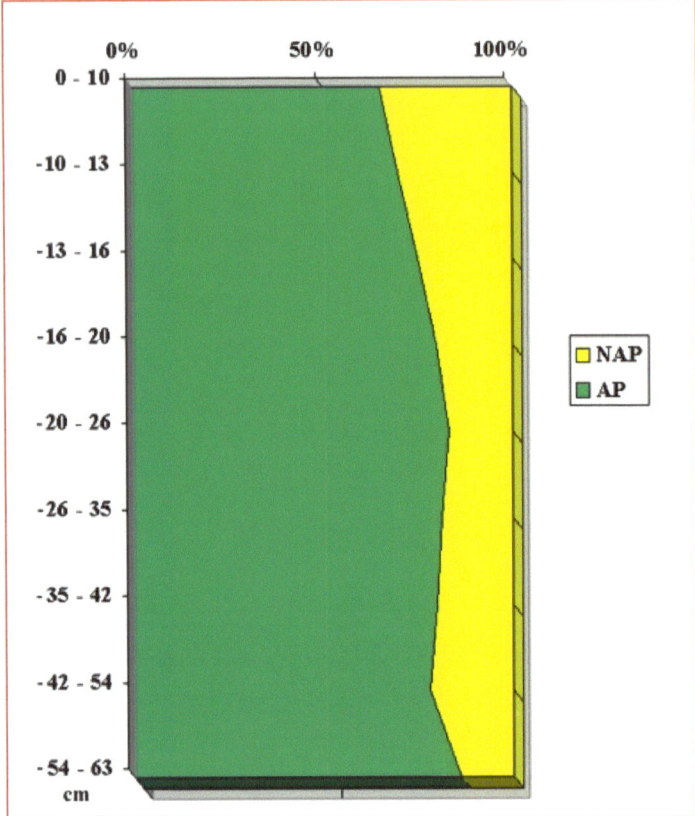

Fig. 43. SU PY09H9: AP/NAP diagram.

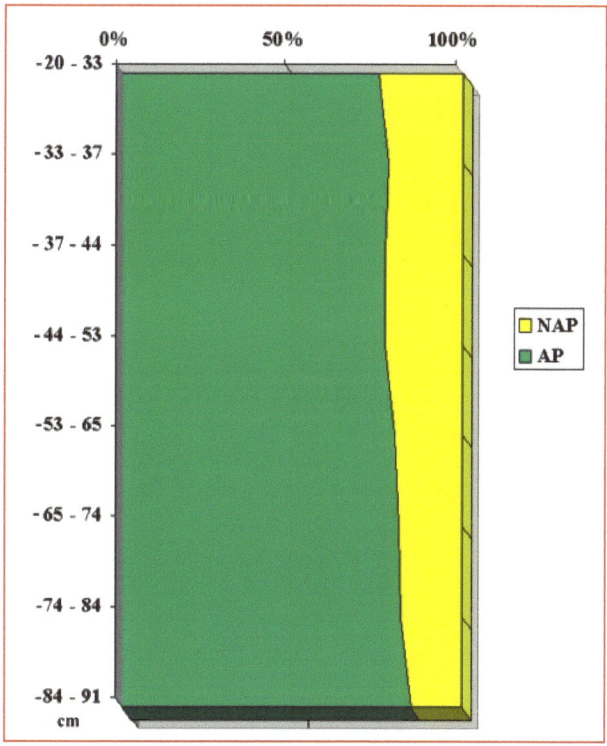

Fig. 44. SU PY12C10A: AP/NAP diagram.

The AP/NAP diagram of SU PY09H9 (Fig. 43) shows the AP component decreasing twice, from -42 to -54 cm and from -16 to -20 cm, throughout the palynological record, probably due to the increase in arable land. In the AP/NAP diagram of the balk section of SU PY12C10A (Fig. 44), unlike the diagram shown in Fig. 42, the NAP component is distributed more gradually, without areas of consecutive decreases.

In the deeper levels of SU PY12C10A, from -54 to -63 cm and from -35 to -42 cm, the distribution of the most representative biomes appears to remain in the same proportions, exhibiting the features of what is on the whole a well-balanced environment (Fig. 46).

Subsequently, from -26 to -35 cm and up to the present-day ground level, the Irano-Turanian, Mediterranean and streamside biomes gradually contract, while the farm crops, the Maloidae species and the garigue show a significant percentage increase. The stratigraphic levels of SU PY12C10A from -84 to -91 cm and from -65 to -74 cm (Fig.46) show a biome distribution that differs from the one appearing in the stratigraphy of SU PY09H9 (Fig. 45).

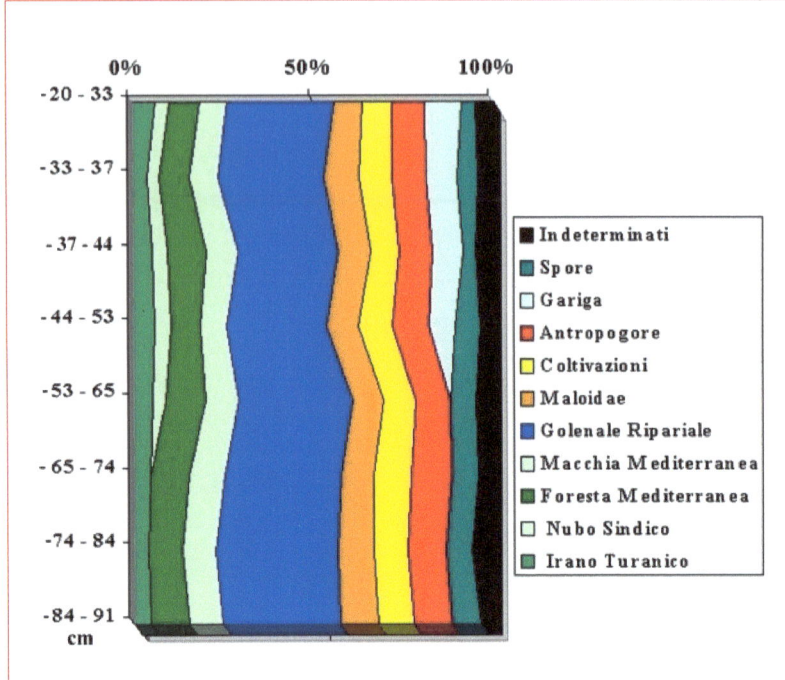

Fig. 45. SU PY09H9: Distribution of the phytogeographic elements

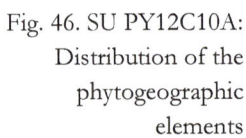

Fig. 46. SU PY12C10A: Distribution of the phytogeographic elements

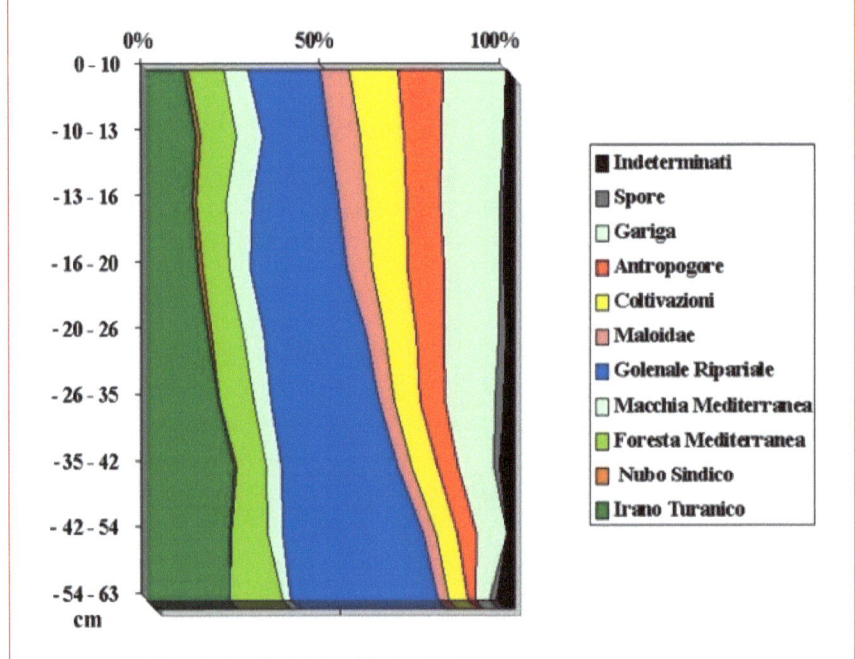

The streamside element is the one most represented, while the Irano-Turanian and the Mediterranean elements significantly reduce their presence throughout the paleopalynological sequence. From -53 to -65 cm and -20 to -33 cm, all the elements present decreases that do not affect the qualitative ratios of the characterized biomes, but in quantitative terms attest to the gradual development of the garigue (well documented on the Mesaorya plain, historically the Cyprus area most affected by human activities), which is made up mainly of *Quercus coccifera* L.,

Olea europaea var. *sylvestris* MILL. and Amaranthaceae Chenopodiaceae. The initial phase of the garigue could document the earliest deforestations and the earliest agricultural activities that proceeded in accordance with the seasons, as documented by the paleoseeds found at Pyrgos (Lentini and Belgiorno 2012), Marki Alonia (Adams and Simmons 1996), Khirokitia (Miller 1984) and Cape Andreas Kastros (Van Zeist 1981).

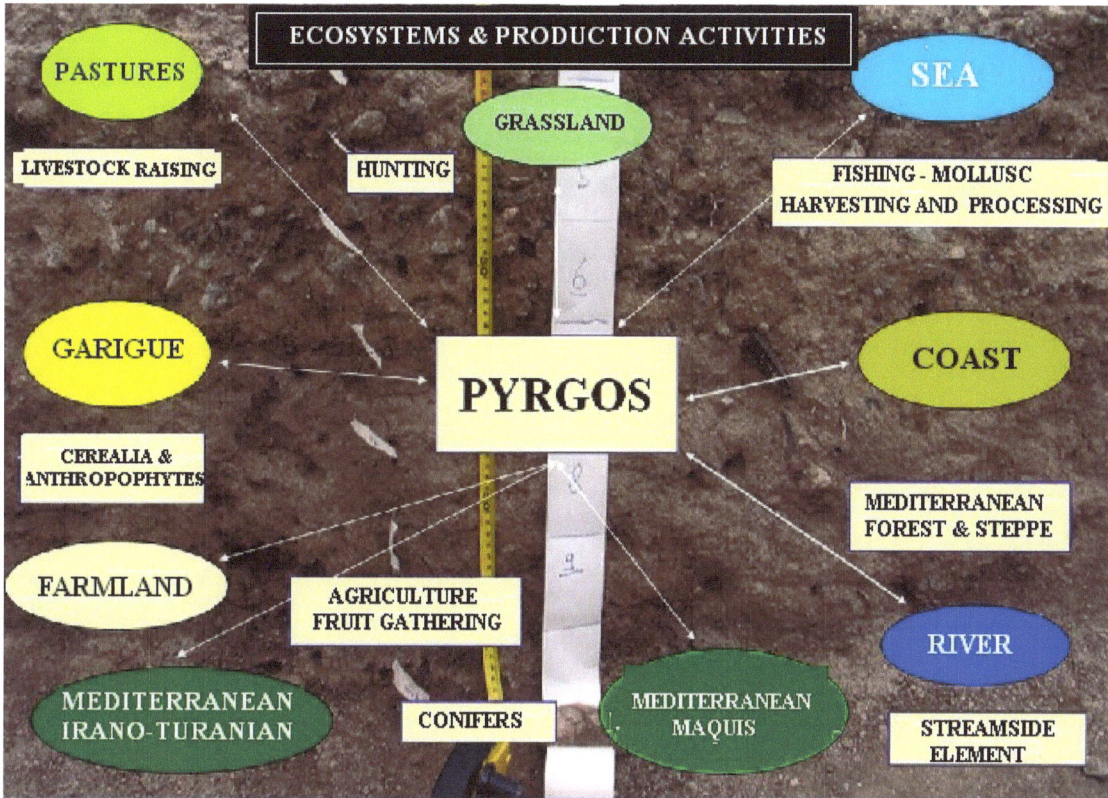

Fig. 47. The main environments revealed by paleopalynological investigations at Pyrgos Mavrorachi

Our investigations concerned an agricultural context in which non-farming activities were also pursued in well-organized nitrophile environments in which were present all the synanthropic elements (buildings, metal-working activities, textile weaving and dyeing, production of wine and olive oil, selection of officinal species, distillation; Belgiorno 2009) that form a "particular combination" of essential variables in an advanced production system characterized by continuous seasonally-based processes and highly structured ways of organizing labour in a humid climate where the great availability of water probably encouraged the development of these activities.

Our paleopalynological investigation of two stratigraphic sections dating from the Bronze Age and yielding a wealth of information, though limited to a single archaeological area because of the lack of comparative studies on Cyprus, can constitute an initial contribution to the definition of certain aspects of the natural landscape, of climate changes, and of the main human activities that helped shape the environment and the territory in this part of the island.

REFERENCES

-Adams R. and Simmons D. 1996: Archaeobotanical remains, in Frankel D. and Webb J.M., *Marki Alonia, An Early and Middle Bronze Age Town in Cyprus, Excavations 1990-1994*, 223-226, Forlag P.A., Jonsered.

-Belgiorno M.R. & Lentini A. 2005: L'industria tessile del sito preistorico di Pyrgos/Mavrorachi (Cipro), *Informatore Botanico Italiano*, vol. 37, 1, 894-895.

-Belgiorno M.R. & Lentini A. 2008a: I colori del sito preistorico di Pyrgos-Mavrorachi (Cipro), *Colore e Arte: Storia e Tecnologia del Colore nei Secoli* a cura di -Bacci M. A.i.A.r., Patron Editore, Bologna,169 - 178.

-Belgiorno M.R. & Lentini A. 2008: Sostanze terapeutiche dal sito preistorico di Pyrgos/Mavrorachi (Cipro). Indagini tossicologiche preliminari, *Atti del IV Congresso Nazionale di Archeometria*, a cura di. D'Amico C, vol. IV, 751-761, Pàtron Editore, Bologna.

-Belgiorno M.R. 2009: *Cipro all'inizio dell'Età del Bronzo, Realtà Sconosciute della Comunità Industriale di Pyrgos/Mavrorachi*, Gangemi Editore, Roma.

-Belgiorno M.R. & Lentini A. 2010: Origini e sviluppo dell'industria tessile a Pyrgos/Mavrorachi (Cipro), durante il II° millenio a.C., *Atti VI Congresso Nazionale di Archeometria "Scienza e Beni Culturali"*, a cura di Riccardi M.P. e Basso E., Patron Editore, Bologna 1 – 13.

-Belgiorno M.R. e Lentini A. 2010: Monitoraggio aerobiologico dei pollini, spore e microresti vegetali, nell'area archeologica di Pyrgos/Mavrorachi (Cipro), *Il Monitoraggio costiero Mediterraneo: Problematiche e Tecniche di Misura*, a cura di Benincasa F., CNR-IBIMET, 257-276, Firenze.

-Belgiorno M.R. & Lentini A. 2012: Il vino più antico del Mediterraneo, *Darwin*, 47, 18 - 25.

-Bonifacio E. & Falsone G. 2005: Rimozione di carbonati, sostanza organica ed ossidi di ferro, in: Adamo P. (Ed.), *Metodi di analisi mineralogica del suolo*, Roma.

-Campana A. e Medioli Masotti P. 1981: Bartolomeo Sacchi il Platina, (Piadena 1421-Roma 1481), *Atti del Convegno Internazionale di studi per il V centenario (Cremona, 14-15 novembre 1981)*, Antenore (1986), Padova.

-De Candolle M. Alph., 1883: *Origine des Plantes Cultivées*, vol. I, Librairie De Victor Masson, Paris.

-Della Loggia R. 1993: *Piante officinali per infusi e tisane. Manuale per farmacisti e medici*, Organizzazione Editoriale Medico Farmaceutica, Milano.

-Dioscoride Pedanius: *De Materia. Medica*. Plants from Dioscorides' «De materia medica», (Touwaide A. and De Santo Natale G., ed. 2009).

-Dioscoride, *Codex Julianae Aniciae*.

-Donato G. 1984: Cosmetics in ancient time, In: Donato G. e Bisogno P. *Aphrodite's Scents: Aromatic Journey Experimental Archaeology* I, 7-13, Roma.

-Donato G., Branca M.E., Rallo A. 1975: *Sostanze odorose del mondo classico*, Venezia.

-Donato G., Hensel W. and Tabaczynski S. 1986: *Teoria e pratica della ricerca archeologica*, vol. I, Ed. Il Quadrante, Roma.

-Evans M. 1991: *Herbal Plants History and Uses*, Studio Editions Ltd., London.

-Fejgi M. 1989: *Spot Test in Organic Analysis*, Seventh Completely Revised Edition, Elseveir, Amsterdam.

-Figueredo G., Chalchat J.C. and Pasquier B. 2005: A study of the Mediterranean oregano populations: Chemical composition of essential oils of *Origanum cordifolium* Monbret et Aucher from two populations in Cyprus. *Journal of Essential Oil Research*, 17, 638-641.

-Flourentzos P., Belgiorno M.R. and Lentini A. 2005: *Cyprus in the prehistory of wine*, MAE Ambasciata d'Italia a Nicosia.

-Georgiades C. 1992: *Flowers of Cyprus. Plants of Medicine*, vol. I, Third Edition, Loris Stavrinides and Son Ltd., Nicosia, Cyprus.

-Greig, J. 1989: *Archaeobotany*. European Science Foundation, 4, Strasbourg.

Grimm, E., 2002: *Tilia and Tilia Graph*, Newsletter Illinois State Museum, Springfield, Illinois, USA.

-Gücel S., Ozturk, M., Yucel E., Kadis C. and Güvensen A. 2009: Studies on the trace metals in the soils and plants growing in the vicinity of copper mining area Lefke, Cyprus. *Fresenius Environmental Bulletin*, 18 (3): 360-368.

-Hanbury A., and Serra J. 2001: Mathematical morphology in the CIELAB space, *Image Anal. Stereol.*, 21 (3), 201-206.

-Hatcher H., Tite M.S. and Walsh J.N. 1995: A Comparison of Inductively Plasma Emission Spectroscopy and Atomic Absorption, Spectrometry on Standard Reference Silicate Materials and Ceramics, *Archaeometry*, 37, 83-94.

Hodgson, E., 2004: *Tossicologia Moderna*, EdiSES S.r.l., Napoli.

-Johansson L., Xydas C., Messios N., Stoltz E., and Greger M. 2005: Growth and Cu accumulation by plants grown on Cu containing mine tailings in Cyprus, *Applied Geochemistry*, 20 (1): 101-107.

-Jonsson J. A. 1987: *Chromatography theory and basic principles*, Marcel Dekker, New York.

-Kadereit J.W. 1986: A revision of *Papaver* section Argemonidium, *Notes of Royal Botanical Garden*, Edinburgh 44, 25-43.

-LARN fonte Società Italiana di Nutrizione Umana: 1996.

Lehninger, A.L., 1989. *Principi di Biochimica*, Zanichelli, Bologna.

-Lentini A. & M.R. Belgiorno 2008: Palaethnobotany investigations at the site of Pyrgos/Mavrorachi, Cyprus, *International Symposium on Archaeometry*, Kars H., Meyers P. and Wagner C.A. Editors, 37, 296-297.

-Lentini A. & Belgiorno M.R.: 2012a. Archaeobotanical investigations at Pyrgos-Mavrorachi (Cyprus), preliminary results, Society of Cypriot Studies, *Proceedings of the IV International Cyprological Congress*, Edit by Andreas Demetriou and Leventis Foundation, Nicosia, 573 – 588, with plates, 90 -102.

-Lentini A. and Belgiorno M.R. 2012b: Investigations on a Bull's Head from Pyrgos/Mavroraki (Lm) to Design the Biodiversity of Cyprus in Early Middle Bronze Age, *Euromed 2012, Progress in Cultural Heritage Preservation*, Edited by: Ioannides M., Fritsch D., Leissner J., David R., Remondino F., and Caffo, R., Multi-Science Publishing Co. Ltd, Brentwood, 187 – 193.

-Lentini A. & Nelli M. 2008: Schede delle specie officinali identificate nel sito Preistorico di Pyrgos/Mavrorachi (Cipro), in Belgiorno M.R., *Mavrorachi – Dal 2000 ad oggi quattromila anni di profumo*, Gangemi Editore, Roma,110-135.

-Lentini A. and Scala G. 2004: Fragrant substances and therapeutic compounds, In: Belgiorno M.R., *Pyrgos/Mavrorachi <Advanced Technology in Bronze Age Cyprus>*, 45-47, CNR Bureau President's, Nicosia.

-Lentini A. & Scala G. 2006: Aromatic and therapeutic substances from the prehistoric site of Pyrgos/Mavrorachi (Cyprus), In: Belgiorno M.R., *Cyprus Aromata, Olive Oil in Perfumery and Medicaments in Cyprus 2000 B.C.*, 219-243, Edizioni Eranuova, Perugia.

-Lentini A. e Scala G. 2007: Sostanze odorose e terapeutiche dal sito Preistorico di Pyrgos/Mavrorachi: indagini chimico tossicologiche e archeo botaniche preliminari, In: Belgiorno M.R. *Il Profumo di Afrodite e il Segreto dell'Olio*, 87-109, Gangemi Editore, Roma.

-Lentini A. 2005: Archaeobotany brewing and winemaking in Mediterranean basin and TransCaucasus area, In: Flourentzos P. Belgiorno M.R. and Lentini A. *Cyprus in the Prehistory of Wine*, MAE Ambasciata d'Italia a Nicosia (Cyprus), 11-16.

-Lentini A. 2009a: New archaeobotanical data on the cultivation of *Vitis* ssp. at Pyrgos/Mavrorachi, in: *Notes of Kinyras, Since 4th Millennium B.C. and Evidence from Erimi*, Cyprus Wine Museum and Department of Antiquites Museum, Nicosia, 56 - 73.

-Lentini A. 2009b: Preliminary archaeometric analysis of some organic contents of Erimi necropolis, in *Notes of Kinyras, Since 4th Millennium B.C. and Evidence from Erimi*, Cyprus Wine Museum and Department of Antiquites Museum, Nicosia, 74 - 77.

-Lentini A. 2009c: Tra Archeologia e Archeometria, Archeologia e Paesaggio Naturale: Indagini archeobotaniche e fisico chimiche, in: Belgiorno M.R. *Cipro all'inizio dell'Età del Bronzo, Realtà Sconosciute della Comunità Industriale di Pyrgos – Mavrorachi*, Gangemi Editore, Roma, 129 - 187.

-Lentini A. 2010: Scents in the ancient civilizations of the Mediterranean basin: archaeometric studies on Cleopatra's officine (En Boqeq, Israel) and on Pyrgos/Mavroraki's perfumery (Cyprus), in Belgiorno M.R., Lazarou Y. and -Lentini A. *Perfume de Chypre, The role of Aphrodite's island in the history of the Mediterranean scents*, F. Lazarou Investiment LTD, Nicosia, 105 - 153.

-Lentini A. 2013: L'isola dei tulipani, *L'Isola*, 72, 13-14, Vele Bianche Ed., Napoli.

-Lowe J.J. 1996: Analytical method in pollen analysis, Institute of Earth Sciences Vrije Universiteit, *Scientific Papers n° 12*, Amsterdam.

-Meikle R.D. 1985: *Flora of Cyprus*, vol. II, Bentham-Moxon Publishers, Kew.

-Meriaux S. 1957: *L'analyse granulometrique par densimetrie*, "Association Française pour l'Etude du Sol" 91, pp. 928-944.

-Miller N. 1984: Some plants remain from Khirokitia, Cyprus: 1977 and 1981 excavations, In: Le Brun A. (èd.), *Fouilles récents à Khirokitia (Chypre)*, 1977-1981, 183-191, ERC, Paris.

-Mills J. and White R. 1989: The Identity of the Resins from the Late Bronze Age Shipwreck at Ulu Burun (Kas), *Archaeometry*, 31/1: 37-44.

-*Munsell Speciality for Color Coding Chart*,1999. Macheth Division Kollmorgen Corporation, Baltimore (Maryland).

-Pandeli K.Z. 1998: *The Medical Plantis of Cyprus*, Printco Ltd., Larnaca.

-Pedretti M. 1986: La valeriana, *Erboristeria Domani*, 5, 18-24.

Perfumi M., Arnold N. and Tacconi R., 1991: Hypoglycemic activity of Salvia fruticosa Mill. From Cyprus, *Journal of Ethnopharmacology*, 34, 135-140.

-Plinio il Vecchio, *Naturalis Historia*, Rizzoli (1999), Milano (a cura di Ferri S.).

-Reagent M., Colinart S., Degrand L. and Decavallas O. 2001: Chemical alteration and use of beeswax through time: accelerate ageing tests and analysis of archaeological samples of various environmental contexts, *Archaeometry*,43, 549-569.

-Quezel P. 1979: Les écosystèmes forestiers crétois er chypriotes. *Chroniques intern*, RFF, 31.

-Saltini A. 1984: *Storia delle scienze agrarie*, vol I, Edagricole, Bologna. (Columella, *De re rustica*, coedizione Museo Galileo - Fondazione Nuova Terra Antica).

-Snyder L.R and Kirkland J.J. 1982: *Introduction to High-performance Liquid Chromatography* Chapman and Hall, New York.

-Teofrasto, *Historia Plantarum e Cause Plantarum*, Edizioni Panini F.C., 2001, Modena.

-Townsens T., Solo-Gabriele H., Stook K., and Hosein N. 2003: Copper concentrations in soil under earth, *Soil and Sediment Contamination*, 12, 779-798.

-Villavecchia V. e Eigenmann G. 1973: *Nuovo dizionario di merceologia e chimica applicata*, vol. IV, Hoepli Editore, Milano.

-Traverse A. 2007: *Paleopalynology*, Second Edition, Springer, New York.

-Wayne G., Landis and Mingh-Ho Yu 2004: *Introduction to Environmental Toxicology: Impacts of Chemicals Upon Ecological Systems*, CRC Press, Boca Raton, Florida.

-Weiss E. & Kislev M.E. 2004: Plant remains as indicators for economic activity: a case study from Iron Age Ashkelon, *Journal of Archaeological Science* 31, 1, 1-13.

-Wyble D.R. and Fairchild M.D. 2000: Prediction of Munsell Appearance Scales Using Various Color Appearance Models, *Color Res. Appl.*, 25, 132-144.

-Yadun S.L. and Evron M.W. 1994: Late Epipalaeolithic wood Remains from El Wad Cave, Mount Carmel, Israel, *New Phytologist*, 127, 2, 391-396.

-Zeist W.van 1981: Plant remains from Cape Andreas Kastros (Cyprus). Appendix VI., 95-99, in Le Brun, A., (ed.) *Un site néolithique précéramique en Chypre Cap Andreas Kastros. Recherche sur les grandes civilisations.* Mémoires 5, Editions ADPF, Paris.

-Zohary M. 1973: *Geobotanical Foundation of the Middle East*, vol. 2, Fischer Verlag, Stuttgart, Swets and Zeitlinger, Amsterdam

5. TEXTILES QUALITY AND SPINDLE WHORLS TYPE: NEW DATA ABOUT SPINNING TECHNIQUES IN CYPRIOT MIDDLE BRONZE AGE

Federica Gonzato & Alessandro Lentini

1. Spindle Whorls: Function and Typology (Federica Gonzato)

The archaeological site of Pyrgos (Belgiorno 2009) offers the opportunity to carry out an archaeometric investigation of Bronze Age textile evidence. In 2003, during the excavation season, twenty spindles-whorls were found in the textile area G7 (Belgiorno 2004). In the following years, spindle whorls have been detected all around the excavation area and the evidence in 2009 were distributed as follows: five specimens from F5/7 (a living unit); eight from E5/7 (a living unit); three from F9 (main crossing street); eight from G8 (area in connection with the textile sector); one from H7 (a secondary storage/service room); two from H9 (storage winery); one from I6 (central room with olive press and perfumery); two from I8/9 (large metallurgical area); four from K7 (coppersmith workshop); four from M/L5 (a working area with two basins in connection with metallurgy.

The spindle whorls have been classified by shape (conical, biochemical, spherical, truncated and cylindrical), type (fabric technology and surface treatment, height, diameter, weight, size and inclination of the central perforation, use-wear) and chronologically, starting from Philia phase to MC II (Gonzato 2008) (Fig. 1).

As for the weight, Pyrgos evidence offers a wide range of sizes, confirming the use of different spinning technologies, in relation to the type of fibre and the result to achieve, as this paper aims to show. Indicatively, weight from 5 to 30 gr. has been considered light; from 30 to 60 gr. has been classified as medium; from 60 to 90 gr. heavy, and over 90 as very heavy.

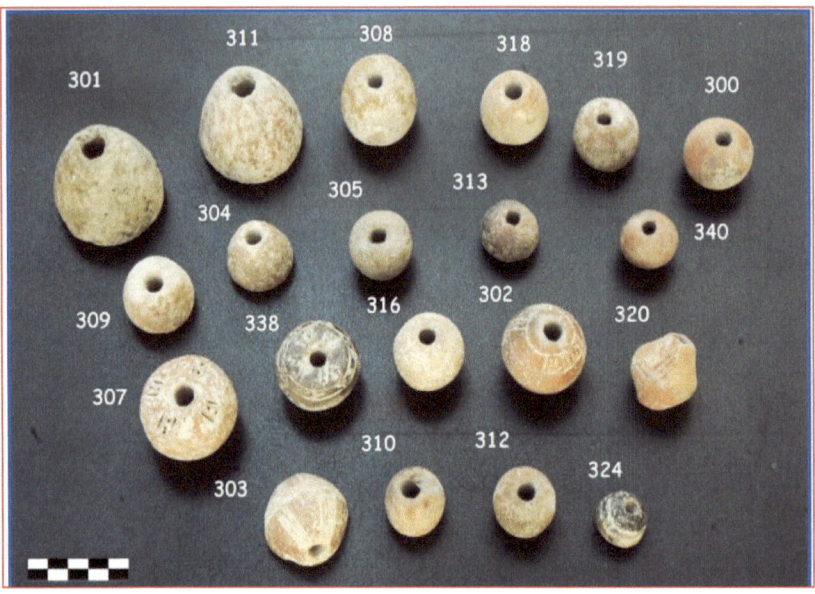

Fig. 1. Spindle whorls from Pyrgos-Mavroraki.

Even if spinning could be carried out only with fingers, the use of a spindle with a whorl allowed to accelerate the process and obtain a regular, continuous yarn, spun with the necessary device to keep fibres together, which required a different treatment (Barber 1991, 42). The use of a spindle stick increased the speed and the addition of a whorl prolonged the rotation, increased the tension, and guaranteed a constant spinning speed (Fig.2).

Fig. 2: Cypriot lady spinning (around 1950): from the original photo on the wall of a private house.

It is evident that the weight and diameter of whorls influenced the result. This is the reason it has already suggested to use the Moment of Inertia (M) as a basic parameter to compare whorls of different type and material, because this value expresses the tendency of a body to maintain a constant speed in movement (Mistretta 2007). The basic formula $M=1/2\ mr^2$ (where m expresses the mass and r the radius) is suitable for objects with uniform thickness, as cylindrical/flat whorls but, since tools from Pyrgos presented more complex forms, it is preferable to consider the relation between weight and diameter, which are in general directly proportional. With whorls of similar diameter, some difference is due to the varying density of clay and inclusion.

Incised decoration on whorls can regularly be found in association with specific fibres as *Tortrix viridiana*, *Urena*, *Hibiscus*, *Asbestos* (plus one single recurrence with *Hyphaena thebaica* MART.), which were considered high-quality and prestigious fibres in antiquity. For this reason, as a working hypothesis, it is possible to suppose that this "value" was recognized and displayed through decoration on specific tools to spin certain fibres; it is even more interesting to know that qualified artisans could perform this task, if we accept the idea that specific decoration could refer to specific workers (Mogelonsky and Bregstein 1996, 212).

Speaking of textiles, it is important to underline that the case of more fibres associated to a single whorl could be due basically to two situations: either different materials were spun together, or the same whorl was used twice for different fibres. A final consideration is possible if we consider a textile sample with piliferous bulbs presenting an unclear cut: it is likely that no sharp blade was used in sheep hearing (Fig. 3).

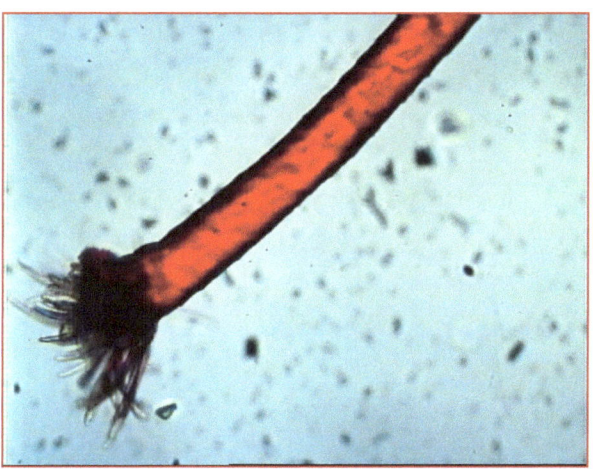

Fig. 3. Fibre of wool (40X) from Pyrgos/Mavroraki spindle whorl.

2. Analysis: Materials and Methods (Alessandro Lentini)

The fibres and organic materials found were the subject of chemical and morpho biometric analyses to obtain a detailed definition of their origin and evolution. The features examined have been compared with fibres from the same species of different collections. The fibre and woven materials were treated with a solution of glycerine and 50% bi-distilled water.

The fibres and woven materials, all of which were particularly deteriorated, were consolidated with a 5% vinyl Acryl Nitrile emulsion. The morpho biometric study of the different fibres was done using an image analyser. The images, remotely sensed by the optical video-microscope, were acquired in true colour.

Fibre Vegetali	NUMERO	%	BLU	NERO	ROSSO	VERDE	INCOLORE
Gossypium ssp.	150	16,304	56	0	0	36	58
Urena lobata	20	2,1739	0	0	0	8	12
Asclepias ssp.	62	6,7391	0	0	0	0	62
Calotropis sp.	25	2,7174	0	0	2	0	23
Tilia ssp.	18	1,9565	0	0	0	0	18
Lygeum spartium L.	16	1,7391	0	0	0	0	16
Cannabis sativa L.	21	2,2826	0	0	0	0	21
Urtica dioica	24	2,6087	0	0	0	0	24
Typha ssp.	16	1,7391	0	0	0	0	16
Hibiscus ssp.	45	4,8913	21	0	0	0	24
Arundo donax L.	20	2,1739	0	0	0	0	20
Genista ssp.	20	2,1739	0	0	0	0	20
Stipa ssp.	18	1,9565	0	0	0	0	18
Linum usitatissimum L.	28	3,0435	0	0	0	14	14
Genista ssp.	45	4,8913	2	0	0	18	0
Totale	528	57,391	79	0	2	76	346
Fibre Animali							
Lana	297	32,283	55	52	38	106	46
Seta (*Tortrix viridiana*)	15	1,6304	0	0	0	0	15
Totale	312	33,913	55	52	38	106	61
Fibre Miste							
Lana ligusta	1	0,1087	1	0	0	0	0
Fibre Minerali							
Amianto (Asbestos)	30	3,2609	0	0	0	0	30
Fibre Alloctone							
Hyphaena thebaica MART.	16	1,7391	0	0	0	0	16
Crotalaria ssp.	12	1,3043	0	0	0	0	12
Totale	28	3,0435	0	0	0	0	28
Fibre poco rappresentate							
Sciurus vulgaris L.	13	1,413	0	13	0	0	0
Talpa europea L.	6	0,6522	0	6	0	0	0
Totale	19	2,0652					
Indeterminate	14	1,5217	0	0	0	0	14
Totale	932	100	135	71	40	182	492

Table 1 (by A. Lentini originally in Italian): Characterized textile fibres from Pyrgos, reported percentages for groups of provenance and colours.

We initially examined 932 morphologies (Table1), of which 150 of cotton (Gossypium ssp.), the most relevant of the vegetable fibres with fibres of Asclepias ssp. (62) and Hibiscus ssp. (45), and 297 filaments of wool, the main animal fibre.

2.1 Wool is a textile fibre that originates from sheep skin. It is rich in proteins and contains large amounts of keratin. It has an extremely complex structure, consisting of two, or more often three, different types of cellular clusters, which form transversal sections and are concentrically distributed. The net effect of this complex construction is a flaky exterior and a porous interior. In this zone, the cuticle cells have an elongated form, that can be distinguished in ortho and para. The disposition of these two components causes the curliness of the fibre (Paddok 1960). During its growth, a waxy mixture of lanolin lubricates the fibre.

There are two distinct types of wool fibres – woolly and bristly – whose difference depends on the type of follicles used. If the fleece contains more of the woolly fibre, it has a greater value. The area of the animal from which the wool is taken is also important to determine its quality. The shoulders and the back give the most valued wool fibres. The flanks produce fibres that are fine and valued. The other areas of the animal produce the bristliest and irregular fibres. The fineness varies between 10 and 70 microns.

2.2 Wild silk - Tortrix viridana *L., Leporinely - Tortricidae Family*- Filamentous micro remains with thickened margins and circulated terminal portion forming obtuse angles.

Thanks to the recovery of some morphological structures, that constitute the unitary edges of the reticular plan, it is possible to identify the typical interlacing generated from the winding of the silk cocoon of the Leporinely Tortrix Viridiana L. Chrysalides.

2.3 Cotton fibres are made of hair produced by the growth of individual cells, part of the epidermis of seeds contained in the capsular fruit of some plants of the Gossipium. Cotton is a monocellular seminal vegetal hair (Wingate 1974). When viewed longitudinally through a microscope, cotton appears as a flattened tape with slightly raised edges. This tape spirals and changes the direction of its torsion at the so-called longitudinal zones. In some case, there are thin stripes together with a reduced lumen along a thin line towards the fibre's centre. It is fundamentally composed of non-lignified cellulose. Its thickness varies from 1 to 4 microns.

2.4 Hybiscus *ssp.* – It has a flattened tubular morphology with fibres spilling out from a main trunk and from the branches; its fibres are highly visible. The presence of swamps and marshlands characterize its environment. It is cultivated for its fibre, extracted from the stalk, and is used in the fabrication of sails (Wild 2001). Asclepias ssp. has a cylindrical morphology with a large empty canal and thick cuticles (Poma 1970). Asclepias graeca is ideal for making ropes, and Asclepias syriaca is often used for making low quality textiles. Asclepias vincetoxicum is widespread in the Mediterranean (Zohary 1973). Not easily spun, the plant was used almost exclusively for padding. Fibres that can be spun, obtained from the stalk, are also of little value. These fibres are glossy, yellowish white, with very thin, lignified walls.

2.5 Lygeum spartium *L.* - Some fragments of Lygeum spartium L., with borders jutting out for the expansion of the parenchymal tissue, and Halpha ghedima are materials typically used to make bags and straw mats. Through soaking, one may obtain spinnable fibres with a ribbon-like morphology and few transversal stripes.

2.6 Calotropis *ssp.* - Pectin consolidates the bundle of filaments. The morphology, typical of the Calotropis (Garner, 1949), is characterized by frequent dots on the cuticle. The most frequently used are Calotropis gigantea L. (Giant milkweed), Calatropis procera and Gompocarpus fructicosa L. AITON (Swallow-wart). The fibres obtained from the last species are like silk (vegetable silk).

2.7 Cannabis sativa L – It has a tubular morphology with oblique, transversal septa and fibrils protruding from the cuticle. The fibre always shows a faded area on its surface. Cannabis' fibre is well-known (Barber 1991). In fact, it is one of the most resistant natural polymers, which has always been used in the manufacturing of sails and hawsers, various types of ropes, clothing and paint canvases.

2.8 Urena lobata, is a Malvaceae, with long, glossy, and fine filaments. It is used for the manufacturing of ropes and light textiles. In ancient Greece (Pekridou Gorechki 1992) a fibre was produced from the Malvaceae family, always quoted in literature in generic terms but never found in excavations; for this reason, the recovery of Urena can be considered significant.

2.9 Asbestos has medium-large fibres, flattened with a pointed extremity. The fibre has a central canal with semi-diagonal septa that correspond to various discontinuous growths alternating with a secondary channel. The fibres can be free in a friable matrix or weakly bonded. It is almost famous for being easily spinnable and it was the finest and precious fibre of antiquity. It was called "live linen" or "Koapas linen" (Pliny the Elder), from the mines of Amiondos and Dimmata in the island of Cyprus where it is obtained. All the fibres analysed have a Mediterranean origin (Lentini 2009).

3. Conclusion (Federica Gonzato and Alessandro Lentini)

It is known that long and elastic materials could be spun through medium/big whorls (about 30-100 gr. indicatively), while shorter ones were worked with light spindle whorls (Ryder 1968, 81). If we consider data from Pyrgos (Fig. 4), wool was spun with heavy and very heavy whorls. As for the wide range of weights of whorls recorded in association with wool (from 37 to 130 gr.), it is interesting to note that hair of different lengths characterized sheep's fleece, depending on the part of the body sheared: hair from the back is normally longer than that coming from the legs or belly. This requires different spinning technologies and, therefore, different types of spinning tools. Samples of Linum give two different parameters, too, from light/medium to heavy whorls.

Evidence of silk has been found, together with Hibiscus, inside two spindle whorls of similar weight, n° 335 and 303, catalogued as heavy whorls, according to the characteristics of these vegetable micro remains. From the statistic table, it comes out that constant weight whorls (25/26 gr.) were used to spin Genista. Something similar happened with Asbestos (21 gr.), a material whose fibres could be selected in different length, depending on the final effect to achieve. Plinius recalled Asbestos as a textile that could be compared to flax, but was more precious. Interesting is the case of Calotropis: even if we are dealing with two evidences only, we suppose that different weights of whorl used to spin this material, 32 gr. For spindle whorl n° 320 and 100 gr for n° 330, were functional to the result, since Calotropis was usually used to produce ropes of different kinds, for nautical equipment.

Spindle whorls connected with Gossypium cover a range from light to medium weight, with two heavy examples, while Hibiscus ssp. normally required from medium to heavy whorls.

The two spindle whorls associated with Urtica are very light (6 and 15 gr. respectively); Urtica offered the possibility to obtain two different yarns, comparable with cotton if spun with "S" torsion, or with wool if done with "Z" direction. At last, Urena was spun through light/medium whorls; it was a very precious material used to obtain iridescent effects.

Item	Context	Type (Crewe 1998)	Period	Preservation	Decoration	Weight	Height	Max D	TAXA
331	E6	Ic3 emispherical/cylindrical	ECI-II	1/2	-	6,0	1,3	2,7	Urtica dioica
323	E6	IIa3 biconical	Philia	complete	-	14,0	2,3	2,8	Gossypium - Asclepias
324	K7	IIc3 biconical/spherical	Philia	>2/3	incised	15,0	2,1	2,6	Urtica dioica
325	I7	IId0 biconical	Philia	complete		16,0	2,1	3,0	Gossypium
342	K7	Ib4 conical	MCI-II	1/6	incised	18,0	2,5*	1,8*	Urena lobata
329	F7	IVa1 cylindrical	ECI-II	1/2	-	20,0	2,2	2,5	Typha
337	E6	IId3 spherical	ECIII-MCI-II	1/2	-	20,0	2,0	3,1	Stipa Tilia - Asclepias
340	G7/8	IIb3 biconical/spherical	ECIII	complete	-	20,0	2,7	3,1	Gossypium - Asclepias
310	I9	IIIb5 truncated biconical/spherical	MCI-II	complete	incised	21,0	2,5	3,1	Asbestos
312	G8	IId1 spherical/cilindrical	ECIII-MCI/II	complete	incised	21,0	2,7	3,1	Asbestos
313	G8	IIIc5 truncated biconical/spherica	ECIII-MCI/II	complete	-	22,0	2,3	3,2	Gossypium
348	H9	III ? truncated biconical/spherical	ECIII-MCI/II	<1/2	-	25,0	2,4	3,0	Genista - Typha
305	K7	IId6 spherical	ECIII-MCI/II	complete	-	26,0	3,0	3,4	Gossipium - Asclepias
306	E5	IIa2 biconical	ECI-II	1/2	incised	26,0	2,9	3,2	Halpha ghedima - Arundo donax L.
315	G8	Ib4 conical	MCI-II	1/2	-	26,0	2,6	3,2	Genista - Typha
346	F9	IId4 biconical	ECI-II	1/2	-	28,0	2,7	3,3	Gossypium
304	D7	Ia4 conical	MCI-II	complete	-	31,0	2,8	3,6	Linum
320	L5	II3 conical with concave sides	ECI-II	complete	incised	32,0	3,6	3,4	Calotropis ssp.
326	M5	IId3 spherical	ECIII-MCI/II	1/2	-	35,0	3,3	3,3	Gossypium - Asclepias
300	G7	IIc3 biconical	ECIII	complete	-	36,0	3,3	3,9	Linum usitatissimum L.
328	H7	Ib4 conical/hemisferical	MCI-II	1/2	incised	36,0	2,6	3,7	Cannabis sativa L.
309	F5	Ia1 conical	MCI-II	complete	-	37,0	2,7	3,7	Wool - Linum
319	F9	IIId5 truncated biconical/spherical	MCI-II	complete	-	37,0	3,9	3,7	Wool - Linum
349	F9	IId4 biconical	ECI-II	1/2	-	38,0	3,1	3,7	Gossypium - Cannabis
318	F9	Ib6 conical	ECIII-MCI/II	complete	-	39,0	3,2	3,7	Lana
332	E6	IIIc- truncated biconical/spherical	ECIII-MCI/II	<1/3	incised	40,0	2,7*	3,3*	Halpha ghedima - Arundo donax L.
333	E7	IId- spherical	ECI-II	1/4	incised	40,0	3,2*	2,6*	Urena lobata
334	E7	Ib- conical	MC I-II	1/4	incised	40,0	2,2*	3,3*	Urena lobata
345	I3	IId5 biconical/spherical	ECIII-MCI/II	1/2	-	40,0	3,1	3,8	Gossypium - Cannabis
339	G7/8	IVb cilindrical	ECIII-MCI/II	1/2	-	42,0	3,3	3,8	Gossypium .
347	F9	Ia1 troncated conical	ECIII-MCI/II	1/2	-	42,0	2,7	?	Gossypium - Asclepias
316	M5	IIc2 biconical/spherical	ECIII-MCI/II	complete	incised	45,0	3,6	3,8	Hibiscus
314	G8	Ia6 conical	ECIII-MCI/II	<1/2	-	46,0	3,4	3,7*	Stipa
327	I8	?	ECIII-MCI/II	<1/4	-	50,0	3,3*	3,1*	Lygeum spartium L.
343	F9	Ib1 conical	ECIII-MCI/II	<1/2	incised	55,0	3,1	4,1	Hibiscus
336	E7	Ib6 conical/spherical	ECI-II	1/2	-	56,0	2,9	4,2	Gossypium - Asclepias
338	G7/8	IIIb6 truncated biconical	ECI-II	complete	incised	60,0	3,0	4,4	Wool
344	H9	IIId6 truncated biconical/spherical	ECIII-MCI/II	1/2	incised	68,0	3,6	4,2	Hyphaena thebaica MART.
302	H9	IIc2 biconical	MCI-II	complete	incised	69,0	4,3	4,4	Wool
317	M5	IIId6 truncated biconical/spherica	ECIII-MCI/II	complete	incised	70,0	3,9	4,3	Wool
321	F7	Ib6 conical	ECIII-MCI/II	<1/2	-	70,0	4,4	4,1*	Linum usitatissimum L.
308	H9	Ib6 conical/cilindrical	ECIII-MCI/II	complete	-	74,0	4,1	4,2	Wool - Crotalaria
335	F9	IIIc5 truncated biconical/spherical	ECIII-MCI/II	1/2	incised	88,0	3,2	4,9	Hibiscus - Tortrix viridiana
303	F7	IIc2 biconical	MCI-II	>1/2	incised	90,0	4,2	4,4	Hibiscus - Tortrix viridiana
322	F6	Ib6 conical	ECIII-MCI/II	1/3	-	90,0	4,3	4,1*	Linum usitatissimum L.
341	E6	Ib4 conical	ECIII-MCI	<1/3	incised	90,0	4,2*	3,6*	Gossypium - Asclepias
330	I6	IIId7 ? Spherical	ECIII-MCI/II	<1/3	-	100,0	4,7*	4*	Calotropis
307	D7	IIId6 truncated biconical/spherical	MCI-II	complete	incised	103,0	3,6	5,0	Hibiscus
301	I7	Ia4 conical	MCI-II	complete	-	130,0	4,6	6,2	Wool
311	I8	Ia4 conical	ECIII-MCI/II	complete	-	133,0	4,9	5,1	Wool

Fig.4: Data Base of spindle whorls from Pyrgos-Mavrorachi. Numbers marked (*) refer to the measure of the fraction found; whorl weight given in bold refers to complete spindle whorls, while, if written in italic, means that the weight is reconstructed.

REFERENCES

-Barber E.J.W. 1991: *Prehistoric* Textiles*: The Development of Cloth in the Neolithic and Bronze Ages with special reference to the Aegean*, Princeton University Press.

-Belgiorno M.R. 2004: *Pyrgos-Mavroraki. Advanced Technology in Bronze Age Cyprus*, NicosiaTheopress.

-Belgiorno, M.R. 2009: *Cipro all'inizio dell'età del Bronzo*, Roma: Gangemi.

-Garner W. 1949: *Textile Laboratory Manual*, London: Publishing Company.

-Gonzato F. 2008: Textile Production in Early and Middle Cypriot Bronze Age: the Pyrgos-Mavroraki Case, in Proceedings of theIV International Cyprological Congress, Nicosia.

-Lentini A. 2009: Origini e sviluppo dell'industria tessile, indagini archeobotaniche, in Belgiorno M.R. (ed), *Cipro all'inizio dell'età del Bronzo*, 153-165, Roma: Gangemi.

-Mistretta V. 2007: Analisi funzionale dei manufatti relativi alla filatura e alla tessitura provenienti dall'insediamento del Bronzo Finale di Fonte Tasca (Archi, Chieti), in: *Annali dell'Università degli Studi di Ferrara*, 87-90.

-Mogelonsky M.K. & Bregstein L.B. 1996: Spindle Whorls, in J.E. Coleman et al. (eds), *Alambra: A Middle Bronze Age Settlement in Cyprus*, 205-217. Jonsered: Studies in Mediterranean Archaeology 118.

-Paddok K. 1960: *Textile Fibres and Their Use*, vol. I, Calcutta: Atma Ram.

-Pekridou Gorechki A. 1992: *Come vestivano i Greci*, Milan: Rusconi.

-Ryder M.L. 1968: The origin of spinning, in *Textile History* 1, 73-82.

-Skinkle J.H. 1949: *Textile Testing*, vol. 1, Bombay.

-Wingate I.B. 1974: *Fairchild's Dictionary of Textiles*, New York: Fairchild Publications.

-Zohary M. 1973: *Geobotanical Foundation of the Middle East*, vol. 2, Stuttgart: Gustav Fischer Verlag.

6. EXPERIMENTAL ARCHAEOLOGY FOR PYRGOS/MAVRORAKI AND THE RESEARCH ON LOOM WEIGHTS

Angelo Bartoli and Concetta Cappelletti

1. What is Experimental Archaeology

Experimental archaeology was established in Scandinavia towards the 1860 and since then as an interesting means of knowledge of the past has made its way with experiments that, together with studies more purely theoretical, have contributed in a fundamental way to the understanding of the techniques and methodologies pertaining people through the ages that preceded us.

For John Coles, one of its founders. "Experimental archaeology is trying to play through the experiments, in the closest possible material conditions, tools, objects and buildings of the past, and the circumstances under which they are degraded and destroyed...", thus providing a "way, the only, to examine the opinions of archaeologists on human behaviour in the past" (J. Coles 1981).

Using the experimental Galilean method, experimental archaeology has become a complementary discipline of archaeology, able to recommend a trial, a test, a methodology to verify interpretations, theories, and conclusions.

In practice, we start from the observation of the phenomenon, play and study the laws that govern it, then we move to the study and analysis of a culture, of its archaeological environmental and socioeconomic level in which it developed.

It continues with the remaking artefacts, ancient techniques to address the actual experimentation, using materials, methods, and knowledge of the time to realize an object or replay a technology. The tour ends with the processing of data obtained during the trial, the study of the result and comparing it with the original.

Experimentation research on techniques and production methods of antiquity examines the characteristics for every different geographical area trying to understand the specific uses and identify the circumstances in which such artefacts have degraded and destroyed.

2. Collaboration with ITABC-CNR.

The collaboration with ITABC-CNR started in 2005 about the excavation of Pyrgos-Mavroraki in Cyprus. The digging had already unearthed part of a multipurpose industrial complex dating from the early second Millennium BC rich in elements that have aroused the interest of Antiquitates and have begun a large sequence of research, testing and applications of experimental archaeology which covered various production contexts. Analysing retrospectively the experiments carried out we realized the high importance of the results obtained.

In fact, the site of Pyrgos, turns out to be a rare chance for the conservation status of perfectly readable, because an earthquake of the 2nd millennium BC sealed the layers. The taking of direct knowledge of the site and the exchange of Archaeology, Ethnoarchaeology and Archaeometry data. Metallurgy, oil production, fragrances and textiles have been the productive sectors considered for archaeological experimentation.

The first experiments were performed in February 2006, directly at Pyrgos and covered the functionality of ovens for the reduction of copper, an activity witnessed by the abundance of waste and copper slag in each sector brought to light (Fig. 1).

Fig. 1: Pyrgos February 2006: experiments for the reduction of copper using olive oil.

Importance was given to the Central existence of a mill to produce olive oil and its use during the different stages of metallurgical production: archaeometric analyses land use certificate of the furnaces of which have reported the presence of olive oil (Fig. 2).

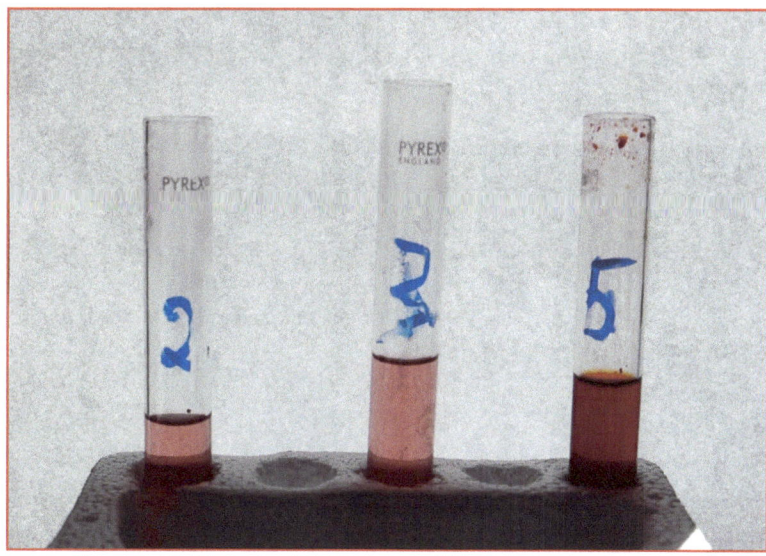

Fig. 2: Results of Feigl test made on the site by A.Lentini (June 2006) of the ashes found in furnaces ns.2,3 and 5.
Colour red conferms the high presence of olive oil.

4.1 Oil perfumes

Archaeometric analyses (Lentini 2007) have provided useful elements for reconstruction, through experimentation, fragrances in use in Cyprus 4000 BP. Starting from the ancient sources (Pliny, Theophrastus, Dioscurides), reproducing the forms useful techniques identified vascular and recovering species encountered by the organic residue analysis of ceramics, different useful experiments were made to understand the times, features and problems. The experimental path has broadened the appeal of extraordinary discovery perfume factory of Pyrgos.

The equipment consists of aryballoi, alabastra, stills, grinding stones, Pestles and mortars were repeatedly exhibited, in 2006 at the Museum of the Olive tree in Trevi in Umbria, in 2007 at the Capitolini Museum, in 2008 at the Officina Profumi Farmacia Santa Maria Novella in Florence and then in the Etruscan Museum at Rocca Albornoz in Viterbo and Festival of Science at Genova, accompanied by the smells of fragrances recreated from Antiquitates, renamed Athena, Hera, Artemis, and Aphrodite (Fig. 3).

Fig. 3: Athena, Hera, Artemis, and Aphrodite oil fragrances recreated by Antiquitates

The particularity of the perfumes discovery at Pyrgos, attracts the attention of the scholar, not so much for the understanding of the production techniques of perfumes in the Bronze Age, as for testing fragrances in vogue 4000 BP.

4.2 During the months of May-August, we organised at Antiquitates the experimentation on the technique of extracting fragrant oil maceration in warm, as in use in so-called "factory of fragrances" of Pyrgos. After a careful study of the methodologies used in the past, based primarily on pottery typology, and reproduced, attention focussed on technique that seemed to be the most special and interesting. Some sources make it known that this is a very old technique whose origins date back to Egypt.

Sources related historical age of Theophrastus, Pliny the Elder and Dioscurides, which have comparisons in the administrative records of the Mycenaean Linear B tablets of the second half of the second millennium BC, tell about maceration, the perfume extraction by soaking plants in water and olive oil. Through a series of pits, just like those found on the site of Pyrgos, we put "in heat" containers with precise proportions of rain water, olive oil and parts of scented plants. By maceration of these substances in the water, maintained at a temperature such that they rot and do not boil, they got rid the essential oils contained in the plant itself, which were gradually to join by osmosis to oil vessel on the surface. The technique involved a period of approximately 5 days, during which the oil acquired increasingly smell of the herbal substance and the water evaporated. Attention during the trial has focused on this technique widely attested on the site of Pyrgos, considering the high number of pits, 14 in all, arranged in no order in a privileged position close to the olive press.

According to the physical characteristics of the area of Pyrgos on "perfume factory," pits have been recreated (Fig. 4) with the intention to experiment with this technique and specially to understand the difficulties that the people faced at a time when the instruments were essentially made of stone.

Fig. 4: Antiquitates, artificial mound with two pits and jugs for the 1st test.

Inside the "Antiquitates" was created an artificial mound of fine soil the size of 1.95 m x 1.55, in which there are two pits almost circular shape (a 54 cm in diameter and 20 cm deep the other 51 cm in diameter and 18 cm deep). Both were covered inside with coarse sand to create a thermal insulator. The pits of Pyrgos are covered with basalt pebbles and coated with lime and talc, the famous asbestos of Cyprus (magnesium silicate), but difficult to find it in our area has led us to use the sand, with similar heat resistance capacity.

As recently suggested by Maria Rosaria Belgiorno coating the pit with pebbles of basalt needed to accumulate the necessary heat for maceration, in fact fired pebbles of basalt retaining the heat even for 14 hours, are used by different ethnic groups in the world to warm liquids and cook food in containers of organic material such as pumpkins and pockets of skin.

In each pit were found the ashes of the fire lit before placing the pots. We used hot ashes from simple charcoal. As material for the preparation of the ointment we employed plants of botanical species available in the Cyprus forest. These were pressed using stone millstones and pestles (Fig.5)

Fig. 5: Stone mill and pestle used to press the plants.

The result of the shredding was a moist mash, to which we have taken away the fibrous part, which already gave a characteristic odour. This result demonstrated the importance of this task as a necessary step in various stages of perfume production. The mixture obtained was poured into long necked jugs like the Pyrgos' (Fig. 4).

It is important that the mixture just did is placed into the container with the water and olive oil, not to disperse the odoriferous substances emitted by the plant after the grinding. We used distilled water (rainwater alternative used in the past) and olive oil, following the recipes of the Roman period. From the hearth was then picked up a portion of hot ashes and placed under and around the jug and the pot containing the mixture. We calculated with a thermocouple (model IEC 584 CR-ALK and HANNA HI-type thermometer 93530) the temperature of the embers at the time of collection that was still of 230° C, despite the coals were outdoors for about an hour. Finally, the pot was covered and sealed with sand up to his neck, leaving out only the mouth (Fig. 6).

Fig. 6: 2nd test of maceration with a pot: Sequence of measuring the weight of ingredients and control of temperature

Experimentation has clarified more directly what were the difficulties related to such delicate steps, what were the errors that you could incur and how essentially a 'specialization' in identifying appropriate times and temperatures to the success of a quality product.

It is to be noted that, much later examples of perfume production made with the same procedure, found at Delos, 3rd cent. BC and in Pompeii, 1st cent. AD, hint at what was important to isolate the container from the direct heat. The container, in fact, placed in a sort of platform covered with soil, sand, and manure with the insulating function, never entered direct contact with fire positioned lower.

To produce the ointment, we waited all water vaporises completely, more than five days reported in the literature. Although the procedure was not identical, we wondered if the five days were an absolute or relative time to the need to evaporate the water, or if it was a "standard" time dictated by the need to keep the essence as possible soaking in oil.

3.4. Distillation.

This technique, better known and widespread than the first, historical and archaeological finds numerous references that clarify better the functionality of ceramic elements and methods of extracting the fragrant water.

The four clay elements of the distillers found at Pyrgos were reproduced: a cooking pot, a head of steam with tubular spout for the steam, a jug collector with the neck of the size for inserting the spout and a basin of cold water for placing the collector and facilitate condensation of steam. The whole corresponds perfectly to the well-known still apparatus with onion head. Essence this time were oregano flowers and rose petals, finely chopped, and measured using a calibrated container in volume equal to one litre of water. The flowers were then beaten on millstones, to free the odorous substances and added to water.

For the fire charcoals were used and positioned the distillation apparatus over a stand like the horseshoe-shaped pottery of Pyrgos.

Fig. 7: Starting distillation sealing spout into the neck of the jug with a cotton rag tied with a rope to avoid steam dispersions.

We then sealed the interlocking of the spout into the neck of the jug with a cotton rag tied with a rope so that there were no steam dispersions (Fig. 7). However, we have found that separating the spout from the collector neck, drops of condensation coming out anyway.

It is therefore evident that the distillation process is facilitated, but not activated by the cooling of the collector into the basin with cold water.

3.5. Results.

The results drawn from experimentation on techniques of production of fragrances found in Pyrgos technically may be considered positive, since experimental evidence have facilitated the understanding of the basic steps of both production systems, and above all have defined margins of time and temperatures to obtain a quality product (Fig. 8).

Fig. 8: Collecting fragrant water with drops of essential oil after distillation.

Inevitably, however, the trial opens new questions looking for answers. Given that both tested techniques come from the same archaeological context, we must wonder if they were interrelated to each other. In other words, whether scented water produced by distilling was used to produce scented oils. If so, this might suggest that the ancients were also mixing fragrances. As we learn from modern cosmetics, any perfume requires a base, meaning a substance that does not alter the composition of the perfume but keeps its fragrance intact. It may be that distillation was used to produce perfume bases, whereas maceration was used to make scented oils that would remain stable over time.

All this is reflected in the plants identified in Pyrgos like coriander, pine resin, the oak and the Laurel considered in the cosmetic bases for perfumes. From the comparison of the experimental with the archaeometric analysis results the substances discovered at Pyrgos could in some way lead to new hypotheses about the ancient production processes.

These questions Will probably never be answered satisfactorily unless new written or archaeological sources become known and help form new theories and solutions

4. The research on loom weights

In the study of Pyrgos, as in every production-site, it is essential to focus the attention not just on the material findings, but moreover of the craft involved in its production cycle. Studying the ancient phases of any craft should always involve experimental archaeology and serious restitutions. The experimentations will be the key to deepen the comprehension of past crafts. Very reliable archaeological and Archaeometry data, good comparisons and a perfect knowledge of the context create together excellent conditions for the experimental research. In the 2006 a furnace has been discovered in square Py I9-a. Inside the furnace there still were 76 loom weights made of simple pressed earth (Fig. 9).

Fig. 9: Furnace full of loom weights found in Py I9-a, 2006 excavation season.

We focused our attention on the methodology employed in the production of the loom weights, starting from the find about 75 of these weights still being in a furnace.

This finding suggested that production of these objects was performed directly *in loco*, strictly connected to the needs of textile industry. Because of this necessity, the production methodology had to be very practical and rough materials had to be very easy to find.

4.1 Archaeometry

- Loom weights found on the dig have various sizes (between 10 cm in diameter and 15 cm in height).
- All archaeometrical analyses were carried on by the Institute of Technologies Applied to Cultural Heritage (ITABC) of the Italian National Council of Research (CNR) under the supervision of Alessandro Lentini.
- The colleague Lentini found out that the dough of which are lead loom weights was mostly composed of clay-earth, rich of inclusions.
- It was noted also the presence of organic material, such as a quantity of sulphur (originated by dung or animal fat).
- In the middle of the loom-weights is present a piece of stone or other material (such as a pottery processing discard), with a weight function for the verticality of the wire.

4.2 Rough Materials

To procure materials has been the very first step of this experiment. Unfortunately, the experimentation was not held in Pyrgos or nearby, but at the Centre for Experimental Archaeology Antiquitates in Italy, so it has been impossible to use the same rough materials employed for the original weights. Our selection has been oriented to those substances which use to have the same consistence, composition, and functionality characteristics.

- <u>Clay</u>: we choose two different kinds of raw clay to test their effects on the production:
  1) the first kind of clay was collected in the territory of Vetralla[114]. It was dark red-brownish, rich of inclusions and rather coarse in texture.
  2) the second kind of clay was collected in the territory of San Giovenale[115]. It was yellowish, with a finer texture and less inclusions than the other.
- <u>Animal fat</u>: we choose this material instead of dung. We melt the lard and we filtered it. This is a very fatty substance rich in proteins (892 Kcal e 99% fat).
- <u>Stone</u>: we collected the stones from the creek (Vesca) which runs along the borders of Antiquitates. We crushed them obtaining pieces in regular sizes between 3 cm and 5 cm in height and 1 cm thick.
- <u>Earth for covering</u>: we collected the earth that is commonly found around Antiquitates. It is a clay-sand, earth rich of inclusions of sub-centimetric sizes

4.3 Reproduction methodology

A simple autoptic analysis allowed us to understand that loom weights were hand-made one by one mixing elements together with fingers. Very impressive is the discovery of a weight found next to the furnace, unfinished and still bearing the imprint of the fingers. A sort of curve flint tool was employed to give the weights a rounded and regular profile.

---

[114] Vetralla is a small town in Viterbo province (Italy), near the site of Antiquitates.
[115] The territory of the famous archaeological site occupied since the bronze age and famous for its Etruscan settlement, next to the site of Antiquitates.

Fig. 10: Raw clay from Vetralla   Fig. 11: Raw clay from San Giovenale

We didn't establish a constant quantity of clay for each weight because of the number of variables such as the inner stone, the correct mixing of the elements, etc.Clay was hand-mixed with pork lard to reach a homogeneous dough. The presence of the lard gave to the dough a shining and viscous aspect. Shaping the weights as the original ones (tall, with round base and flat bottom, light central fairing, and rounded apex), a stone (5x1 cm) has been inserted from the bottom. Using a very liquid barbotine we try to regulate and smooth the surface of the weight, then we cover the weight with the clay-sand earth all over the external surface.

Finally, we obtained the holes in the upper part of the weight for the passage of the wire, simply using a thin and regular wood stick. At the end of this work the sizes of the reproduced weights were various in height, largeness, and weight. Weights were prepared for the drying process which should be very slow and gradual because of the presence of internal stones which may cause injury in the clay in drying. To avoid a too violent drying due to the seasonal temperatures, a black plastic film covered weights. We reproduced 32 loom weights in two hours of work.

5. Classification of the reproduced weights

After two days, circa, weights were examined and divided by the different quality of clay and drying effects. They have been individuated 3 groups:

1) group A: weights made of clay from Vetralla, which after 10 days of drying presented several injuries, come of them very deep.

2) group B: weights made of clay from San Giovenale, which after 10 days of drying didn't present any injury or break.

Divided in this way, weights have been signed and numbered, weighed (with a normal scale calibrated to 5 kg with signs every 25 g) and measured (with a common calibre and 25 cm ruler).

5.1 Group A: 29 weights reproduced

These weights, after the first phase of drying, appear brown to reddish. During the manipulation of clay, it appeared inhomogeneous, probably because hand-worked and not perfectly purified.

The mixture appears composed by compact and hard lumps, which has gotten nevertheless the same composition of the softer part of the mixture.

The paste made of clay and lard appears slick and bright. After just two days, weights present small breakings at the base in correspondence of the stone. Breakings have been plugged with barbotine, polishing the surface.

After the preliminary drying under the black plastic film, despite all the tricks and tweaks used to keep the them intact, the weights made with the clay from Vetralla present several breakings, the most deep of them located near the base, in some case showing the internal stone.

5.2 Group B: 13 weights reproduced

These weights appear light yellowish. During the processing phase, the mixture appears homogeneous in texture, without any lumps or impurities. The colour difference had been already clear from the beginning. The lard made the mixture more compact.

In contrast with the Group A, these weights, after two days of drying, didn't present any breaking and the surface appears very compact, keeping this aspect for a long time.

6. The baking technique

Fig. 12: Rounded open air furnace made of tuff blocks.

The archaeological context directly suggested the cooking technology, as the weights were found inside an oval open-air furnace. Open air baking requires a long period of preparation, not only for the research of combustible, but most of all for the maintaining of the fire and for the cooling phase of the process.

For the cooking of the weights we used an open-air furnace we already use to have at Antiquitates. 11 small Tuff blocks of different sizes, border it. The external diameter is 2,30 m; the internal diameter (combustion area) is 1 m circa; the height is 25 cm on borders (Fig. 12).

Nearby Antiquitates' site we collected the combustible: a big quantity of dry straw, dry twigs and barks. A big pot-bellow was employed for stoking. The entire process took 4 hours of work. The use of the open-air furnace requires a division of the work in more phases, proceeding very gradually. The artefacts were disposed initially around the furnace to guarantee a better drying and a gradual assumption of heat. The process requires a gradual approach toward the centre of the furnace and the embers in direct contact with flames.

Fig. 13: Looms positioned inside the rim of the furnace, ready to be fired.

Exactly as in the original Pyrgos furnace, big fragments of pottery were inserted in the furnace among the weights. This pottery was functional to keep and radiate the temperature inside the furnace. After 1.15 hour, weights have been accosted to the heat, from the top of the tuff blocks to the internal space of the furnace.

Fire has been newly alimented with combustible and oxygenated with the pot-bellow.

After about one hour, when the flames were lower, weights were placed one by one on the hot embers, among the fragments of pottery. After that everything was covered with a big quantity of dry straw, wood, and bark, let burn for 30 minutes high heat fed from time to time with more wood and straw.

At the end of this process the furnace could cool gradually. After 2 hours, circa we tried to extract the weights one by one from the furnace, not yet completely cooled.

6.1 Baking results

Group A (Fig. 14)

The difference of weight after the baking ranges from 5 to 25 g.

In the case of weight n° 20 the breaking of the base motivates the consistent loss of weight.

The colour changed after the baking, the weights now appear maculated, from the brown, blackish (parts which were directly in contact with flames) to the reddish, following the usual shades of pottery.

All the exemplars presented clear breakings on the entire body, and sometimes lost entire pieces of pottery.

The same breakings were evident during the preliminary drying phase, and this certainly contributed to the bad baking of the weights.

Fig.14: Looms of Group A after firing.

Fig. 15: Looms of group B after firing.

Group B

The difference of weight after the baking ranges from 10 to 25 g.
Even in this case the colour of the artefacts appears maculated, from the blackish to the brown. Weights don't present any breaking on their surface, they remained intact showing a more compact mixture than the ones belonging to Group A.

The presence of the internal stone didn't influence the result of the baking.

Conclusions

Pyrgos' loom weights, production experimentation was useful for several reasons.

-First, the experimentation helped us to understand how important was the direct functionality of the weights' processing, reduced to a few essential gestures. This was both valid for the collecting of the rough material both for manufacturing and baking technique.

-The choice of the clay kind proved essential for the success of the entire process.

-The comparison between the Vetralla's clay and the San Giovenale's one has shown clearly how many problems could cause a bad choice of the rough material: Vetralla's clay is inadequate for this kind of work.

REFERENCES

-Barber E.J.W. 1991: *Prehistoric textiles. The development of cloth in the Neolithic and Bronze Ages with special reference to the Aegean*, Princeton University Press.

-Coles J. 1981: *Archeologia sperimentale*, Longanesi, Milano.

-Feigl, F. And Anger V. 2009: Spots tests in organic analysis, 7th ed., elsevier, Amsterdam.

-Garner W. 1949: *Textile laboratory manual*, Publishing company, London.

-Hort A. translator, 1916: "*Theophrastus: Enquiry into Plants*", volume II.Series: Loeb Classical Library, New York and London, Putnam's Sons and Heinemann.

-Plinio il vecchio. *Naturalis Historia*, Rizzoli (1999), Milano.

-Wellmann M. translator 1958: *Pedanii Dioscoridis. De Materia Medica I*. Berlin: Weidmann verlag.

7. EXPERIMENTAL ARCHAEOMETALLURGY AT PYRGOS-MAVRORAKI: THE PILOT-EXPERIMENTS

Angelo Bartoli & Marco Romeo Pitone

Abstract

A peculiarity of Pyrgos' metallurgical context is the proximity of the furnaces to the Olive Press Room and to several huge pithoi for the storage of olive oil.

This fact, added to a very unusual shape of two furnaces and to the scarcity of charcoal recovered in the combustion chambers of furnaces, produced some considerations about the nature of the fuel employed in the metallurgical process. The hypothesis of an eventual use of the olive oil (and its processing residue) has been tested by preliminary experimental trials which created a solid base to design a more accurate and scientific research protocol for the future investigation of Pyrgos-Mavroraki by Experimental Archaeometallurgy.

1. Experimental Archaeometallurgy and Pilot Experiments[1]

The best way to materially test hypothesis drawn on ancient crafts and their operative processes is experimental archaeology.

The application of experimental archaeology has been recognized as an essential field of the archaeometallurgical studies since the birth of this discipline [2].

An accurate experimental plan, made of several series of experiments dedicated to specific

---

[1] This paper sums up the presentations held by Angelo Bartoli at the Conference for the 70th Anniversary of ITABC-CNR in Rome, and at the seminar "Archaeometry and Charm: gender, copper and music of silk" in Nicosia in 2013. The entire paper represents the effort to record all the notes about the several experiments Angelo Bartoli carried out on Pyrgos' metallurgy, within the ITABC-CNR PYRAME Project. His first experiments and hypotheses motivated Marco Romeo Pitone to carry on the research, which is now part of his PhD project at Newcastle University. Angelo Bartoli, founder of the Centre for Experimental Archaeology Antiquitates, prematurely left us on the 25th of February 2014, and this paper is dedicated to his memory.

[2] A significant prove of this early interest for Experimental Archaeometallurgy is represented by an old thesis on copper smelting furnaces from Timna, submitted yet in 1977 at Newcastle University under the supervision of Prof. R. F. Tylecote by P. J. Boydell (1977).

questions, can test the validity of a certain hypothesis, or even to stimulate the drawing of new ones. Experimental protocols can be designed for almost every metallurgical field, since the ore mining (Timberlake 2007) to the ore's smelting (Fasnacht & Senn 2001; Pryce et al. 2007; Girbal 2013; Timberlake 2013) and the casting and refining of an artefact (Barbieri et al. 2015), to even the last use (applying experimental archaeology to the study of use-wear analysis) of the same artefact (Dolfini & Crellin 2016; Heeb 2014; O'Flaherty 2007; Molloy 2004).

An effective example of the importance gained by experimental archaeometallurgy is shown also by the several conferences, workshops and summer schools organized all around the world dedicated to this discipline[3]. One of these events dedicated to experimental archaeometallurgy which gained a great success for a series of reasons is undoubtedly the HMS 2010 conference organized by David Dungworth and Roger C. P. Doonan at West Dean College, Sussex. The proceedings of this conference (Dungworth & Doonan 2013) represent an up-to-date state of the art of this specific field of archaeometallurgy.

The characteristics of every single experimental research protocol depend on different factors among which is essential to remind: the hypothesis we want to test, the specific questions we want to look for an answer to and the archaeological and analytical data we have.

In addition, before engaging in an articulate scientific project, it is not rare to take into consideration pilot experiments, sometimes carried out with the help of "archaeo-technicians". Archaeo-technicians are not necessarily archaeologists, but they are usually provided with the right practical skills required to materially deal with the craft, subject of the research.

A pilot experiment is a preliminary trial experiment which is designed taking care, where possible, of the major quantity of archaeological/archaeometric data available, but also inspired by a certain grade of practical experience in a determined field. This kind of experiment is very useful to guide the design of a scientific research protocol in on a promising direction, avoid losing time (energies and money) on eventual even more accurately designed, but ineffective experiments.

As pointed out by Cunningham et al. (2007: v-vi), pre and pilot experiments are functional to add an experiential element to the research, that leads, in our opinion, to a fundamental heuristic value of the project. These kinds of experiments of experiments should be taken into the account before to design the experimental protocol dedicated to a specific question.

Several pilots-experiments have been carried out on Pyrgos' archaeometallurgy by Angelo Bartoli and his Team at the Centre for Experimental Archaeology "Antiquitates"[4], with the aim to give a start to the construction of an experimental protocol for the investigation of Pyrgos' archaeometallurgy.

It was decided to start testing the functionality both two main furnace's shapes (the shaft structure interpreted as a smelting furnace and the small pit-furnaces with carburetor) and the use of olive oil as an additive fuel to reach high temperature in less time.

Operational timings, temperatures, quantity of ore used and metal obtained, (the) amount of fuel employed were recorded, but because of the preliminary heuristic nature of these pilot-

---

[3] All the major international conferences dedicated to Archaeometallurgy are usually provided with a specific session dedicated to Experimental Archaeology (Archaeometallurgy in Europe, Historical Metallurgy Society Meetings...etc.) In Italy, the Centre for Experimental Archaeology Antiquitates (www.antiquitates.it) has been organizing several international conferences dedicated to different archaeometallurgical topics investigated by experimental archaeology since 2003 (the last one occurred in 2014).

[4] At the Centre an exposition-corner of the Open-Air Museum has been dedicated to Pyrgos. The Centre, strongly believing in the value and "mission" of the educational and communicative aspect of experimental archaeology, dedicated also through the years several expositions to the site of Pyrgos-Mavroraki seen by an experimental point of view (www.antiquitates.it).

experiments, no specific protocols were applied.

The most relevant result has been mostly to prove the efficiency of olive oil as a fuel for metallurgical processing.

2. The archaeological context

The pilot-experiments presented in this paper were carried out primarily considering the results from two main areas of the site: Northern and Southern Sectors.

Traces of smelting were identified in the Northern Sector of the site (H-I-J/2-3-4) (Belgiorno 2009: 78-79).

The best-preserved smelting furnace was found in J4, it had got a shaft-shape with a base made of big grey basalt blocks and the cylindrical walls in white limestone blocks. The stones were consolidated using mud as mortar. The furnace measures (in its actual condition) about 50 cm in height with an internal diameter of about 25 cm. It is not easy to say if the furnace were totally open on a side (in a horseshoe shape) or if it used to have just a small door at the base.

Large carbonaceous levels were recovered in this sector, which could be interpretable as the remains of roasting beds or as the result of the cleaning of the furnace after its use.

The excavation of the surrounding area still needs to be completed[5], but the presence of big grinders (Karageorghis & Belgiorno 2005: 51), the considerable quantity of crumbled ore and slags in the archaeological record and the shape of this furnace seems to suggest that this area of the settlement was dedicated to the smelting of the ores (Belgiorno 2009: 79-80)[6].

Samples rich in carbonaceous traces have been taken from the internal walls of the furnace and will be analysed to testify the presence of metal and eventually try to identify what kind of fuel was used to run the reactor.

The Southern Sector shows the remains of a different kind of furnace. A large quantity of small pit-furnaces, possibly used with crucibles, with an internal diameter of about 20 cm and a maximum deep of 30 cm has been recovered leaning on a bench (maybe, as mentioned before, part of a previous ancient structure). A mud-brick usually surrounded the furnaces circle up to 30 cm, even if it is not always easy to recognize it, considering that a lot of this /these pits seem to obliterate previous similar structures.

Two main shapes are recognizable within this pit-furnaces' category: the simple hemispherical pit, dug into the soil and a sort of twined furnaces, composed by two different pits combined, maybe one for the crucible and one for an eventual bellow. Both the types show a lateral hole linked with the external, used possibly for the ventilation of the "combustion chamber" (Karageorghis & Belgiorno 2005: 51).

The stratification of these furnaces usually shows, beyond the carbonaceous levels, also a burnt red earth level, which testified the presence of high temperatures within the specific context.

The crucible was positioned inside the pit and covered up to the border, as testified by the absence of high temperature traces only on the external walls of the majority of the crucibles found. Most these furnaces were found covered by a large stone lid (Belgiorno 2009: 82) and two of them presented an unusual peculiarity. Buried among the mud-bricks ring around the pit, it has been recovered a small juglet, heavily marked by the high temperatures, with its spout facing the "combustion chamber" and its belly, broken toward the upper surface of the earth-

---

[5] The structures proceed beyond the excavation borders.
[6] According to the preliminary analysis of the archaeological remains from the Northern Sector, other three different furnaces (probably built in sequence) were recognized by the high temperature traces, carbonaceous levels, slags and a circle of stones near the northern limit of the sector, in I-H2 (Belgiorno 1999: 58-59).

ring. This artefact has been interpreted as a sort of "carburetor" used to drop olive oil into the furnace as a fuel, after it had been started with some normal wood or charcoal. Olive oil has got a high calorific power and could have been used to reach high temperatures sooner (Belgiorno 2009: 83).

3. The pilot-experiments

3.1 Archaeometry

There is no need to stress on the importance of a serious plan of archaeometric analyses to obtain the basic data to employ in the design of an experimental protocol. Within the "Pyrame" project, the Research Team of the ITABC-CNR conceived to dedicate a specific attention to the archaeometallurgical finds (Belgiorno 2000).

Waiting for a systematic plan of analyses[7], a series of preliminary archaeometric considerations was published in a few papers: analyses have been carried out both on artefacts (Giardino et al 2002) and slags from Pyrgos-*Mavroraki*.

Giardino initially (2000: 23), and then in collaboration with Rovira (2007) carried out preliminary slag-analyses (ED-XRF; XRD; OM; SEM-EDX; FTIR) on 5 slags from the Northern Sector (H-I-J/2-3).

The analyses suggested that mainly sulphide copper ores were used in the smelting process performed at Pyrgos. The external feature of the most of Pyrgos' slags appears inhomogeneous, but characterized by very visible greenish veins and copper prills. No liquidous features were identified and the several rough shapes recovered suggest that the slags have been solidified within the furnace (Giardino 2000: 21). The presence of magnetite seems to suggest an oxidizing atmosphere in the furnace (Giardino & Rovira 2007: 3).

Other archaeometric analyses were made in the laboratories of CNR which allowed to suggest that the ores employed for the smelting used to pertain to mixed charges from the Mavroraki area, considering the very similar bulk composition between them and the slags recovered in the site (Belgiorno et al. 2012: 31). On this occasion a possible furnace for the processing of precious metals has been possibly recognized (Belgiorno et al. 2012: 31-32).

Gas-Chromatography revealed that the huge *pithoi* found in the Press Room used to contain oily residues diagnosed with the presence of palmitic, stearic and oleic acids, characteristic of olive oil (Belgiorno 2009: 50). The possible common link of the entire Pyrgos' workshop was suggested to be the production of the olive oil, used not only in the food processing, but also for several other purposes among which the possibility to employ it as a fuel in the metallurgical process (Belgiorno 2009: 83; Lentini 2009: 135 Belgiorno et al 2012: 29).

Other scholars suggested a similar hypothesis on the use of olive oil and its processing residues (Betancourt 2006: 186) and new archaeometric analyses will be planned considering the very recent works of some of them (Braadbaart et al. 2016).

The pilot experiments, on the one hand, have demonstrated the possibility to reach high temperatures with olive oil in the reconstructed furnaces, on the other hand stimulated further archaeometric investigations to endorse the application of this hypothesis on the Pyrgos' case.

Anyway, all the archaeometric analyses carried out until now on the archaeometallurgy of Pyrgos-*Mavroraki* were intended, as well as the pilot experiments we are going to briefly present, as to produce the essential considerations necessary to design a more articulated and specific archaeometric project.

---

[7] Which is now part of a PhD project carried out at Newcastle University by Marco Romeo Pitone, funded by the Northern Bridge Doctoral Training Partnership.

3.2 Rough Materials

The very first step of this research has been to procure materials. The experiments have been carried out both on autochthonous Cypriot ores (basaltic copper ores with malachite formations present in the site's surroundings) and on allochthonous ores (malachite from Congo).

Only one pilot experimentation has been carried out in Cyprus by the Antiquitates' Team, with the possibility to use rough materials from the site's surroundings to build the furnace and smelt the original ores (Fig. 1). Other pilot experiments have been carried out afterwards by Belgiorno and her collaborators (Belgiorno et al. 2012: 31).

Fig. 1: Copper minerals from the Mavroraki Hill.

The other experiments, which have been carried out in Italy, should be considered most reliable regarding the behaviour of furnaces' shapes and fuel, more than the main result coming from the ore. It is important to remind that in both cases just copper carbonates were used, which are consistently easier to smelt, being richer in copper.

The use of chalcopyrite (attested archaeologically at Pyrgos' workshop) or in general mixed charge was not yet well investigated, nor even at a preliminary research-stage such as a pilot experiment.

3.3 Smelting
The shaft-furnace

The model considered for this test was the shaft-furnace found in J4. The furnace was found with a thick internal layer of earth-lining. No airing conducts were found, except a possible opening facing the sea.

The experiment considered as valid the shape of the furnace recovered on the site as the original one, but it is not to be excluded that what we see today is just what remains of the furnace's basement, which could eventually have an upper portion of the walls made simply by mud-bricks, as the coeval general architecture of the settlement suggests.

To build the furnace the same materials recovered during the archaeological excavation have been used: basalt blocks (for the base), limestone blocks bound by a simple earth-mortar (for the cylindrical walls). The internal room had a cm25 diameter and was 35cm high.

The furnace has been built facing the direction of wind.

Fig. 2: Angelo Bartoli making the first smelting experiment.

The autochthonous ore was used for this experiment: malachite formations on green *basaltina* has been crumbled and put in a normal modern pottery vase used as crucible.

After starting it with a few small branches, olive oil has run the furnace, gently added from a small opening on the top of it, using a small bowl (Fig. 2). The temperature reached (measured with a thermos-couple chrome-vanadium IEC 584 CR-ALK and a thermometer HANNA HI-93530) was 850° without the aid of any artificial airing.

The fusion-conglomerate obtained was composed by a black silica matrix, containing copper drops (Fig. 3). Albeit no archaeometric analyses have been systematically carried out yet on the experimental conglomerates, they appear very like the original ones. The very surprising result of this pilot experiment was to validate the hypothesis of the use of olive oil to reach temperatures useful for the smelting operations, without any artificial air adding in this case.

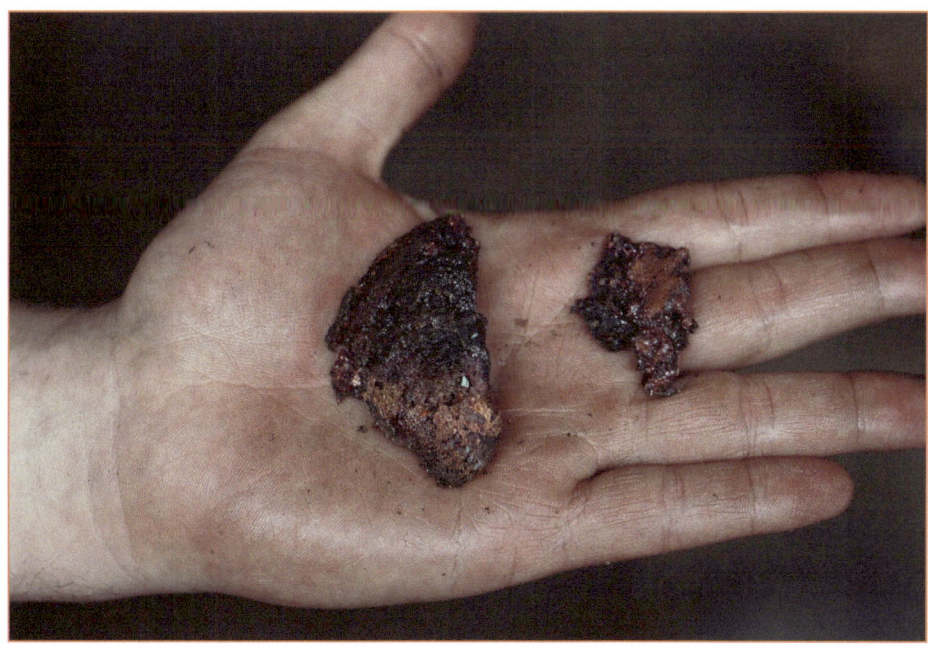

Fig. 3: The fusion-conglomerate composed by a black silica matrix, containing copper drops.

The pit-furnace

This pilot experiment was carried out at the Centre for Experimental Archaeology Antiquitates in Italy in 2006-2007, in the presence of authorities from Italy and Cyprus, including the Cypriot Ambassador Stavros Epaminondas, the General Director of the CNR Angelo Guerrini and the Press Director of the CNR Marco Ferrazzoli (Fig. 4).

Fig. 4: Cypriot Ambassador Stavros Epaminondas interviewed by an ANSA reporter.

This furnace has been reconstructed, several times, considering the original structure found in J7 (Belgiorno 2009: 83), characterized by the presence of a small juglet inserted in the earth ring of the furnace, reversed with the spout facing the combustion chamber, and with an intentional breaking on the portion of the belly wall which faces the top. The juglet shows clearly the traces of the exposures to high temperatures.

The experimental pit was carved in the local tuff (to substitute the Pyrgos' bedrock), with two airing channels connected to two leather bellows. The base of the ring is 55 cm large and 25 cm tall. The internal combustion chamber has got a cm 18,5 diameter and it is 22 cm deep.

The opening of the two airing channels into the combustion chamber are 6 cm large and positioned on the lower part of the walls, connected by two channels (40 cm and 80 cm), each one ending in two more channels (99 cm, 123 cm; 69 cm, 64 cm) linked to 4 leather bellows[8] with wooden handles (Fig. 5).

Fig. 5: The experimental furnace with two air channels connected to two leather bellows.

The juglet's spout (facing the combustion chamber) has been placed between the openings of the two airing channels. To drop the olive oil in this sort of carburetor a common reed was used, so that it was possible to maintain a minimum distance from the furnace.

As this was a pilot experiment with the aim to test the efficacy of olive oil as a fuel, the choice to place the juglet's spout right in the middle of the two airing channels' openings revealed to be particularly significant, since this put in strict connection the oil, the fire and the oxygen. This made the most of the combustive capabilities of the olive oil.

---

[8] The presence of the channels in the original context seemed to point to the use of bellows, but this aspect is still under study. We would like to remember that Kassianidou (2011: 45-46) suggests that the introduction of bellows (and touyeres) on the island could be datable to the beginning of Late Bronze Age.

On the frontal wall of the furnace a small door was created with a cm12 diameter: both the top opening and the vertical door of the furnace were provided with stone[9] lids (the top lid had a small central hole as found in Pyrgos' evidence, probably used to check the combustion chamber during the process).

A small crucible realized in clay, sand and *cocciopesto* was used to contain the ore (Fig. 6).

Fig. 6: Position of the crucible inside the furnace.

After the crucible filled with 480 gr of crumbled malachite was put in the combustion chamber, the fire in the furnace was started with small dry wood's pieces, dry leaves and straw.

In this first phase, both two main openings (the top one and the vertical door) were left open.

Using the bellows the archaeologists reached a 300/400° temperature, necessary to pre-heat the entire structure avoiding thermal shocks.

After this phase, the top opening was closed, while the vertical door was left open to allow adding more "starter-fuel".

At the end of the pre-heating phase the vertical door was also closed. The next step was starting the slow addition of the olive oil through the reed inside the "juglet-carburetor", which permitted to reach in a small time the temperature of 1350/1380°[10] (Fig. 7). It was possible to maintain this temperature constant for about 30 minutes, consuming about 3.25 l of olive oil.

The result found in the crucible, at the end of the experiment, was a blackish amalgam within which they were recovered about 350 gr of small rough copper lumps.

Another similar kind of fuel could leave the same traces detected for olive oil by Gas Chromatography (Belgiorno 2009: 50), represented by the main fatty acids characteristic of olive

---

[9] Instead of the original Cypriot calcarenite, the local *peperino* was used to this purpose.
[10] Detected with a thermocouple IEC 584 CR-ALK provided with a thermometer HANNA HI-93530.

oil (palmitic, stearic and oleic): the discard of the olive processing (also called crude olive cake, gift, pomace[11] or, in Italian, *Sansa*) that is mainly composed of a mixture of olives' skins and cores semi-crushed.

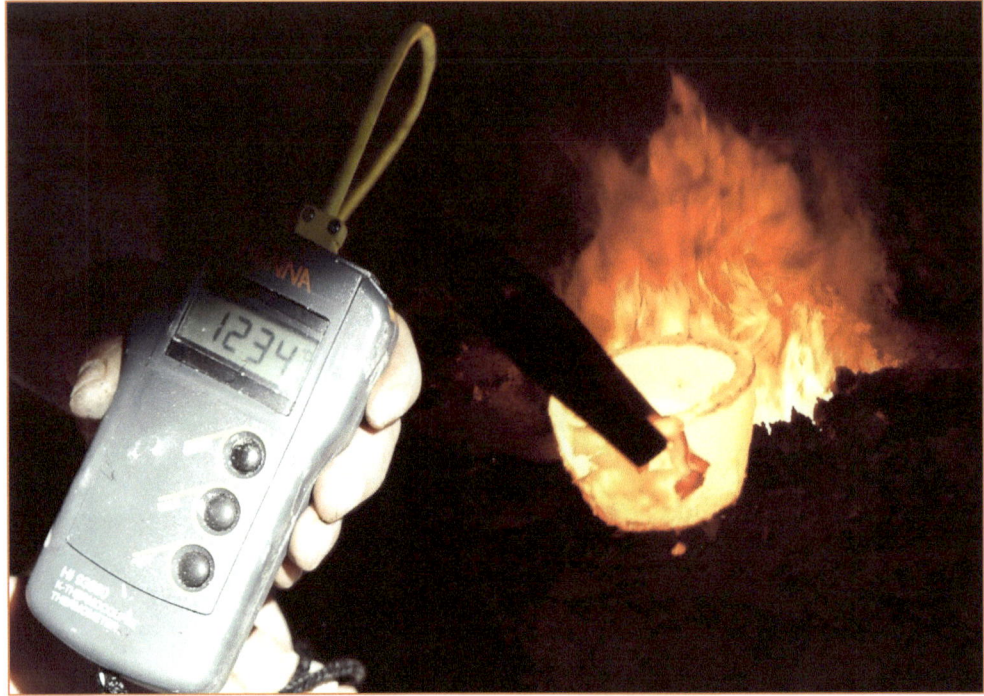

Fig. 7: Control of the temperature with the thermocouple.

For this reason, this kind of fuel has been tested, without any success (the temperature reached was not sufficient to reduce the ore).

A last attempt has been done using horse-dung embedded with olive oil[12], because of traces of dung seemed to be recovered during the preliminary analysis of samples from the furnaces. Even in this case it was not possible neither to reach the ideal smelting-temperature, neither to maintain it steady.

Conclusions

The preliminary experimental study carried out on Pyrgos' archaeometallurgy underlined the great potential of this kind of research on the site.

Pilot experiments demonstrated that in a re-built metallurgical context like the original one, the processing of copper ores with the use of olive oil as a fuel additive was possible. The pilot experiments enlightened three main aspects:

1. The olive oil has been demonstrated to have twice the calorific value of coal.
2. Olive oil reduces considerably the time requested by smelting.
3. The temperature has been maintained steady more easily, even in lack of oxygen, while other fuels usually decrease the temperature any time the combustion chamber is refilled with them.

All the preliminary data informally collected during the experiments and all the observations

---

[11] Braadbaart et al 2016: 3.

[12] A particular use of dung is described by Gowland (1899) in regard of the Nepalese smelters (Timberlake 2013: 135)

carried out can play an essential role in the prosecution of the research. The results of these initial studies asked for a more accurate and systematic long term plan of research to dedicate to Pyrgos' metallurgy.

From the knowledge acquired from the previous experimental work, it has appeared interesting to set a complete experimental plan dedicated to this subjected, ruled by a strict scientific research protocol. This plan will be designed following the most recent tendencies of experimental archaeology (Shimada 2005), to produce valuable data for a sensible comparison with the archaeological data. The main research questions will cover the following topics: the thermo-physical behaviour of the copper ores, the treatment of it to extract the metallic copper, the shape of furnaces and the fuel employed.

A long-term focused project seemed to be the most appropriate way to design a complete research protocol on this topic, employing Field-Archaeology, Archaeometry and Experimental Archaeometallurgy to attempt to reconstruct the complex copper ore processing performed during the Early and Middle Bronze Age at Pyrgos-*Mavroraki*. With this aim one of the authors is carrying out a PhD project entitled "Reconstructing Early Cypriot Metallurgy: the case of Pyrgos-*Mavroraki*" at Newcastle University[13] funded by Northern Bridge Doctoral Training Partnership, in collaboration with ITABC-CNR of Rome and the Director of the Italian Mission at Pyrgos-*Mavroraki* Dr Maria Rosaria Belgiorno.

The project implies a complete plan of archaeometric analyses on Pyrgos' finds.

Great importance will be given to the systematic study of the slags (from the different metallurgical areas of the site) with the aim of categorizing them (also recognizing to which step of the operative process they belong such as roasting, smelting or melting/casting) and establishing the exact composition of the ore-charge, the possible shape of furnaces (tracing the different grade of red/ox atmosphere developed in different shapes of furnace), the temperature reached by them and the fuel used. All these information have been recorded by the compounds present in the slags at the moment of their formation and can be detected combining multiple types of archaeometric investigation such as: OM, SEM-EDX, XRF and Gas Chromatography.

In addition to the slag analysis, on-field analyses will be carried out by pXRF on the remains of the different types of furnaces and other metallurgical artefacts will be analysed such as crucibles, nozzles, moulds and grinders.

After the collection of all the archaeological and archaeometric data it will possible to draw a series of hypotheses which will be tested by Experimental Archaeometallurgy, designing from time to time a specific protocol.

Among the others, the main objects of the future reconstructions will be devoted to understand the management of the multiple steps of the *chaine operatoire* and their relations with the different furnaces' shapes and the identification of which fuels were employed and how.

The experimental material results will be analysed by the same methods used for the archaeological finds, to be matched with them.

At the end of the research we will be hopefully to shed light on the still obscure raise of early metallurgy in Cyprus.

---

[13] Under the supervision of Dr Andrea Dolfini, Dr Alasdair Charles (Newcastle University) and Dr Benjamin Roberts (Durham University).

REFERENCES

-Barbieri M., Cavazzuti C., Pellegrini L. and Scacchetti F. 2015: Experiencing visible and invisible metal casting techniques in the Bronze Age Italy, in Kelm R. (ed) *Archaeology and Crafts. Experiences and Experiments on traditional Skills and Handicrafts in Archaeological Open-Air Museums in Europe*, 94-102.

-Belgiorno M.R. 2000: Project Pyrame 1998-1999: Archaeological, Metallurgical and Historical Evidence at Pyrgos (Limassol), in *Reports of the Department of Antiquities Cyprus*, 1-17.

-Belgiorno M.R. (ed) 2009: *Cipro all'inizio dell'Età del Bronzo. Realtà sconosciute della comunità industrial di Pyrgos*-Mavroraki, Roma, Gangemi.

-Belgiorno M.R., Ferro D. and Loepp D. 2012: Pyrgos-Mavroraki in Cypriot metallurgy, in Kassianidou, V. and Papasavvas, G. (eds) *Eastern Mediterranean Metallurgy and Metalwork in the Second Millenium BC*, 26-34.

-Betancourt P.P. 2006: Ch. 14: Discussion of the Workshop and Reconstruction of the Smelting Practices, in Bentacourt, P. P. (ed) *The Chrysokamino Metallurgy Workshop and its Territory* (Hesperia Supplement 36), Athens, 179-189.

-Boydell P. J. 1977: *Experiments on copper smelting based on early furnaces found in Southern Palestine*, thesis submitted for the degree of M.Sc in Metallurgy at the University of Newcastle-Upon-Tyne.

-Braadbaart F., Marinova E. and Sarpaki A. 2016: Charred olive stones: experimental and archaeological evidence for recognizing olive processing residues used as fuel, in *Vegetation History and Archaeobotany* (on-line publication) doi:10.1007/s00334-016-0562-2.

-Cunningham P., Heeb J. and Paardekooper R. (eds) 2007: *Experiencing Archaeology by Experiment. Proceedings of the Experimental Archaeology Conference, Exter 2007*, Oxford, Oxbow Books.

-Dolfini A. and Crellin R. J. 2016: Metalwork wear analysis: The loss of innocence, in *Journal of Archaeological Science, 66*, 78-87.

-Dungworth D. and Doonan R. C. P. 2013: *Accidental and experimental Archaeometallurgy*, HMS Occasional Publication No 7, London, The Historical Metallurgy Society Ltd.

-Fasnach,t W. and Senn, M. (2001), Experimental copper smelting at Agia Varvara - Almyras a contribution to the controversy af Ancient iron production in Cyprus, in *Archaeologia Cypria* (vol. IV), 129-133.

-Giardino C. 2000: Prehistoric copper activity at Pyrgos, in *Reports of the Department of Antiquities Cyprus*, 19-32.

-Giardino C., Gigante G. E. and Ridolfi S. 2002: Archaeometallurgical inverstigations on the Early-Middle Bronze Age finds from the area of Pyrgos (Limassol), in *Reports of the Department of Antiquities Cyprus*, 33-48.

-Giardino C. and Rovira S. 2007: Pyrgos-Mavroraki (Cyprus): Copper Smelting Slag of the Beginning of the Second Millennium BC, in *Proceedings of the 2nd International Conference "Archaeometallurgy in Europe 2007"*, file 153 (digital pubblication PDF), 1-8.

-Heeb J. 2014: *Copper Shaft-Hole Axes and Early Metallurgy in South-Eastern Europe: An Integrated Approach*, Oxford, Archaeopress.

-Karageorghis V. and Belgiorno M. R. 2005: Primi esempi di tecnologie agricole e industriali nell'Età del Bronzo a Cipro, Roma.

-Kassianidou V. 2011: Ch. 5: Blowing the Wind of Change: the introduction of bellows in Late Bronze Age Cyprus, in Betancourt, P. P. and Ferrence, S. C. (eds), *Metallurgy: Understanding How, Learning Why. Studies in Honor of Jmaes D. Muhly*, Philadelphia, INSTAP Academic Press, 41-47.

-Lentini A. 2009: Archeologia e paesaggio naturale: indagini archeobotaniche e fisico chimiche, in Belgiorno, M. R. (ed), *Cipro all'inizio dell'Età del Bronzo. Realtà sconosciute della comunità industrial di Pyrgos*-Mavroraki, Roma, Gangemi Editore, 128-187.

-Molloy B. 2004: Experimental combat with Bronze Age weapons, in *Archaeology Ireland, 18(1)*, 32-34.

-O'Flaherty R. 2007: A weapon of choice: experiments with a replica Irish Early Bronze Age halberd, in *Antiquity, 81*, 423-434.

-Pryce T.O., Bassiakos Y., Catapotis M. and Doonan R. C. 2007: "De Caerimoniaes" Technological Choices in Copper-Smelting Furnace Design at Early Bronze Age Chrysokamino, Crete, in *Archaeometry 49 (3)*, 543-557.

-Shimada I. 2005: Experimental Archaeology, in Maschner, H. D. G. and Chippindale, C. (eds), *Handbook of Archaeological methods*. Lanham, Altamira Press, 603-642.

-Timberlake S. 2007: The use of experimental archaeology/archaeometallurgy for the understanding and reconstruction of Early Bronze Age mining and smelting technologies, in La Niece S., Hook D. and Craddock P. (eds) *Metals and Mines. Studies in Archaeometallurgy*, 27-36.

-Timberlake S. 2013: From ore to artefavt: smelting Alderley Edge copper ores and the casting of a small copper axe, in Dungworth, D. and Doonan, R. C. P. (eds) *Accidental and Experimental, HMS Occasional Publication No 7 Archaeometallurgy*, London, The Historical Metallurgy Society Ltd, 135-142.

8. THE HOUSE OF THE GODDESS.
COINS TELL THE CYPRIOT APHRODITE MYTH

Francesca Ceci

2 (Titus) ....cupido incessit adeundi visendique templum Paphiae Veneris, inclitum per indigenas advenasque. haud fuerit longum initia religionis, templi ritum, formam deae (neque enim alibi sic habetur) paucis disserere.
3 Conditorem templi regem Aeriam vetus memoria, quidam ipsius deae nomen id perhibent. ...hostiae, ut quisque vovit, sed mares deliguntur: certissima fides haedorum fibris. sanguinem arae obfundere vetitum: precibus et igne puro altaria adolentur, nec ullis imbribus quamquam in aperto madescunt. simulacrum deae non effigie humana, continuus orbis latiore initio tenuem in ambitum metae modo exurgens, set ratio in obscuro.

P. Corneli Taciti, *Historiarvm liber secvndvs*, 2-3.

Coinage was one of the most powerful resources of propaganda for images of the ancient world, and Rome knew how to use this wisely. Every issue, with its capillary circulation, potentially could reach an unlimited audience at every remote corner of commerce. Iconic patterns could be easily recognizable to users, and through the immediacy of visual language, Rome could present and affirm herself everywhere[129].

Emissions from the Imperial period in the provinces subject to Rome provided some freedom for the choice of iconographic themes to be represented on the back of the various series by local authorities.

While the front side was usually intended for the Emperor or a regional personification, the back could be reserved for specific types, often connected with strongly felt and shared local deities and cultures.

---

[129] Howgego Ch. 1995; Norena C.F. 2001.

The imperial authority always inserted, and promptly, such rituals into its religious system, achieving the dual purpose of respecting the submissive populations and inserting them through the sharing of the rite, under Roman-centric power[130]. This also happened in Cyprus, which became a Roman province in the 58 BC keeping as a rule its religious institutions, first the ancient worship of Aphrodite-Wanassa at Palaipaphos (here called Paphia) administered by a great priest, who played a pan-political function as a recognized symbol of identity of the island[131]. (Fig. 1)

Fig. 1: Aphrodite's Temple at Palea Paphos

The goddess's shrine, which represented the Paphos sanctuary in its entirety, became the image chosen for locally surrendered emissions under the control of the *Urbs*, which probably supported the choice of the iconographic type in accordance with local magistrates[132].

---

[130] Howgego Ch., Heuchert V., Burnett A. 2007.

[131] Tacitus, *Historiae*, II, 3. For the great goddess of Paphos that will later become, from IV century BC Aphrodite: Maier F.G. 1975; Karageorghis J. 1977; Karageorghis J. 2013; for the ancient and modern sources about sanctuary and goddess: Näf 2013, 16-20. Dissertation of Rocelli M. 2014-15, 5, on line, offers an agile summary of the "state of the matter" on the sanctuary.

[132] Price M.J., Trell B.L. 1977; Amandry M. 1993; Parks D.A. 2004; RPC 1992; RPC 1999; Carradice I. 1988, 182-187; Amandry M. 2011; Tsochos Ch. 2014, 201-208. Fundamental is the study of Schwarzer H. 2013, with a reasoned catalogue of all relevant emissions, which is the most complete and up-to-date contribution to the subject, to which I refer for further details. See also pictures and contributions in:
http://kyprioscharacter.eie.gr/en/scientific-texts/details/numismatics/cypriote-coinage-under-roman-rule-30-bc-3rd-century-ad.

This sanctuary was one of the most celebrated and venerated dedicated to Aphrodite in the Mediterranean, a destination of the constant flow of pilgrims from every country and social level, including the imperial family. Around the temple, it was also possible to buy prestige devotional *souvenirs*, such as rings with gems and gold castings representing the site[133] (Fig. 2).

Fig. 2: Gold Ring depicting the Temple of Aphrodite at Palea Paphos, I-II century AD. New York, Metropolitan Museum HTTP://WWW.METMUSEUM.ORG/ART/COLLECTION/SEARCH/243500

Archaeological excavations, which still are underway in the sanctuary area, attest occupation starting in the third millennium BC, and its interregional attendance going on from 1200 BC until the end of the 4th century AD, with testimonies of the various phases and episodes of building and renovations during the centuries, which scholars argue about[134].

The prehistoric origin and the antiquity of the cult[135] emerges from the architectural structure of the shrine, which appears of Middle Eastern origin, back to the Bronze Age. It is a tripartite structure characterized by a central tower with the divine simulacrum positioned in the centre, side by side with two lower rooms, perhaps porches. A semi-circular courtyard precedes the whole, with various furnishings and decorations pertaining to the worship. Although the archaeological excavations have not yet found evidence of such planimetry, the coins of Roman-imperial age, together with the recalled rings and monies, give a great deal of testimony. In favour of the Mediterranean-East derivation also the goddess's simulacrum gives some suggestion: it is an aniconic black stone depicted by literary sources such as a pyramid-shaped basalt block with no human form, whose precise meaning is ignored[136].

But the question of the real adherence to the original templar structure still remains open.

The veneration of stones of various forms and sizes is largely attested in the Mediterranean: like the Apollo's Omphalos, the black stone of Magna Mater / Cibele, the baetyl of Zeus Kasios, the sacred stones of Sardinia, often exposed in sacred open air sites, within a religious koiné of

---

[133] Some precious gold rings are kept at the British Museum in London (with bibliography) (http://www.britishmuseum.org/explore/highlights/highlight-objects/gr/g/gold_ring temple_of_aphrodite.aspx and at Metropolitan Museum of Art di New York (http://www.metmuseum.org/collection/the-collection-online); Maier F.G., Karageorghis J. 1984, pp. 85-86, 11.6. Interesting is the gem, now lost, with Serapis and the Temple of Aphrodite Paphia: Veymiers R. 2005.

[134] In Gardner E.A., Hogarth D.G., James M.R., Elsey Smith R. 1888, the excavations carried out in Palea Paphos have been reported since the end of the seventies of the last century, with previous bibliography. A sum of the archaeological history of the Aphrodite sanctuary is in Karageorghis J. 2005. See also the bibliography of excavations carried out by the University of Zurich in:
www.hist.uzh.ch/static/ag/_DEL_paphos/publications/index.html.

[135] Pausanias, Ἑλλάδος περιήγησις, I. 14.7; VIII, 5.2; Herodotus, Ἱστορίαι, I, 105, attributes the introduction of worship to the Phoenicians and defines the Aphrodite sanctuary in Paphos as the oldest in the Greek world.

[136] Tacitus, *Historiae*, 2, 2-3; C. Max. Tyrius, *Diss.*, 8, 8; Serv., *Ad Aen.*, 1, 274.

Aegean origin extended to the Tyrrhenian, which from the Bronze Age lasted until and beyond the Roman period[137].

Occasionally, archaeological excavations of the end of the nineteenth century at Kouklia/Palea Paphos returned an aniconic black stone recognised as the simulacrum of Aphrodite Paphia,[138] although the details of its discovery have not been precisely reported[139]. This basaltic baetyl identified as the original Aphrodite stone is currently exposed in the Antiquarium set up inside the archaeological area of the sanctuary.

The stone, a semi-pyramidal monolith of local gabbro, 122cm high, very polished due to continuous aspersions, ointments and manual smoothing, corresponds in shape to Tacitus' description. Though there is no absolute certainty of its identification, today the chance to see the stone and its elegant simplicity is a remarkable emotion for any visitor. (Fig. 3)

Fig. 3: Aphrodite stone: a semi- pyramidal monolithic of local gabbro H. 122 cm.

---

[137] Among the numerous contributions on the subject: Carstens A.M. 2008, Zeman K. 2008, Stewart P. 2008. I refer also to the Minoan gems with scenes representing cults of stones, consisting of hugs and contacts with stone: an almost complete review in 2002-2017; relative to the "own life" of the stones: Dasen V. 2014.

[138] It is interesting to note that Kouklia, the name of the town born on the site of ancient Paphos, means "dolls" (*koukles*) probably because the number of human clay figurines found on the site: Myres J.L. 1945, p. 97.

[139] The find of the black stone, still controversial and not well described (Gardner E.A., Hogarth D.G., James M.R., Elsey Smith R. 1888, 200), took place in 1887/8 under the porch of the Roman Stoà. The stone was found buried in a late mosaic floor, underlining the chronology in relation to the Roman phase and its religious upheaval not far from its original position. Myres J.L. 1945 states that the stone was found in 1913 embedded in a Roman mosaic floor in the courtyard of a house of Kouklia. The text continues, stating that previous investigations of 1887/8 failed to find it for a few centimetres, adding that you cannot affirm that it was the temple worship simulacrum, and then in 1935 was brought to Nicosia Archaeological Museum.

As mentioned earlier, this stone finds a correspondence in the iconography reported on the Roman moneys coined in Cyprus between the first cent. BC and the beginning of the 3rd cent. AD, under Augustus, Drusus Minor, Galba, Vespasian, Titus, Domizianus, Trajan, Didia Clara, Septimius Severus, Julia Domna, Caracalla, Geta and Gordian III[140]. To them, we must add a late-Hellenistic Ptolemaic emission attributed to Cleopatra VII (47-30 BC), with an eagle on the right[141]. The coins were struck in the Island and perhaps even in Rome, under the enthroned emperor and under the municipal authority of Cyprus. On the reverse, they celebrate the main glory of the country, the temple of Aphrodite Paphia, which represents the island's identity.

The specimens on behalf of A. Plautius Procos struck under Augustus and those of Drusus Minor are written in Latin while the rest is in Greek. On the right side, there is the Emperor's profile, while the reverse is dedicated to the unmistakable sacred tripartite structure of Aphrodite Paphia's temple, preceded by a semi-circular fence, whose appearance was subdivided by studies in four variants. Architectural distribution differs from the usual Greek and classic template planimetry with right angles and suggestions for the curved line, an Aegean matrix, which lasts for more than 200 years until the imperial emissions (Fig. 4).

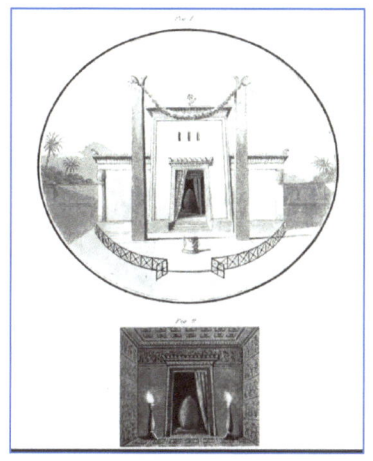

Fig. 4: Reconstruction of the shrine of Aphrodite on the basis of Numismatic iconography (by Münter, Hetsch 1824).

With a variety of stylistic differences, including meticulous detail rendering and extreme stylisation, the coins depict a tripartite building which is accessed by a semi-circular fence, perhaps paved, with a low entry gate, usually ported or symbolized by a Semicircle, sometimes confused with the rim of the coin as in some examples of Drusus, Vespasian, Titus and Gordian[142]. The inner area can be free or with a table and three circular elements, perhaps symbolizing votive gifts (Severi family, Gordian III), and sometimes bird-nesting, probably the doves of the goddess (Vespasian, Domitian, Didia Clara, all Severi, Gordian III)[143].

The sanctuary has the central part highest of its sides; in the middle, there are a sort of windows, surmounted by the crescent moon and sun, symbols of the religiousness connected

---

[140] Please refer to the detailed analysis of all the emissions from the temple of Aphrodite Paphia to Schwarzer H. 2013, who considers the architectural differences in the temple possibly attributable to episodes of reconstruction following the earthquakes reported by the sources, such as those of 15 BC. and 77 DC (Schwarzer H. 2013, 24-25).

[141] Schwarzer H. 2013, 21-22.

[142] Schwarzer H. 2013, Taff. 6-8, nn. 2, 4, 8, 10, 12, 23.

[143] Certainly, they are the famous Aphrodite's doves: *Iginus* in the *Fabula* (CXCVII) dedicated to Aphrodite tells of the doves hugging until Venus came out from the egg. For the presence of the doves in the Paphos sanctuary: Bates W.N. 1932, discusses the presence of dove decorations in churches nearby the Aphrodite shrines (and Welz K. 1959).

with the Great Goddess. Sometimes the forehead has "horn" endings, recalling second-millennium-style clay models from funerary contexts, and the temple model from Lemnos of the 7th century BC preserved in the National Museum of Athens[144]. Often two birds are present, probably referred to Aphrodite's holy doves.

In two side rooms, which we can interpret as open porches, sometimes with festoons or garlands, stand two very high censers[145]. At the centre, there is the ancient baetyl/simulacrum of the goddess, probably with an altar outdoors, covered with a canopy of perishable material, which Tacitus describes outdoors, but not wet by the rain[146].

Money items coined under various emperors are different: while still maintaining the same typological pattern, they may report changes of the sanctuary architecture over the centuries, or different indications of magistrates responsible for the issue and perhaps also for the dissimilar artistic skills of the engravers.

Under Augustus, the model resembles the Ptolemaic pattern: the temple is simple, with the triangular stone under a canopy and two incense burners at the sides. The front yard is paved with slabs enclosed in a semi-circular area along which the Latin legend runs[147]. Under Augustus and then Drusus minor son of Tiberius, on the reverse of the bronze coins of the island appears Zeus Salaminios with the stone of Aphrodite Paphia and legend in Latin letters[148] (Fig. 5).

figs. 5: Drusus bronze coin under Tiberius, 23 AD, right: CAESAR DRVSVS Head of Drusus. reverse: temple of Aphrodite Paphia to the right of Zeus Salaminios figure. www.cngcoins.com/Coin.aspx?CoinID=318246

Under Vespasian, the temple appears in a simplified form, marked by a high central architectural element embracing the stone, while the two lateral wings are intended or recall colonnade porches. (Fig. 6)

fig.6: Tetradacma (silver) of Vespasianus, Paphos Cyprus. 76-77 AD.
(© Coin Archives, Gorny and Mosch 160, 9 October 2007, lot 2015)

---

[144] For Cypriot models: Frankel D., Tamvaki A. 1973; for Lemnos: Price M.J., Trell B.L. 1977, 149, fig. 270.
[145] Zaccagnino C. 1998, 54.
[146] Tacitus, *Historiae*, II, 3.
[147] RPC 1999, 3906.
[148] Issue of 22/23 AD, Hill G. 1904, 74, 6-7, RPC 1999, 3921-26.

In silver tetra-drachmas of Titus, who personally went to visit the shrine in 69 A.D.[149], the tripartite temple has two side windowed rooms; the semi-circular courtyard is suggested by the perlated rim of the coin or the curve movement edge[150] (Fig. 6).

It should be noted that Titus' silver emissions of 79/80 A.D. have an ear of corn below the temple and they lack the semi-circular enclosure[151]. The subject celebrated on the coin, perhaps refers to a donation of corn made by the emperor to the shrine or to the island, in memory of auspices that the Oracle of the Temple of Aphrodite had predicted, confirming the favour of the goddess to large fates awaiting the Emperor[152].

The coins made under Trajan are the most linear and stylized, in them the temple architecture becomes a composition formed by the triangle of the sacred stone and by slender garlanded piers, while a simple curved line delineates the semi-circular courtyard[153]. (Fig.7)

Fig. 7: Dupondius Traianus, 112-117 AD:
(© Coin Archives, Classical Numismatic Group MBS 66, 19 May 2004, lot 1222).

The coins minted under the Severi[154] are rich in details and denote the engraver's attention to portray a realistic composition of the shrine: the holy place is formed by a circular area enclosed by a fence "according to the Roman style", paved with large rectangular slabs. Here we can find birds, two globes or a rectangular element of uncertain identification, which we can interpret as the already mentioned votive gifts or functional objects of any kind. (Fig. 8)

Fig. 8: Copper coin Septimius Severus 193-211AD
(www.wildwinds.com/coins/ric/septimius_severus/_cyprus_SNGCop_89.).

---

[149] Tacitus, *Historiae*, II, 2-4; Svetonius, *Titus*, 5.
[150] RPC 1999, 1809.
[151] Schwarzer H. 2013, Taf. 7, Nr. 13.
[152] Tacitus, *Historiae*, II, 2-4; Svetonius, *Titus*, 5.
[153] Hill G. 1904, 38; Schwarzer H. 2013, 23.
[154] Hill G. 1904, 54-63.

The Shrine consists of a main structure within which, surrounded by a frame probably pertinent to the front door, there is the sacred simulacrum. Above, there is a multiple window flat and finally between the two extremities of the building a sun and a crescent emerge. The whole seems to allude to a close relationship between Aphrodite Urania/Cipria and Astarte.

The sides of the main entrance had two porches of which we can recognize the side columns that support a coffered roof (or a wooden arbour?), where two birds rest. Over the porch roof, two censers rise, suggesting the diffusion of aromas inside and outside the building[155].

Fig. 9: a-b: Bronze coin Caracalla 198-217 AD.(*Encyclopaedia Biblica*, IV, Toronto 1903).

It should be noted that in some coins of Caracalla the stone seems to have two small lateral appendages like arms as to connote more human form the aniconic simulacrum[156] (Fig. 9 a-b).

As for wholeness, we mention the currencies of Asia (province) in which the sanctuary of Aphrodite Paphia appears: emissions on behalf of Hadrian (Pergamum in Mysia and Sardis), Severus Alexander, Maximinus the Thracian, Gordian III and Philip the Arab of Sardis (in Lidia), where the inscription on the reverse refers explicitly to the sanctuary of Paphos. We wonder if it is a tribute to one of the most important Mediterranean shrines, or it refers to the picture of another temple of Aphrodite Paphia repeating the same plant and Cypriot identification[157]?

The question that all coins with the Temple of Aphrodite at Paphos pose to us concerns the appearance of the shrine in Roman times. If it is truly represented or whether it is a reminiscence of an archaic structure remained in the tradition[158], only the archaeological findings can give a definitive answer to this question.

---

[155] One of the first and most impressive reconstructions on numismatic basis is in Münter F., Hetsch G.F., 1824, Figg. 1-2. See the virtual reconstruction of the sanctuary in Ceci F., Lauro V. 2016.
[156] Hill G. 1904, 62-63.
[157] Hill G. 1904, 62-63; Burnett A. 1999, 145; Schwarzer H. 2013, 31-34.
[158] Maier F.G. 1982, 767-777.

REFERENCES

- Amandry M. 1993: *Coinage Production and Monetary Circulation in Roman Cyprus* (Bank of Cyprus Cultural Foundation), Nicosia.
- Amandry M. 2011: Chypre, in *Proceedings of the XIVth International Numismatic Congress*, Glasgow, 89-99.
- Bates W.N. 1932: Aphrodite's Doves at Paphos in 1932, in *The American Journal of Philology*, 53, 3, 260-261.
- Burnett A. 1999: *Buildings and Monuments on Roman Coins*, Ann Arbor.
- Burnett A., Amandry A., Carradice I. 2006: *Roman Provincial Coinage*, I, *From Vespasian to Domitian (AD 69-96)*, London-Paris 1999 (2006ed).
- Carradice I. 1988: The coinage of roman Cyprus, in Tatton-Brown V. (ed.), *Cyprus and the East Mediterranean in the Iron Age*, Londres.
- Carstens A.M. 2008: Huwasi rocks, baityloi and open air sanctuaries in Karia, Lilikia and Cyprus, in *Olbia*, XVI, 73-93.
- Ceci F., Lauro V. 2016: *La casa della divinità: la ricostruzione virtuale in 3D del tempio di Afrodite Paphia a Palaipahos (Cipro) sulla base della monetazione provinciale romana. Una proposta interpretativa* in A. Russo Tagliente, F. Guarnieri (a cura di), *Santuari mediterranei tra Oriente e Occidente. Interazioni e contatti culturali*, Roma, 358-361.
- Dasen V. 2014: Sexe et sexualité des pierres dans l'antiquité gréco-romaine, in *Micrologus' Lybrary*, 60, 195-220.
- Hill G. 1904: *Catalogue of the Greek Coins of Cyprus*, London.
- Frankel D., Tamvaki A. 1973: Cypriot shrine models and decorated tombs, in *Australian Journal of Biblical Archaeology*, 2, 39-44.
- Howgego Ch. 1995: *Ancient History from Coins*, London and New York, cap. IV.
- Howgego Ch., Heuchert V., Burnett A. 2007: *Coinage and Identity in the Roman Provinces*, Oxford University Press, Leipzig.
- Karageorghis J. 1977: *La grande déesse de Chypre et son culte*, Lyon.
- Karageorghis J. 2005: *Kypris, the Aphrodite of Cyprus: Ancient Sources and Archaeological Evidence*, Nicosia.
- Karageorghis J. 2013: Images de la Grande Déesse de Chypre entre 1600 et 600 a.C., in *Pasiphae*, 7, 115-123.
- Gardner E.A., Hogarth D.G., James M.R., Elsey Smith R. 1888: Excavations in Cyprus, 1887-8. Paphos, Leontari, Amargetti, in *Journal of Hellenic Studies*, 9, 147- 264.
- Maier F.G. 1975: The Temple of Aphrodite at Old Paphos, in *Report of the Department of Antiquities Cyprus*, 69-80, Nicosia.
- Maier F.G. 1977-2013: Ausgrabungen in Alt-Paphos auf Cypern (*Herausgegeben im Auftrag des Deutschen Archäologischen Instituts*, 1-8).
- Maier F.G. 1982: Der Tempel der paphischen Aphrodite in der Kaiserzeit, in G. Wirth, *Romanitas-Christianitas. Untersuchungen aus Geschichte und Literatur der römischen Kaiserzeit. Johannes Straub zum 70. Geburtstag am 18. Oktober 1982*, Berlin 767-777.
- Maier F.G., Karageorghis V. 1984: *Paphos. History and Archaeology*, Nicosia.
- Myres J.L. 1945: The Black Stone on the site of the paphian Temple at Kouklia, in *Annual of the British School at Athens*, 41, 97-98.
- Münter F., Hetsch G.F. 1824: *Der Tempel der himmlischen Göttin zu Paphos*, Kopenhagen.
- Näf B. 2013: *Testimonia Alt-Paphos*. Darmstadt.

- Norena C.F. 2001: Coins and Communication, in M. Peachin (ed.), *The Oxford Handbook of Social Relations in the Roman World*, Oxford University Press 248-268.
- Parks D.A. 2004: *The Roman Coinage of Cyprus. Nicosia* (The Cyprus Numismatic Society), Nicosia.
- Price M.J., Trell B.L. 1977: *Coins and their Cities*, London.
- RPC 1992: Burnett A., Amandry A., Ripollès PP., *Roman Provincial Coinage*, I, *From the death of Caesar to the death of Vitellius (44 BC-AD 69)*, London-Paris, 576-580
- RPC 1999: Burnett A., Amandry A., Carradice I., *Roman Provincial Coinage*, I, *From Vespasian to Domitian (AD 69-96)*, London-Paris (ed. 2006), 576-580.
- Rimmel B. 2002-2017: *The Minoan Epiphany. A bronze Age Visionary Culture*, 2002-2017, in http://biroz.net/words/minoan-epiphany/
- Rocelli M. 2014-15: *Il santuario di Afrodite a Paleopahos*, Università Cà Foscari Venezia, aa. 2014-1025, on line 839835-1173526.
- Schwarzer H. 2013: Heiligtümer der Aphrodite Paphia in der antiken Münzprägung, in *Boreas*, 36, 19-46.
- Stewart P. 2008: Baetyls as statues? Cult images in the roman Near East, in *The Sculptural Environment of the Roman Near East*, Leuven, 297-314.
- Tsochos Ch. 2014: Das dreiteilige Heiligtum der Aphrodite in Palaepaphos und die baitylos-Darstellungen auf zypriotischen Münzen der Kaiserzeit, in Graen D., Rind M., Wabersich H. (Hrsg.), *Otium cum dignitate. Festschrift für Angelika Geyer zum 65. Geburtstag* (BARIntSer 2605), Oxford, 201-208.
- Veymiers R. 2005: Sérapis au sanctuarie d'Aphrodite Paphia. À propos d'une gemme disparue de la Collection Petrie, *in Acta Orientalia Belgica*, XVIII,. 339-356.
- Welz K. 1959: Die Tauben der Aphrodite, in *SchMünzBl*, 9, 34, 33-37.
- Zaccagnino C. 1998: *Il thymiaterion nel mondo greco*, Roma.
- Zeman K. 2008: The Aegean origin of the aniconic cult of Aphrodite in Paphos, *POCA 2005. Postgraduate cypriot Archaelogy* (BAR I.Series 1803), Oxford, 61-64.

The houses of the goddess. Coins tell the Cypriot Aphrodite mith